PREJUDICE REDUCTION AND THE SCHOOLS

Prejudice Reduction and the Schools

JAMES LYNCH

CASSELL
LONDON

NICHOLS PUBLISHING COMPANY
NEW YORK

First published in Great Britain in 1987 by:
Cassell Educational Limited
Artillery House
Artillery Row
London SW1P 1RT

British Library Cataloguing in Publication Data
Lynch, James
   Prejudice reduction and the schools.
   1. Education—Social aspects
   2. Prejudices
   I. Title
   370.11'4   LC192

   ISBN 0-304-31384-X

Published in the United States of America and Canada by:
Nichols Publishing Company
PO Box 96
New York, NY 10024

Library of Congress Cataloging in Publication Data
Lynch, James
   Prejudice reduction in schools
   Bibliography: p.
   Includes index
   1. Education sociology—Great Britain
   Racism—study and teaching—Great Britain
   I. Title
   LC 192.2.L966   1987 370.19'0941   87-12223

   ISBN 0-89397-283-5

Typeset by M C Typeset Ltd
Printed and bound in Great Britain by Mackays of Chatham Ltd

Last digit is print no: 9 8 7 6 5 4 3 2 1

Contents

List of Tables and Figures

Acknowledgements

It would not have been possible for me to write this book without the support and co-operation of a number of persons and organisations, whose rôle I should like to specifically acknowledge. First I wish to express my appreciation to Sunderland Polytechnic for granting me a one-term sabbatical leave to complete the research for this book. Secondly, I should like to record my deep gratitude to my friend and colleague, Professor James A. Banks, for his unselfish encouragement and professional support during the writing of this book and for providing me with a 'safe haven' at the University of Washington, where I had the peace, the opportunity and the resources to undertake what turned out to be a very complex task. I also owe a debt to the three anonymous 'clearance readers' who made such critical yet helpful and constructive comments when reviewing the book for publication. Lastly, it gives me particular pleasure to thank my wife, Margaret, for her part in the preparation and critical appraisal of the typescript and, as always, for her enthusiastic support for my endeavours.

Seattle, Washington
July 1986

JAMES LYNCH

Introduction

This book has been written from a perspective which emphasises the responsibility of all members of society to work for the eradication of discrimination, the amendment of prejudice and the removal of socially dysfunctional attitudes. The greater responsibility for this task lies with the majority society, not minorities. The overall aim of the book is, therefore, to show that an education for prejudice reduction is possible. Such education is based on the acquisition of principles of social justice and respect for all persons, which may be implemented through discourse, decision and action. Without underestimating the role of the wider society, and especially such powerful norm-building influences as the media, the book concentrates on the role and function of schools and teachers in the task of prejudice reduction. It starts from the premise that, in order to combat any form of prejudice, teachers need to know how it arises and why.

The author recognises the inadequacy of current approaches to prejudice reduction and seeks to offer an alternative, more positive and optimistic perspective for teachers. In the book attempts are made to show how they can examine their own practices in the light of new criteria which are more appropriate to a multicultural society. For, insofar as strategies to eradicate prejudice in British society are focused on members of ethnic minorities, either predominantly or exclusively, they are unlikely to greatly affect either the level of prejudice in the broader society or the socially reproductive function of education in this respect. Yet, the literature of multicultural education is replete with exhortations addressing that very goal, almost as though it were in some way an acceptable proxy for strategies aimed at tackling the root problem: the tenacious and endemic commitment of much of British social life to the perpetuation of structural, institutional and personal prejudice and discrimination. To explain the tenacity and complexity of racial and other prejudices, multifactor, interactive explanations are necessary which take into account four major influences: personality, social structure, culture and environment. Only in this way, it is argued, will teachers be able to build into their professional lives, and particularly their teaching/learning strategies, both cognitive and affective means for the reduction and eradication of prejudice. That task is seen in this book as a central aspect of the teacher's role, a continuing function of education and the school system, coterminous with formal education.

One of the difficulties inherent in the task of pulling together the relevant literature for the book has been the widely disparate traditions within which prejudice reduction has been analysed and discussed. These range from the predominantly psychological work of post-war authors such as Adorno and Allport through the work of the

Intergroup Education Movement and the recent work by authors in the field of moral education, such as Kohlberg, to authors such as Banks who have written predominantly within a multicultural education paradigm. While the international literature in these fields is voluminous indeed, there has been relatively little work in the United Kingdom, apart from the still unsurpassed early work of Stenhouse and his colleagues and followers. This neglect of the contiguous and precursor traditions has opened the way for new initiatives deriving from a reaction to the vagueness and apparent inefficacy of multicultural education. Encouraged by neo-Marxist macroanalysis of British schools and education, such initiatives have become current under the overall label of anti-racist education, including short experiences and activities called 'racism awareness training' (RAT).

There are a number of problems, however, with such a formulation and the analysis which it implies. Firstly, the focus is too narrow, insofar as it seeks the goal of prejudice eradication within a very short timespan and across only one form of prejudice. It is necessary to consider the mutually reinforcing nature of, for instance, racism, sexism, credism, classism and handicap prejudice, as well as their social and cultural pathology. Secondly, its advocates are largely neglectful of the aetiology of current knowledge about prejudice. How it is acquired and worked out into the very essence of society and its underlying value positions and, thence, into the structure and regulatory mechanisms of that society is, for the most part, disregarded. Thirdly, it tends to be political, confrontational, accusatory and guilt-inducing in its approach, to an extent that it is likely to be unacceptable to the vast majority of teachers in schools. In that sense, it might be described as out of line with the main-stream educational enterprise. Fourthly, in a way which is inimical to the very ethic of a multicultural democracy some racism awareness programmes have sought to be coercive. In doing this they encompass an ideology committed to propaganda rather than an educational enterprise appropriate to a democratic society, where change comes by persuasion and appeal to reason rather than compulsion. Nor, for that matter, does the ideology offer a thought-out moral basis for behaviour and decision within a context where there is a pluralism of values, some of which may be inappropriate to a multicultural society and many of which are in conflict, but where often two 'goods' may be in competition. It provides no basis for the resolution of such conflicts other than by authoritarian or imposed means. Fifthly, it neglects the fact that prejudices are continually created and recreated within a pluralist society, by dint of the fact that individuals are socialised into different values and perceptions of roles by the different families and cultural groups into which they are born. Prejudice reduction is, thus, a continuous requirement in a culturally diverse society. Lastly, the philosophy of such approaches has been essentially nihilistic, insofar as it focuses either on unrealistic macropolitical revolutionary change, for which the schools are as instrumentally unsuited as the broader society stubbornly unwilling, or on the achievement of long-term cognitive and affective gains by short-term means. This alternative flies in the face of all the current evidence and past experience with regard to how people learn, how they acquire their attitudes and how their attitudes and behaviours may be changed.

For me, therefore, antiracism, antisexism and opposition to prejudice as a whole, are a necessary but insufficient condition for tackling the problem of unacceptable prejudice in society and school. Such an essentially negative formulation needs to be topped up with the active commitment to action for the replacement of unhealthy attitudes which is fully compatible with a culturally pluralist society that espouses and implements human rights and respect for persons, even if it does so imperfectly. This task is essentially one of controlling public behaviour by legislation and regulation, and of changing unhealthy personal and social attitudes by an education which has, as one of its central aims, the initiation of learners into healthy moral attitudes by rational means and which includes the combating of prejudiced attitudes. For, whereas all prejudices are attitudes, clearly not all attitudes are prejudices. Thus, while teachers and schools are not omnipotent, nor are they impotent in the task of correcting prejudiced attitudes such as racism. Schools do not have to continue to reflect inflexibly the power relations and prejudices of a wider society while waiting for some kind of millenial conversion. They can both combat and, in many cases, counteract those values and actively educate for alternatives, which are more compatible with life in a culturally diverse democracy.

In this sense, I agree with Cummins (1986) when he states that while legislative and political reforms are necessary conditions for effective change they are insufficient in themselves. Cummins argues that what is needed in addition, to supplement and amplify political change, is a redefinition of the role of the educator and the school, with regard to their interaction with minority students and communities. And, for me an essential corollary of that focus is a sharpened professional role *vis-à-vis* the attitudes and moral behaviour of all students. This task involves teachers in a redefinition of their role and an increased recognition of their responsibility for prejudice reduction and eradication as new goals for education in a democracy.

Recognising the inadequacies of current approaches, therefore, it is the aim in this book to offer an alternative, positive and more optimistic perspective on how teachers in schools may re-examine their own professional theory and practice in the light of extended criteria appropriate to a multicultural society. At the nucleus of such a recognition is the acceptance of the central, but not exclusive, responsibility of schools for the reduction and, if possible, the eradication of socially damaging and unacceptable prejudices. In this sense, the book is concerned with supporting teachers in combating racism, sexism, credism and classism as virulent and specific manifestations of the propensity of society to discriminate on irrational and illogical grounds. The book addresses the need of teachers for support in the process of absorbing new values into their everyday professional work and the essentially moral nature of their task is recognised.

In this context, education for prejudice reduction is an integral part of education, seen as the induction of learners into moral behaviour by means of rational strategies and towards greater rational sophistication. As Habermas (1983) asserts, rationality is the means by which individuals may claim validity for their case and which enables them to engage in rational disputes for the resolution of competing claims. It is this pursuit of rationality by means of strategies which appeal to reason that enables learners to increase their cognitive sophistication. Thereby they may cope with alternative validity claims, judge the truth content of conflicting assertions, arguments and situations, resist intolerant responses and recognise the distinction between relative and absolute differences. Decisions in education, as in the wider society, if they are to be considered to be moral, need to be underpinned by generally accepted principles based on the need for respect for persons and free expression of individual needs and interests. There is no doubt that these two demands, the individual and the social, represent a dilemma for all societies, but particularly those that are democratic and culturally pluralist. One means of resolving this dilemma in the form of general principles has, however, been suggested by Keller and Reuss (1985). Such principles would include the acceptance of the need to legitimate proposed courses of action; of the need for balance, fairness and mutuality in their applicability and in the effort and sacrifice of all; of the obligation to anticipate the consequences of actions and omissions; and, of the application of consistency of judgement, including willingness to take the part and the role of others — what is referred to as reversibility.

I am well aware that it is no easy matter to ask teachers to understand and to undertake this crucial role in prejudice reduction. Nor can it be an easy, short-term matter to enable them to extend the criteria by which they judge their own professional fairness and effectiveness. On the other hand, it really is a question of the extension and refinement of the distinctive role of a teacher as it is currently seen in Western democracies, namely the initiation of children in schools into moral behaviour and attitudes by rational means rather than by indoctrination and other coercive measures. Looked at this way, the teachers' task is to morally empower their pupils to discard existing prejudices and to resist the absorption of new ones, and to enable pupils to become morally autonomous as well as socially responsible.

Such an education is fully appropriate to a culturally diverse society capable of preparing pupils for life in a democracy where there is a pluralism of, often competing, values and views. Not all such values and views are equally valid and the need, therefore, arises to differentiate, on rational principles, between those which represent legitimate divergence, and those which are inconsistent with moral behaviour in a multicultural society. Whilst the former are to be welcomed and encouraged the latter must be rejected. Among these latter are surely those which manifest prejudiced attitudes and discriminatory behaviour, such as racism, sexism, credism and classism.

The structure of this book is, I hope, fairly easily understood and followed. In chapter 1, I seek to explain briefly the reasons why cultural pluralism has become an issue in Western society in general and for education in particular. The ideals proclaimed by democratic societies are contrasted with the widespread operative marginalisation and victimisation of ethnic minorities, particularly visible minorities. The *legitimation crisis* consequent on this cultural and ethical dissonance is explained and examples are given of the alternative strategies which have been attempted — varying from coercive measures such as legal discrimination and apartheid, through attempts to solve the issue technocratically by disguised strategies of assimilation, such as intercultural education, to pluralist strategies involving dialogue and discourse, aimed at achieving greater congruence between declared and operative values. The chapter concludes with an overall picture within which concerns current in the United Kingdom over anti-racist and anti-sexist education are located, pointing to the need to legitimate them as base-lines for more sophisticated, pluralist and effective strategies in both political and educational sectors.

Chapter 2 then seeks to firmly locate prejudice reduction as a central concern of any commitment to multicultural education. The relationship of credism, sexism and racism to prejudice, stereotyping and discrimination are considered and the importance of social climate at societal, systemic and institutional levels is emphasised. Classism is advanced as explanatory of a substantial proportion of other forms of prejudice, necessitating advances in social status as a prerequisite for an advancement which is inhibited by prejudice in a classic vicious circle. The relationship between self-concept and prejudiced attitudes is explored and the importance of social contact in the form of positive intercultural relations in enabling people to emerge from ethnic captivity is emphasised, subject to explicit conditions. From these considerations a set of principles is devised against which teachers may develop the activities proposed in the central part of the book in their own schools and classrooms.

In chapter 3 the extensive literature on prejudice acquisition and reduction is described and analysed. Four major theoretical domains of prejudice acquisition: individual personality needs, social structure, cultural context and environment are derived from the previous literature. An extensive, international overview of the literature is assigned to these categories and they are, in turn, honed for their societal, systemic, institutional and individual professional relevance. Prejudice reduction is defined and interpreted into a categorisation of approaches (reaching forward in a preliminary way to chapter 6) as a function of the overall survey of the literature. Definitions and diagrammatic representations are provided and the chapter concludes with principles for educators and policy makers.

Chapter 4 seeks to identify the dynamic factors involved in effective schools — 'effective' being defined as those which successfully tackle prejudice reduction as well as pursuing major academic objectives. The importance of a holistic approach is contrasted with current initiatives which address individual components of the social system. Research on the powerful function of the school ethos and the way in which the school policy and structure communicate institutional norms and values are highlighted; as is the way in which such factors as racial climate often affect the achievement of minority students more than that of majority students. The need for co-operative incentives and control structures in pursuit of low school anxiety, high self-esteem and field independence, and thus heightened academic performance, is advanced. The chapter includes examplars of school policies and concludes with institutional checklists and criteria for multicultural education and prejudice reduction.

Within the institutional context set by the previous chapter, the central concern of chapter 5 is to provide, explain and detail a flexible model approach to developing a curriculum attentive to the need for schools to contribute to prejudice reduction and, therefore, for individual components of the curriculum to do likewise. A seven-part curriculum strategy for prejudice reduction is introduced and the crucial importance of the prescanning of the target population, their cultural biographies and cognitive styles is emphasised. The seven components of the model are then clarified. The iterative relationship between the first step and all succeeding components of the strategy is then illustrated in outline, and each component is discussed in greater detail, as a preparation for the succeeding chapter. Reference is made to the need to address not only cognitive increments but also the affective and behavioural dimensions and to aim for increased self-esteem, moral maturity and an improved ability to assess social situations objectively and higher levels of intellectual functioning in each of the epistemological domains of the curriculum. The groundwork is prepared for the next chapter and its central focus on pedagogical strategies for prejudice reduction. Chapter 5 concludes with a diagrammatic representation of the model and its components and a tentative specification of criteria and principles is proposed.

Following the model introduced in chapter 5, 12 major approaches to prejudice reduction are introduced from which teachers may compile their own integrated teaching strategy. In each case, a brief description is given of the approach and details of the research and/or other appraisals available. The limitations and, in some cases, dangers of the approaches are also referred to. Particular emphasis is placed on the central importance of co-operative learning approaches, for multicultural education more broadly and for successful prejudice reduction. Reference is made to major conditions such as the need for equal status contact, co-operative incentive approaches, student team learning and the multi-ethnic composition of the working groups, and attention is drawn to the potential negative effects if such strategies are perceived as unsuccessful. Evidence concerning the importance of social and racial climate, previously introduced at school level, is now retrieved for its relevance to the classroom level. Suitable approaches are argued to be productive of high self-esteem, a low degree of prejudice, and low learning anxiety, combined with a high sense of personal efficacy. They are seen as part of a cycle leading to higher academic performance, provided that a wide variety of culturally sensitive stimuli and culturally fair assessment are utilised. The chapter concludes with a verbal résumé and a diagrammatic presentation of the 12 approaches.

In chapter 7, the important function of resources, including teaching materials, in prejudice reduction is linked to the advancement of criteria for their selection, utilisation and evaluation. A range of sources of information on prejudice reduction from the United Kingdom and abroad is described and 'trace' details are given. Some more detailed exemplifications are given to illustrate the kinds of packages available and the need for caution in their utilisation. The role of the library and school librarian are discussed. The material in the chapter is supported by categorisation by source, year and title in an extensive bibliography.

The succeeding chapter, chapter 8, identifies the pivotal role of staff development in any institutional, curricular or pedagogical attempt to achieve prejudice reduction. Current and past approaches are described and evaluated and reference is made to their piecemeal nature. Identifying interdependence, collegial judgement, self and institutional evaluation and the importance of both extended professional criteria for judgement and reference group enhancement, as central platforms of the institutional policy and practice in this sphere, an outline model of staff development needs is proposed. Content, strategies and principles are checklisted for consideration and discussion.

The concluding chapter seeks to collate the threads of the overall argument and development of the book. A brief and coherent résumé is given of the content, and areas for further work and action are identified. Teachers are encouraged to draw on the book as an initial resource for steering their teaching more firmly towards prejudice reduction.

The book is intended to fill a gap in the literature available to teachers and student teachers in the field of multicultural and anti-racist education. It is meant as a contribution to the current discussion of the ways in which racism, sexism, credism, classism and other forms of prejudice may be reduced and, if possible, eliminated through the deployment of deliberate and systematic school and classroom policies and practices. It is sought, through the book, to build up suggestions for principles and practice from analyses of literature, appraisal of research guidelines and descriptions of existing 'good practice' in a number of different countries. *Prejudice Reduction and The Schools* is aimed at helping teachers to improve their own professional practice and to extend their criteria for professional judgement, by means of a consideration of the literature, both theoretical and empirical, in the field of prejudice acquisition and reduction. Throughout the book, the onus is placed on the reader to review the evidence critically and actively to build up his or her own case-law, rather than to receive the material presented in the book as any kind of pre-packaged wisdom. The purpose of the book is thus more educational than political, although reference is made in the earlier chapters to the need for broader social and legal action if progress is to be made towards the elimination of prejudice. Teachers are seen as goodwilled professionals, concerned to improve the way they function professionally. It is to assisting that process of professional improvement that this book is dedicated rather than to constructing hopeless scenarios for recriminations, guilt and eventual Utopian revolution. At the heart of the book is a commitment to the active pursuit of justice through education, not a mere celebration of rhetoric about that goal.

REFERENCES

Cummins, J. (1986) Empowering minority students: a framework for intervention, *Harvard Educational Review*. **56**(1) 18–36.

Habermas, J. (1983) *Moralbewusstsein und Kommunikatives Handeln*. Frankfurt: Suhrkamp Verlag.

Keller, M. and Reuss, S.(1985) 'The process of moral decision-making — normative and empirical conditions of participation in moral discourse', in Berkovitz, M. and Aser, F. *Moral Education: Theory and Application*. Hillsdale, NJ: Erlbaum.

Chapter 1

Democratic Values and Discrimination

INTRODUCTION

In this chapter, I want to set the scene for the more detailed educational considerations in the rest of the book. In that sense, the chapter seeks to offer a macro analysis of the social and cultural changes which have led to many Western democratic societies perceiving themselves as culturally pluralist. I want to argue that this newer perception has led them to begin a more systematic re-examination of both their social organisation and their educational provision to bring them into line with the democratic values they espouse. Further, I want to suggest that new societal values and ideals can only be created by taking full account of that pluralism and with the full contribution of all groups. For, only in social policies which are fully attentive to their cultural pluralism can democratic societies find the opportunity for the peaceful change and dynamic creativity which are so essential to their future (Myrdal, 1944). I do not wish, thereby, to imply that such policies will erase competing claims for resources or legitimacy but rather, that they will provide a means to make such conflicts creative. As the major institutional structure for the transmission of culture, the school and its teachers are at the very core of making this process work, by providing children with the necessary values, attitudes, knowledge and competences.

In the face of their 'new found' racial, ethnic, cultural, religious and social-class diversity, no Western democracy has yet been successful in fully attuning its social and educational policies to democratic values. This is nowhere more obvious than in such fields of public policy as education. The gap between democratic ideals and social reality has caused a crisis of legitimation which can only be resolved by discourse. Put simply, this means that confidence in the ability of existing ideals, values, procedures and institutions to resolve the newly perceived problems has waned and only multicultural dialogue can establish fresh norms appropriate to the cultural diversity of society and necessary for the resolution of its problems. For example, there is currently a marked contrast between the ideals proclaimed in Western democratic societies, such as equality of educational opportunity, and the reality of the treatment — economic, social and educational — of minorities, particularly visible minorities, which is one of social discrimination, victimisation and educational and economic marginalisation. Thus, increased ethnic diversity in Western societies has focused attention on the institutionalised and personal hostility, rejection and violence which minority groups are having to face in the various forms of prejudice. These phenomena represent not only oppression and victimisation of ethnic minority groups and an infringement of the human rights avowed in a democratic society, but also a major challenge to the ideals and values of those societies and the institution entrusted with the transmission of those ideals: the school. But while intergroup conflict is inevitable — and is indeed a source of creative change — discrimination and victimisation are unacceptable. Society needs to take broader social and legal measures to counter them, and educational institutions have a crucial role in overcoming such intergroup and interpersonal behaviour and attitudes. Schools, thus, have an important role in helping children to prevail over those aspects of their inherent enculturation and socialisation which may lead them to act in a discriminatory way against other individuals and groups and in combating those broader social influences which may facilitate prejudiced values and actions.

The argument of this first chapter is therefore that the schools and teachers have a central role to play in closing the credibility, or legitimation, gap by systematic and deliberate policies and practices: policies and practices which not only reflect cultural pluralism but also tackle democratically the central problems of prejudice and discrimination on terms of mutual acceptability and interest to all cultural groups. This task must be seen as a central aim of multicultural education, and I am using the shorthand term *prejudice reduction* to describe it. Teaching for prejudice reduction is crucially a matter of changing existing attitudes and encouraging the development of new ones fully congruent with the ethical basis of a pluralist democracy. Such a pursuit is essentially the provision of bases for moral attitudes, decisions and actions; that is, attitudes, decisions and actions which are fully compatible with cultural pluralism as seen in the school system, its structure, values, procedures and curriculum.

CULTURAL PLURALISM

But to return to the question of the circumstances that have led most Western democratic societies to begin, over the last fifty years, to perceive themselves as culturally pluralist and to the responses they have made in their social and educational policies. Culture is defined by anthropologists as the ways in which individuals and groups perceive, believe, emulate and behave (Goodenough, 1976). No two persons will have exactly the same cultural biography. We all do, however, have more or less the same biological apparatus, and the cultural 'capital' of that biography enables us to make our biological apparatus function for us in society. So culture is a very important determinant of human behaviour and human difference and diversity and of the way in which we relate to each other in school and society.

There are a number of major definitions and approaches to cultural pluralism, but, put simply, it means that there are many legitimate ways of perceiving, believing and behaving, into which children are inducted by their families and their communities. Teachers need to take these differences into account in their teaching and other professional activities, as in their personal relationships. The name for the process of acquiring a culture from birth, for example, learning to communicate in the language of our surroundings, is *enculturation*. Human beings acquire not only knowledge and competences, however, but also social and vocational roles. This process is usually referred to as *socialisation*. Such roles may be very different in different societies and cultural groups among which perceptions of such social roles as wife, mother, sister and brother may differ very widely from those experienced by teachers.

In any classroom, then, a teacher will have children from a diversity of cultural backgrounds, some more markedly different from each other and some less so. Many will have different perceptions of important social roles, values and structures from those of the teacher. Each child will have undergone a unique process of both enculturation and socialisation. There will, though, be many similarities and much overlap and all will be using very similar innate capacities: their biological heritage. Taking into account, in their teaching, the diversity of cultural backgrounds of all learners, teachers need to seek ways which will afford all children equity and equality of educational opportunity. It would clearly be invidious and unfair for them to act otherwise. For that goal to be effectively reached, however, teachers have to make sure that neither they, nor pupils, nor the schools are discriminating negatively against pupils because of their cultural and social backgrounds. Further, they will need to aim to engage all cultures in the classroom in the content, style, language, approaches and motivation, assessment and reward strategies of their teaching.

Often the very process of acquiring one culture involves the development of attitudes and values antipathetic to other groups and individuals, their values, actions and perceptions. Such attitudes have the potential to lead to behaviour which is unfair or hostile to those other groups and individuals and may even infringe their human rights. Schools and teachers have the task, not only of trying to resolve conflicting demands, but also of combating those prejudiced attitudes which may be detrimental to social and educational equity. This struggle must be represented in the values procedures, organisation and curricula of schools and teachers. That process is called *prejudice reduction*.

The cultural microcosm of the classroom is likely to have only a small selection of the cultural diversity or *cultural pluralism* existing in the broader society: the presence within a single nation state of a variety of different groups with different cultural biographies, deriving from such factors as language, ethnicity, religion, race and social class. Some writers refer to these smaller groupings as *microcultures* (Gollnick and Chinn, 1986). These they then contrast with the *macroculture* which represents the core of universal traits which shape the major institutions and organisations of society. These core values, or *universals*, provide the cultural bridges whereby one group may communicate and negotiate with another and all groups and individuals may define what they have in common. Moreover, as not all individuals and groups will see 'eye to eye' all the time, these universals provide both the means whereby the legitimacy of conflicting claims to resources, rewards and opportunity in society may be determined and the process and criteria for the resolution of conflict in ways compatible with a culturally diverse, democratic society. In the United Kingdom values inherent within that macroculture would include:

- a common language;
- social justice;

- rights to a private life and property;
- the rule of law;
- equality between the sexes;
- equality before the law;
- equality of educational opportunity;
- respect for persons, their language, culture and ethnic backgrounds;
- the right to economic satisfaction;
- acceptance of rational discourse for the settlement of conflict;
- peaceful competition;
- the eschewing of violent means for problem resolution.

Such common core values of the macroculture are not always effectively operationalised. They may be espoused but imperfectly implemented and they may be subject to change and only partial acceptance. None the less, they represent the framework within which change can be achieved and the means whereby dissenters or victimised groups may achieve greater justice. A majority of members of all macrocultures would probably accept them to some degree or another.

DIFFERENT VIEWS OF CULTURAL PLURALISM

Returning now to cultural pluralism, it should not be assumed that this is a new term. It derives, in fact, from the work of Horace Kallen in the early part of this century and represents a reaction to the previously dominant response to cultural diversity by assimilation (Kallen, 1970). Assimilation represents the aim of the absorption of microcultures into the macrocultural 'melting pot'. Societies espousing policies of cultural pluralism accept that there is no one way of life which is superior to all others, but that a democratic society must, within agreed limits, afford a wide measure of freedom to individuals and groups to engage in and express difference in their language, their dress, their institutions, their family patterns, their norms and values. While it afforded individuals and groups 'equality of difference' the early view of cultural pluralism has, however, been criticised for not placing sufficient emphasis on the individual's right to choose whether or not to belong.

More recently Glazer (1977) has set down the development of cultural pluralism, as he sees it, identifying a series of stages in that development. He sees what he calls 'weak cultural pluralism' as arising in the 1940s in reaction to the racism of the Third Reich. In the educational sphere this gave rise to the intercultural perspective of that time and what came to be known as the Intergroup Education Movement. The purpose of this movement was to teach tolerance so that perception of difference would disappear. It was, thus, not only dominated by white liberals in American society, but it was also essentially, if indirectly, assimilationist. Only a few characteristics of the movement still remain in education.

Glazer sees this weak cultural pluralism as having been overtaken by what he calls 'strong cultural pluralism', derived from the experience of victimisation and exploitation of ethnic minority groups. It is more aggressive than the previous phase and is based on the assumption that separate groups should continue to exist as such. It should be an aspect of public policy, in such spheres as education, to assist that maintenance and the creative development of the separate cultures.

Responding to the decline of the assimilationist policy of the dominant Anglo-American group and of its values and ideals, Greenbaum (1974) has drawn attention to the way in which the decline of the Anglo-American ideals, on which society in the United States was founded, has left society without an ideal to guide the socialisation process. Implicit in this lack of an ideal is a gap in moral authority and a lack of clearcut goals for that most important of socialisation processes — education in schools. He castigates the previous dominant ideals for their hypocrisy over the issue of equality — a hope rather than a conviction — and for their inherent racism, as well as for their failure to resolve value contradictions within their own philosophy. He calls for the pursuit of justice and equality through the construction of humane, pluralist institutions and communities and for the development of a more broadly based, universal ideal — an ideal which may be sought in the values of oppressed groups in Western societies and in the Third World.

Now, both of these authors were writing from a predominantly North American perspective. On the other hand, the phases of cultural pluralism which they identify and the parameters within which it may be considered are very similar in most Western societies. There can be no doubt, for example, that society in the United Kingdom responded with policies of assimilation to its rapidly escalating ethnic diversity until the late 1970s. Australia, too, was wedded to its 'White Australia Policy' until well into the post-war period.

Cultural pluralism was, thus, by no means the first nor the only way in which democratic societies attempted to respond to increasing cultural diversity. Some, perhaps most, sought initially to respond by aiming for total assimilation, whereby existing or newly arrived minorities would lose their identities and knowledge of their separate heritage, and become indistinguishable from the majority. There would thus, so the argument went, no longer be cause for prejudice. Of course, in the context of visible minorities, this argument was at least naïve, possibly deceitful. Some countries have adopted policies of separation in housing, welfare, education and other fields either at the same time as, or as alternatives to, assimilation. Examples of both sets of policy options may be found in various sectors of most democratic societies in either contemporary or historical location. In the heyday of American assimilation, there was separate school provision, housing, transportation and much else beside for the American blacks. Both of these strategies, assimilation and separation, have proved incompatible, in the long term, with the declared ideals of democratic societies. But it is helpful to recount them because they represent the two poles within which democratic societies have responded to cultural diversity. In reality, of course, they are ideal typifications and each society fashions different facets of its social life and structure in different ways and at different points between these poles. For example, while some societies have integrated state educational systems, they may at the same time permit and even encourage private and parallel systems to arise, organised on the basis of religion or social class. The United Kingdom and France are examples. Moreover, it is quite conceivable that an individual may belong to several minority groups simultaneously, and may, by free act of will, opt in or out of some structures, activities and opportunities and into others. This freedom is an important, although not absolute, right of citizens.

So, it is important to take great care when using such potentially emotive words as assimilation and separation. Cultural pluralism, as a policy, envisages components of both. An individual may belong to common political and economic structures, while at the same time choosing to remain a member of an ethnic group which may, or may not, elect to live separately from other ethnic groups in a community neighbourhood. Thus, cultural pluralism for that person will need to allow for economic and political participation and inclusion. One might say this is assimilation into mainstream economic and political activity and satisfaction, with permitted cultural, linguistic and ethnic separation. But note, the emphasis is on the choice of the individual; not on coercion or compulsion. A democratic society has to enable individuals to make such conscious choices, while protecting them from unfair competition, victimisation, marginalisation and discrimination on the basis of their race, sex, class and creed.

Gordon (1964), writing within a North American context, has proposed seven 'subprocesses' to the process of assimilation which are useful in alerting us to the various dimensions of that word. These subprocesses range from acculturation into the behavioural patterns of society, through large-scale entrance into primary groups, intermarriage, identification with the sense of unity of the society, through to the absence of prejudice and discrimination by that society and the absence of value and power conflicts between groups, as a manifestation of total absorption.

The problem with such models is that they relate to a goal of ultimate total assimilation, i.e., loss of distinctive identity and consciousness of separate heritage, in all sectors of life and in a way which is incompatible with cultural pluralism. In particular, of course, Gordon's model envisages a progression through various stages to that goal. Moreover, such analyses tend to place the focus on the minority group, which is often, by definition, powerless at a political level. In fairness, writing almost a decade later, Gordon did envisage two kinds of pluralism, *liberal pluralism* and *corporate pluralism* (Gordon 1975). In the first, to paraphase, difference is tolerated but not officially recognised by the allocation of resources to support it. Under corporate pluralism, on the other hand, explicit recognition is afforded to ethnic groups as a defined basis for the allocation of rewards and resources. Bullivant, writing more recently, has endorsed the second of these, arguing the need for ethnic minorities to establish some separate structures and institutions in order to survive (Bullivant 1984). Few writers on cultural pluralism have, however, taken up Greenbaum's point that oppressed groups in the West and in the Third World may be a source of the common ideals of culturally pluralistic societies (Greenbaum, 1974). They thus enrich society and extend its problem-solving repertoire. As Banks suggests, ethnic groups denied full participation in society often act as its moral conscience (Banks, 1986b). Logically, of course, any realistic policy of cultural pluralism must sustain the creative development of minority groups. Part of this development, however, must 'empower' them both socially and educationally, so that dialogue or discourse can take place on an equal basis to agree the common values and ideals which are essential for any society. The alternative would be a kind of cultural exploitation or pillaging of those groups which could not be acceptable or even tenable in the long run. Equally, society at large would have to guarantee and work to correct any discrimination or prejudice against these groups or the necessary 'interlearning' could not take place. Again, given broader legal and political safeguards, this task is one pre-eminently for the school.

Building on the portrayal of the development of ethnic revitalisation movements, documented by Glazer and Moynihan (1975), Banks has shown the way in which such movements, deriving from the Civil Rights Movement and commencing with blacks in the United States, later spread to other Western democratic nations with diverse ethnic populations. In these movements, excluded minority groups have pressed those societies for economic and social equality and thus for their inclusion in the structures of power and opportunity of those states (Banks, 1986a; Banton, 1983). Almost invariably, the cases advanced by minorities have used, as their means of leverage, reference to democratic values. The word *minority* does not necessarily merely denote the size of group. It relates also to the relationship of a group to society's institutions, and its experience of domination, victimisation, discrimination and negative stereotyping, as well as its relationship to economic and political power in the nation.

For real cultural pluralism to exist, Pratte (1979) has suggested, not only is the presence of different cultural groups necessary, a condition which is manifestly fulfilled in the United Kingdom, but there must also be some approximation to equality of political, economic and educational opportunity among groups. An overall commitment to the values and social behaviour of cultural pluralism is also vital. These latter criteria clearly imply that all groups, including majorities, are so committed. Such criteria are equally manifestly unfulfilled in the contemporary United Kingdom. We shall return to this point presently.

It will thus be apparent that while the United Kingdom is a culturally pluralist society in form, it is not yet fully expressive of the philosophy of cultural pluralism in its social structure, procedures and values. There is, thus, a cultural and social dissonance in British society between the diversity of its cultures and the extent to which they are reflected in its institutions, social system and its core cultural values.

MULTICULTURAL EDUCATION

I have already referred to the Intergroup Education Movement and the development of intercultural education in the United States from the mid 1930s, with the particular focus of interrelationship between individuals and groups and the attenuation of racial tension (Taba, Bradley and Robinson, 1952). This movement accelerated after the Second World War but was overtaken by the Civil Rights Movement and the development of ethnic studies, seen as a means of empowering minority students to achieve greater equality through appropriate curricular strategies. These, in turn, lost their exclusive focus on minority youth and began to address the needs of the majority, broadening their concern eventually to include issues of race, creed, sex and class. The movement became known in the United States by the label of 'multiethnic education' and in such countries as Australia, Canada and the United Kingdom as *multicultural education*. This is an umbrella term for a series of different educational strategies. The concept is seen differently by different educators and theorists (Lynch, 1983, 1986a). It is, however, generally regarded as focusing on the special needs of minority-group children, the need for a change in attitude and understanding in the majority and the needs of all pupils to feel creatively comfortable with cultural diversity as the norm.

Within that overall focus, it is usually considered as aiming, by democratic and educational means, at the following three goals:

1. education for a shared political and economic value system;

2.   education for cultural diversity;
3.   education for greater equality of educational opportunity.

It is within the context of this general philosophical approach that this book is written. Multicultural education is here envisaged as an inclusive master concept for the achievement of the three goals. I shall return to this in chapter 2.

A parallel movement to multicultural education, known as *intercultural education*, which originated in European societies, such as France, The Netherlands, West Germany and Switzerland, has also developed and been supported by interregional agencies such as the Council of Europe. In the countries where it has arisen however, this strategy has been predominantly interpreted as a means for the assimilation of immigrants into the dominant culture (Lynch, 1986b). In this it can be seen as an essentially assimilationist strategy which is incongruent with multicultural education and its aims.

In debate about appropriate responses to ethnic diversity and cultural pluralism Banks (1981) has probably made the strongest identification of the third major philosophical tradition, in addition to the assimilationist and cultural pluralist referred to above. He argues that multicultural theorists borrow from both assimilationists and pluralists, but seek to construct social and educational policies in which pupils maintain and develop their primary cultural attachments, while being educated for effective participation in the broader national arena. He envisages a process of *accommodation* or *acculturation* whereby both teachers and pupils maintain separate cultural identities, interacting with each other in creative harmony (Banks, 1986b). He recognises the interdependence of school and society by arguing that both must legitimate and respect the cultures of all concerned and share power before accommodation can take place in the school between teachers and learners.

He points out that all individuals have multiple group attachments and identifications. Beyond this a positive group identification with regional, religious, social class, ethnic and racial groups is seen as an indispensable prerequisite to national and global identities (Banks, 1981). In his writing, Banks has proposed six stages of ethnic and cultural development through which it is necessary for the learner to pass before he or she may be released from cultural captivity to what he calls 'reflective and positive ethnic, national and global identifications' which enable the individual to function in other cultures at home and abroad (Banks, 1981). This concept of cultural progression on the part of the individual from the micro to the macro is seminal to the later chapters of this book and we shall retrieve it in due course. Certainly, for positive intergroup relations to develop, pupils need to be weaned away from ethnic captivity to achieve the intercultural competence envisaged by Banks. The process inevitably involves replacing attitudes inimical to this goal with others supportive of it.

ANTI-RACIST EDUCATION

A number of radical writers have suggested that the school cannot achieve social change. They say, to some extent, strategies of multicultural education have either been misplaced or are an Establishment palliative. This latter, they argue, allows for the continued oppression of victimised groups in capitalist societies and more specifically the perpetuation of prejudice in such forms as racism, sexism and classism. A touchstone for much of the criticism of the importance of schools is to be found in the works of such American writers as Katz (1975), Bowles and Gintis (1976) and Apple (1982). In the United Kingdom, too, some radical scholars see capitalism as the major facilitator of continued inequality and structural racism (Tierney, 1984; Barton and Walker, 1983). But it is predominantly in the United Kingdom, with its more rigid system of social stratification, that a more coherent radical critique of multicultural education has been mounted. Early criticism by Mullard (1980) tended to expand the so-called lifestyles/life-chances dichotomy, which was also coherently argued by Bullivant as a necessary corrective to the early 'folkloric' multicultural education. Banks (1984) has summarised both the conservative and the radical critiques of multicultural education, indicating the need for multiculturalists to take the criticisms seriously, especially those of the radical left. He lists their major criticisms of multicultural education as being that it:

- is designed to make oppressed groups content with the status quo;
- does not promote an institutionalised analysis of the causes of that oppression;
- diverts attention from the real problems and issues;
- focuses on the victims and their characteristics as the problem;
- does not provide a serious analysis of the race and class systems.

(Banks, 1984).

More recently, Mullard has made a major contribution to the radical critique of multicultural education in a difficult pamphlet which was instrumental in the establishment of the National Anti-Racist Movement in Education (Mullard, 1984). In an extensive and detailed theoretical presentation, he typifies multicultural education as having a social focus on ethnic minority groups, a political context set by black migrant status and repatriation and of covertly encompassing and reproducing 'the structually qualified cultural relations of ethnicism to secure a plural cultural order' (Mullard, 1984, pp. 14–17). He calls for a new *orientation* of nearly all whites towards new definitions of reality and of problems (p.43), *observation*, including looking, listening and learning, brought together into an anti-racist oriented relationship (p.46), and *opposition* as the informing principle for anti-racist practice (p.46). These three principles, the three 'o's of orientation, observation and opposition are then applied to six educational situations, or levels, and an agenda of action is proposed. Banks has already drawn attention to the ambiguous nature of the radical critique of multicultural education when its proponents advocate strategies for school reform. He points out that if the school merely reflects the social structure it is futile to try to promote change within it (Banks, 1984, p.60).

Those strategies proposed by Mullard which have not already been incorporated into a more broadly conceived multicultural education appreciative of the limited power of any educational institution to achieve social change, relate to major structural and political changes in society. As such, as Banks points out, they relate to a sphere where teachers have forsaken their professional function and have adopted a political one. Nevertheless, the radical anti-racist critique has led to a number of positive developments in multicultural education, such as:

- increased analysis of the social context;
- renewed focus on the needs of all children;
- acceptance of the need for educational responses to structural and personal racism;
- recognition of the need for greater dialogue and potent participation of all cultural groups;
- new policies and delivery strategies to outlaw racism;
- increased focus on the role of the school in prejudice reduction;
- reform of curricula, assessment and organisation to eradicate racist policies and procedures.

In particular, multicultural educationists are concerned that, as Apter argued some years ago, open and competitive performance in a democracy may actually favour the advantaged and establish its own fixed hierarchy and that there is a direct correlation between 'low scores' and prejudice (Apter, 1977). This is not, however, a good argument for abolishing democracy.

None of the educational strategies proposed by anti-racist writers are *per se* incompatible with a more broadly concerned multicultural education. Most of them are, indeed, already on the agenda, except in the early, primitive, folkloric variety. But it is essential that not only the educational but also the broader social critique is taken seriously and scrutinised for its educational content and implications. In this way, the anti-racist critique can contribute to the development of a more effective multicultural education, not least because it has focused on the way in which discrimination, prejudice and their correlates inhibit and destroy that very intercommunication and interlearning which are so necessary to a pluralist society and to the negotiation of the common core values essential to its survival.

Pulling together the various strands of this chapter, I have sought to give a brief account of the precursor and contemporary responses to cultural diversity which have been formulated and implemented by Western democratic societies. These have ranged along a dimension that we might term *structural inclusion*, the extent to which policies aim at enabling all groups to participate in the educational, political and economic structures of the nation on equal terms. The policy options here represent a continuum from complete separation to complete assimilation. If we contrast that dimension with the sharpness and coherence of educational focus, — whether addressed to specific single issues on a specialised segmental basis or on a systemic basis to aggregative policies — (Janowitz, 1969), we have a two-dimensional typology across which educational policy options in response to cultural diversity may be identified. This typological representation is set out in figure 1.1, where the location of a number of educational strategies is suggested against these two dimensions. From the diagram, it can be seen that cultural pluralism draws on components from both separation and assimilation, as do multiculturalism and anti-racist education. Insofar as they accept the continued existence of democratic structures and values, the major distinction between the three is the specialisation of issues and, therefore, the coherence of policy across the education sector as a whole. Insofar as any strategy does not accept the continuation of democracy then it is in the realm of revolutionary political change and beyond the scope of education and teachers as teachers. It is thus beyond the scope of this book.

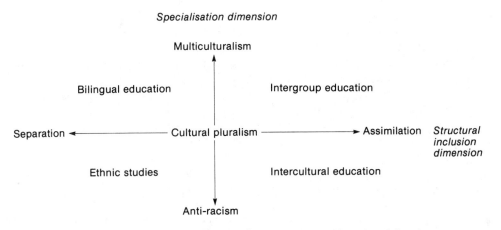

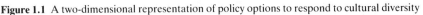

Figure 1.1 A two-dimensional representation of policy options to respond to cultural diversity

Prejudice reduction is a major and indispensable component of any coherent strategy of multicultural education because it is an educational concept, aimed at achieving that greater equality of educational opportunity, which can be frustrated and destroyed by prejudice and discrimination in education and the wider society. In the next chapter, I want to firmly locate prejudice reduction as a central concern of the pedagogy of multicultural education, that is its teaching/learning strategies, as well as broader educational policies and practices. I want to highlight its value as a key concept in combating all prejudice and to indicate a set of principles which may assist teachers in adapting their professional activities to achieve the goal of prejudice reduction.

SUMMARY

In this chapter, I have attempted to introduce the reader to some of the background literature on cultural pluralism. I have aimed identify the development of multicultural education; to contrast it with other proposed educational responses to cultural diversity in democratic societies and to argue the need for prejudice reduction as a central component of any multicultural education committed to democratic practice and the achievement of greater equality of educational opportunity.

ACTIVITIES

1. Read Glazer's article on cultural pluralism, quoted in this chapter. How far do you feel that his account could apply to the development in the United Kingdom? What do you see as being the main distinctions which have emerged between multicultural education in the United Kingdom and the United States?
2. After reading Bank's account of the critics of multicultural education, consider these against Mullard's paper. Do you feel that Banks has dealt adequately with

Mullard's educational proposals? Make a list of the arguments and responses and evaluate them for their relevance to your own institution.

3. Consider the typology towards the end of chapter 1. Against which other dimensions could educational responses to cultural pluralism be considered? Could congruence with democratic values be regarded as one such dimension? If so, what are in your view the common core values of a democratic society? Substantiate for your opinion.

REFERENCES

Apple, M.W. (1982) *Education and Power*. Boston: Routledge & Kegan Paul.

Apter, D.E. (1977) 'Political life and pluralism', in Tumin, M.M. and Plotch (eds.) *Pluralism in a Democratic Society*. New York: Praeger.

Banks, J.A. (1981) *Multiethnic Education: Theory and Practice*. Boston: Allyn & Bacon.

Banks, J.A. (1984) Multicultural education and its critics: Britain and the United States, *The New Era* **65**(3) 58–65.

Banks, J.A. (1986a) 'Race ethnicity and schooling in the United States: past present and future', in Banks, J.A. and Lynch, J. (eds.) *Multicultural Education in Western Societies*. London: Holt, Rinehart & Winston; New York: Praeger.

Banks, J.A. (1986b) 'Ethnic diversity, the social responsibility of educators and school reform', in Molnar, A. (ed.) *The Social Responsibility of Educators*. Alexandria, VA: Association for Supervision and Curriculum Development, (forthcoming).

Banks, J.A. (1986c) 'Multicultural education: development, paradigms and goals', in Banks, J.A. and Lynch, J. (1986), *op. cit.*

Banton, M. (1983) *Racial and Ethnic Competition*. Cambridge: Cambridge University Press.

Barton, L. and Walker, S. (eds.) (1983) *Race, Class and Education*. London: Croom Helm.

Bowles, S. and Gintis, H. (1976) *Schooling in Capitalist America: Educational Reform and the Contradictions of Economic Life*. New York: Basic Books.

Bullivant, B.M. (1984) *Pluralism, Cultural Maintenance and Education*. Clevedon, Avon: Multilingual Matters.

Glazer, N. (1977) 'Cultural pluralism: the social aspect', in Tumin, M.M. and Plotch, W. (eds.) *Pluralism in a Democratic Society*. New York: Praeger.

Glazer, N. and Moynihan, D. (eds.) (1975) *Ethnicity: Theory and Experience*. Cambridge MA: Harvard University Press.

Goodenough, W. (1976) Multiculturalism as the normal human experience, *Anthropology and Education Quarterly*, **7**, November, 4–7

Gollnick, D.M. and Chinn, P.C. (1986) *Multicultural Education in a Pluralist Society* 2nd edn. Columbus, OH: Charles E Merrill.

Gordon, M.M. (1964) *Assimilation in American Life: The Role of Race, Religion and National Origins*. New York: Oxford University Press.

Gordon, M.M. (1975) 'Towards a Theory of Ethnic Group Relations', in Glazer, N. and Moynihan, D. (eds.) *Ethnicity: Theory and Experience*. Cambridge MA: Harvard University Press.

Greenbaum, W. (1974) 'America in search of a new ideal: an essay on the rise of pluralism', *Harvard Educational Review*. **44**(3) 411–440.

Janowitz, M. (1969) 'Institution-building in urban education', in Street, D. *Innovation in Mass Education*. New York: Wiley.

Kallen, H. (1970) *Culture and Democracy in the United States*. New York: Arno Press (Reprint of 1924 edition).

Katz, M.B.(1975) *Bureaucracy and Schools: The Illusion of Educational Change in America*. New York: Praeger.

Lynch, J. (1983) *The Multicultural Curriculum*. London: Batsford.

Lynch, J. (1986a) *Multicultural Education: Principles and Practice*. London: Routledge & Kegan Paul.

Lynch, J. (1986b) 'Multicultural education in Western Europe', in Banks, J.A. and Lynch, J. (eds.), *Multicultural Education in Western Societies*. London: Holt Rinehart & Winston; New York: Praeger.

Mullard, C. (1980) *Racism in Society and Schools: History, Policy and Practice*. London: University of London, Institute of Education (Occasional Paper).

Mullard, C. (1984) *Anti-Racist Education: The Three 'O's*. Cardiff: National Association for Multiracial Education.

Myrdal, G. (1944) *An American Dilemma: The Negro Problem and Modern Democracy*. New York: Harper & Row (Twentieth Anniversary Edition 1962).

Pratte, R. (1979) *Pluralism in Education: Conflict, Clarity and Commitment*. Springfield, IL: Charles C Thomas.

Taba, H., Bradley, E.H. and Robinson, J.T. (1952) *Intergroup Education in Public Schools*. Washington, DC: American Council on Education.

Tierney, J. (ed.) (1984) *Race, Migration and Schooling*. London: Holt Rinehart & Winston.

SELECT BIBLIOGRAPHY: CULTURAL PLURALISM AND MULTICULTURAL EDUCATION

Appleton, N. (1983) *Cultural Pluralism in Education: Theoretical Foundations*. New York: Longman. This book includes a thoughtful theoretical analysis of the concept of cultural pluralism and its implications for schooling.

Baker, G.C. (1983) *Planning and Organizing for Multicultural Instruction*. Reading, MA: Addison-Wesley. This introductory book is designed to introduce educators to multicultural education. Topics include planning and organising for instruction.

Banks, J.A. (1981) *Multiethnic Education: Theory and Practice*. Boston: Allyn & Bacon. This book discusses the historical, conceptual and philosophical issues in multiethnic and multicultural education. It also includes a chapter on teaching strategies for multiethnic education and guidelines for formulating educational programmes that reflect ethnic diversity. It is a standard text in the field.

Banks J.A. (1984) *Teaching Strategies for Ethnic Studies 3rd edn*. Boston: Allyn & Bacon. Teaching strategies, with grade levels designated, and bibliographies for teachers and students are key features of this book. An historical overview and a chronology of key events for all major ethnic groups in the United States are also included.

Banks, J.A. (1985) *Teaching Strategies for the Social Studies 3rd edn* New York: Longman. This detailed and helpful book addresses the case that the major goal of social studies education is to develop the capacity to make reflective decisions. It includes important material on value analysis and clarification.

Banks, J.A. and Lynch, J. (eds.) (1986) *Multicultural Education in Western Societies*. London: Holt Saunders. This book contains original contributions from acknowledged experts writing about their own country and/or region. It includes a conceptualisation of ethnic revitalisation movements, a chapter each on the United States, Canada, the United Kingdom, Australia and Europe and two synthesising chapters, respectively on teacher education and an agenda for change.

Banton, M.P. (1983) *Racial and Ethnic Competition*. Cambridge: Cambridge University Press. This is a well-reasoned and researched book. It presents thoughtful theoretical perspectives on race relations and examples from several nations, including the United States, the United Kingdom and South Africa.

Banton, M.P. (1985) *Promoting Racial Harmony*. Cambridge: Cambridge University Press. This book is a seminal contribution to the field based on research and theoretical work and it continues the tradition set by his previous book.

Barton, L. and Walker, S. (eds.) (1983) *Race, Class and Education*. London: Croom Helm. Radical perspectives on issues related to race, class and education with particular respect to the United Kingdom are presented in this book.

Bullivant, B.M. (1981) *The Pluralist Dilemma in Education: Six Case Studies*. Sydney: George Allen & Unwin. This book includes case studies of multicultural education in Britain, Canada, Fiji, the United States mainland, Hawaii, and Australia. The author also presents a theory regarding the 'pluralist dilemma', faced by all culturally diverse democratic nations.

Cashmore, E.E. and Troyna, B. (1983) *Introduction to Race Relations*. London: Routledge and Kegan Paul. Educators may find several chapters in this book of particular interest, including those on education, ethnicity, youth resistance, and media-racism-reality.

Centre for Contemporary Cultural Studies (1982) *The Empire Strikes Back: Race and Racism in 70s Britain*. London: Hutchinson. Many issues related to race, gender, and social class are examined in this provocative and sometimes stimulating collection of papers.

Clark, R.M. (1983) *Family Life and School Achievement: Why Poor Black Children Succeed or Fail*. Chicago: University of Chicago Press. In this case study of ten families, the author describes family characteristics that facilitate the academic achievement of black students. It is a refreshing alternative approach to the normal deficit theme.

Craft, M. (ed.) (1981) *Teaching in the Multicultural Society: The Task for Teacher Education*. London: The Falmer Press. This book arises from a national conference, held at the University of Nottingham in 1980. Various views on ways to incorporate multicultural dimensions into teacher education are discussed in the papers which comprise the book.

Craft, M. (ed.) (1984) *Education and Cultural Pluralism*. London: The Falmer Press. The essays in this book discuss a range of issues related to multicultural education in the United Kingdom, including languages, home, school and community, assessment and curriculum and ideologies.

Garcia, R.L. (1982) *Teaching in a Pluralist Society: Concepts, Models, Strategies*. New York: Harper & Row. This introductory book on ethnic diversity and American education discusses a range of topics, including schools and their communities, and various models and strategies related to teaching for cultural diversity.

Glazer, N. and Moynihan, D.P. (eds.) (1975) *Ethnicity: Theory and Experience*. Cambridge, MA: Harvard University Press. An outstanding and seminal collection of essays which focus on ethnicity in the United States and in other nations. Martin Kilson, Milton Gordon, Talcott Parsons, and Andrew Greeley are among the contributors.

Gollnick, D.M. and China, P.C. (1986) *Multicultural Education in a Pluralist Society*. Columbus, OH: Charles E. Merrill. Multicultural education is conceptualised broadly in this book, which discusses ethnicity, religion, language diversity, socioeconomic status, sex and gender, age, handicap and giftedness.

Gordon, M.M. (1964) *Assimilation in American Life*. New York: Oxford University Press. This major and seminal book has had an impact upon teaching, research and writing about ethnic groups in the United States. The nature of assimilation and various theories of assimilation and cultural pluralism are perceptively examined by the author. It is a classic and indispensible work.

Husen, T. and Opper, S. (eds.) (1983) *Multicultural and Multilingual Education in Immigrant Countries*. Oxford: Pergamon Press. This book is made up of proceedings of an international symposium held at the Wenner-Gren Centre, Stockholm in 1982. It includes a discussion of the social and psychological aspects of multicultural education.

Longstreet, W. (1978) *Aspects of Ethnicity: Understanding Differences in Pluralistic Classrooms*. New York: Teachers College Press. The author presents an interesting definition of ethnicity and describes a process that teachers can use to study ethnic behaviour in their own classrooms.

Lynch, J. (ed.) (1981) *Teaching in the Multi-cultural School*. London: Ward Lock Educational Books. The chapters in this book are grouped into four sections: theoretical perspectives, curriculum, religious and ethnic background and resources.

Lynch J. (1983) *The Multicultural Curriculum*. London: Batsford Academic and Educational Ltd. This book includes chapters on the teacher and multicultural education, a framework for a multicultural curriculum, the community and multicultural school, as well as sources and guidelines for implementing a multicultural curriculum.

Lynch, J. (1986) *Multicultural Education: Principles and Practice*. London: Routledge and Kegan Paul. This book gives a comprehensive introduction to the field of multicultural and anti-racist education, including extensive reference to international research and writing in the field.

Martin, J.I. (1978) *The Migrant Presence*. Sydney: George Allen & Unwin. This book is an informative and important work on immigrant groups in Australia, written by a perceptive sociologist and one of the foremost authors in Australia to have worked in the field of immigration.

Majoribanks, K. (1980) *Ethnic Families and Children's Achievements*. Sydney: George Allen & Unwin. This is an important study of the relationship between ethclass and academic achievement conducted with a sample of families in Australia.

Ogbu, J.U. (1978) *Minority Education and Caste: The American System in Cross-Cultural Perspective*. New York: Academic Press. In this book, a social anthropologist presents a theory which suggests that a major goal of education in the United States is to prepare minority groups for their caste-like status in society. Comparisons are made with the education of ethnic groups in the United Kingdom, New Zealand, India and Japan.

Philips, S.U. (1983) *The Invisible Culture: Communication in Classroom and Community on the Warm Springs Indian Reservation*. New York: Longman. The author of this study describes patterns of verbal and non-verbal communication among Anglo and Indian children. She describes the conflicts that Indian children experience when they function in their home cultures and in the school.

Ramirez, M. and Castaneda, A. (1974) *Cultural Democracy Bicognitive Development, and Education*. New York: Academic Press. This important book describes ways in which the learning styles of Mexican-American students differ from the learning styles favoured by the schools. The authors suggest the need to improve the match of teaching with students' learning styles.

Samuda, R.J., Berry, J.W. and Laferrière, M. (eds.) (1984) *Multiculturalism in Canada: Social and Educational Perspectives*. Toronto: Allyn & Bacon. A comprehensive collection of papers discussing diverse issues related to multicultural education in Canada are included in this volume.

Samuda, R.J. (1975) *Psychological Testing of American Minorities: Issues and Consequences*. New York: Dodd, Mead. Important psychological and sociological issues related to the testing of ethnic minority groups are discussed in this book.

Thernstrom, S., Orlov, A. and Handlin, O. (ed.) (1980) *Harvard Encyclopedia of American Ethnic Groups*. Cambridge MA: Harvard University Press. This is the most ambitious and comprehensive single volume on the diverse ethnic groups in the United States. It includes a number of thematic essays related to the education of ethnic groups.

Van Den Berg-Eldering, L. and DeRijcke, F.J.M. (eds.) (1983) *Multicultural Education: A Challenge for Teachers*. Dordrecht, The Netherlands: Foris Publications. A group of Dutch and United States' educators and social scientists describe a range of theoretical and political issues in this book which resulted from a conference sponsored by the Dutch government on the occasion of the United States–Dutch Bicentennial in 1982.

Verma, G.K. and Bagley, C. (eds.) (1979) *Race, Education, and Identity*. London: The Macmillan Press. This book contains an informative collection of empirical studies which educators may find useful in their work.

Watson, J.L. (ed.) (1977) *Between Two Cultures: Migrants and Minorities in Britain*. Oxford: Basil Blackwell. This book consists of well-crafted essays on the various ethnic, cultural, and religious groups in Britain.

Weinberg, M. (1977) A Chance To Learn: *A History of Race and Education in the United States*. Cambridge: Cambridge University Press. This well-researched history of the education of ethnic groups in the United States focuses on school desegregation efforts and deals with the education of blacks, Mexican-Americans, American Indians, and Puerto Ricans on the United States mainland.

Wolfgang, A. (ed.) (1975) *Education of Immigrant Students: Issues and Answers*. Toronto: The Ontario Institute for Studies in Education. The papers comprising this book discuss a range of issues, including philosophical and historical perspectives, practical experimental programmes in action, and the results of research.

Wood, D. (1978) *Multicultural Canada: A Teacher's Guide to Ethnic Studies*. Toronto: The Ontario Institute for Studies in Education. In this book, the author describes concepts, teaching methods and materials which teachers may find helpful in permeating their curricula with ethnic content.

Chapter 2

Multicultural Education and Teaching for Prejudice Reduction

INTRODUCTION

In chapter 1, I have outlined the development of multicultural education, setting it firmly within the context of democratic cultural pluralism. I have argued that prejudice reduction must be a central concern of any undertaking to multicultural education which is committed to respect for persons. In this chapter, I want to develop that argument further. I will show, briefly, how multicultural education as an overall managing concept for education within culturally diverse societies fits into generally agreed educational aims. Further, I wish to illustrate how prejudice reduction has to be a central element in any realistic and effective multicultural education. Then I want to identify the relationship between the generic concept of prejudice and discrimination and its specific forms indicating the importance of social climate at various levels. Part of the tendency to prejudice in culturally pluralist societies is seen, in this chapter, as relating to social class and status factors and a classic vicious circle of low status, deprivation and prejudice is identified. The relationship between self-concept and prejudiced attitudes is explored and the role of intercultural contact is highlighted in the process of enabling both individuals and groups to climb out of ethnic captivity. From these considerations an overall set of guiding principles is derived against which teachers may attempt the pedagogies of prejudice reduction in the central parts of the book.

MULTICULTURAL EDUCATION AND THE AIMS OF EDUCATION

In an earlier study (Lynch, 1983), I have argued that a multicultural curriculum derives its aims from the ethical and social imperatives of a democratic, culturally diverse society. By 'ethical imperative' I mean the need to respond to and be guided by the aim of 'respect for persons'; as to the social imperatives, I argue that, because a society espouses democratic values, is characterised by scientific/industrial modes of thought and organisation and offers a broad measure of individual and group freedom, so its curriculum must respond to those dimensions in its aims, processes, content and evaluation. Thus, the specific objectives, curriculum content, teaching/ learning processes and review strategies of a multicultural curriculum may respond in a more co-ordinated way to individual and social needs, including both the 'economic' and 'pluralist'. So I want now to offer a series of fundamental suggestions about the overall aims of the curriculum, as derived from recent official and semi-official publications, and to locate both multicultural education and prejudice reduction within these aims.

A set of broad aims for educational institutions based on recent national and local publications might include six major areas. We might, for example, ask the following questions — does the school assist learners to:

1. develop qualities of imagination, human feeling, inquisitiveness, judgemental and communicative rationality and application (to both tasks and skills)?
2. acquire skills, practical abilities and knowledge appropriate to a culturally pluralist society, employment and recreation?
3. achieve literacy (oral and written), numeracy and sociacy, including intercultural competence?
4. acquire agreed moral bases (values) for behaviour, appropriate to a culturally pluralist society, including an active commitment to legitimate diversity, its creative development and the combating of prejudice and discrimination?
5. develop a critical appreciation of themselves, their community, society and international interdependence, including the social, political and economic orders inherent in these?
6. value the worthy achievements of all individuals and human groups and to seek to contribute to them?

(See, for example, DES, Welsh Office, 1980, 1981; HMI, 1980, 1985; Secretary of State for Education and Science, 1977, 1985; Schools Council, 1981, 1983; ILEA, 1984.)

These very general aims can, of course, be no more than guiding principles for the implementation of opportunities for learning, both formal and informal, that we call a curriculum. Moreover, they are not tidy and separate, but overlap and interact among themselves and with the content of the curriculum. Nevertheless, such broad aims are important, for they provide the declared and agreed parameters within which educational provision and institutions can remain open to rational change, in response to often conflicting demands and pressures from a host of different interest groups. They afford, in other words, a rational means for the reconciliation and processing of a wide range of demands from different interest groups by means of equal discourse and against common criteria which should be widely available. They are a means of deeming certain learning essential for all learners within a culturally diverse society which strives to be open and democratic and to actively combat prejudice and discrimination as part of its 'master aim' for education.

They are not, of course, changeless, and they need to be referenced to a society like the United Kingdom which espouses democratic values, such as the rule of law, basic human rights and participation in social and civic life, although, of course, it does not always succeed in operating them. In other words, a democratic society seeks to promote values such as:

- freedom of communication and association between individuals and groups;
- responsible participation;
- engagement for human rights;
- social justice, e.g., equality of access to education and employment;
- equality before the law;
- a sense of unity and a shared heritage;
- personal and social enterprise and achievement;
- rights to ownership of private property;
- a sense of personal, group and national identity;
- international responsibility;
- economic inclusion;
- mutuality in relationships of individuals and groups.

I have been careful to stress that a democratic society seeks to nurture such values, for I do not wish to imply that it is always successful. Quite the reverse, and, as I indicated earlier, it is in the discrepancy between declared and operative values that the creative fulcrum for social and cultural change is to be found. But it is within the context of these overall aims and supporting values that multicultural education, centrally committed to prejudice reduction and eradication, has to be seen.

It will be recalled that, in chapter 1, three major interactive goals for multicultural education were introduced:

- the creative enhancement, not merely maintenance, of cultural diversity;
- the achievement of greater equality of educational opportunity for all, regardless of sex, race, creed, ethnic background or class;
- the propagation of a sense of shared values, rights and access to political power and economic satisfaction.

One of the major problems in making schooling more responsive to such overall aims is that traditional definitions of the curriculum have rested upon a subject epistemology belonging to pre-industrial societies where education served only a small élite and was shaped to the perpetuation of their values and the exclusion of alternatives. Such a curriculum is clearly unsuited for a society which espouses the values of a culturally diverse, technologically advanced, democracy. Thus, attempts have gradually been made to rethink educational provision in general and the curriculum in particular. The end in mind is not a series of subjects, but teaching/learning processes and situations aimed at particular purposes and guided by particular values towards the achievement of specific selected skills, attitudes and knowledge, taking into account the cultural biography of the learner (e.g. cognitive style, motivational approach, linguistic background, role perceptions, etc.). In short the concept is the socialisation and enculturation process referred to in chapter 1. Now that sounds rather a complex task so let us look again at what that means in terms of teachers' action.

Selection of content — and selection is functionally essential, because not everything from all cultures can be included in school learning — implies a set of principles on the basis of which selection may take place. The decision is, in effect, which learnings are essential to achieve the aims listed above, and what are the criteria for decision. One suggestion for such a process was made by the Curriculum Development Centre in Canberra some years ago. The Centre suggested that a core curriculum for all pupils should:

- focus on the common culture;
- acknowledge the pluralist nature of society;
- include common learning;
- highlight the relevant contemporary aspects of education;
- specify the minimum essential learnings for all;
- define the structure of learning;
- provide common and differentiated learning opportunities;
- indicate the common applied learning tasks.

(Australian Curriculum Development Centre, 1980, p. 15)

Walkling (1980) raises basic ethical issues concerning the principles for the selection of content which will enable fair judgements to be made about what should be included within the multicultural curriculum, what kinds of procedures might be involved and what kinds of purposes such a curriculum might address. Drawing up a series of continua between tolerance and selection in the case of content, between relativism and absolutism in the case of procedures, and between transmission or transformation in the case of purposes, he sets out a typology which clarifies the complexity of decision-making in this area. Using these terms, prejudice reduction strategies are likely to be selective, relativist and transformational.

In Scotland, the Munn Report looked at this issue slightly differently by suggesting four domains concerned with:

- pupil's knowledge of themselves and their social and physical environment;
- the development of cognitive and interpersonal skills;
- the cultivation of appropriate emotional and moral attitudes;
- the nurturing of social competence.

(Scottish Education Department, Consultative Committee on the Curriculum, 1977, pp. 21–23)

and it proposed eight modes of activity, which, if pursued in accordance with the four domains, would constitute essential areas of learning for all pupils.

More recently, the English Inspectorate has proposed what is described as 'one' perspective on the learning and experience which, it is considered, contributes to a rounded education. The well-known and widely-used components are:

- aesthetic and creative;
- human and social (including political and economic);
- linguistic and literary;
- mathematical;
- moral;
- physical;
- scientific and the technological;
- spiritual.

(Her Majesty's Inspectorate, 1985, pp. 16ff)

It will be apparent that each one of these defined areas of learning and experience will have a unique contribution to make to broadly pluralist aims and more narrowly to prejudice reduction. Each will contribute to the skills, attitudes and knowledge of the essential curriculum which is susceptible to acquisition through different learning processes such as:

- listening, speaking, reading and writing;
- observing, analysing, interpreting and judging;
- discriminating, classifying and concluding;
- formulating questions, posing hypotheses, testing them and solving problems;
- imagining, creating and expressing;
- designing, making and testing;
- measuring, estimating and formulating;
- developing physical skills;
- nurturing acceptable personal and social attitudes and values.
- developing social skills such as co-operating, empathising and competing fairly.

(List based on HMI, 1985, pp. 39–40)

But such 'modes of activity' or 'learning processes' cannot be implemented in isolation. They are, rather, embedded in a particular context, school, college, etc., taking into account what we know about human learning and in particular responsive to — one might say interactive with — the needs and characteristics of the learners. In other words, curricular and student facts have to be matched. But what are those facts, how can they be detected and what can the teacher do about them?

In a recent study (Lynch, 1986), I have emphasised that there is more to a multicultural education than culturally diverse content, even though that content may draw on a detailed and up-to-date knowledge of the cultural context of the school. Teachers, it seems to me, need to consider very carefully the teaching/learning strategies which they adopt and their policies for reward and reinforcement both against that cultural context and as a support for the equal educational opportunity of all children. Thus, there are needs in addition to the curricular facts about multicultural content, resources, media and learning environments. There has to be a process of pedagogical matching with functional characteristics of pupils, including their learning background, their cognitive modes, their interpretive competence, their motivation, the values and attitudes of the cultural background from which they come. Moreover, insofar as is possible, there should be some understanding of what might be considered to be appropriate reward and reinforcement strategies. In particular, teachers need to be alert to inappropriate and prejudiced attitudes and behaviour which may be brought to their school experience by children — and teachers.

This is a tall order for teachers. The problem is to avoid the 'I'm treating them all the same' syndrome and to take into account the relevant functional characteristics, without generating the basis for new stereotypes and thus new prejudices as a source of future discrimination. Clearly, there are other factors in addition to ability which control, and sometimes determine, learning and attainment and good teachers are aware of these. By their early and continuing socialisation and enculturation many children are ill-adapted to the structure and general ethos propagated by a school committed to multicultural education. Teachers can help pupils to overcome these disadvantages by trying to pull together the curricular facts when formulating their instructional strategies and attempting to match the two, varying the pedagogical approaches which they adopt, so as to include a multiplicity of different approaches and methods.

Among these different approaches may be the variable use of different stimuli including oral and visual, verbal and non-verbal. A broad selection might be made of cultural artefacts, exemplars and content. A variety of learning experiences might be introduced including peer-group tutoring, collaborative and co-operative group learning along with graduated approaches to skill requirements based on a diagnostic and reflective progression by the child which emphasises and rewards success across a spectrum of different concepts of reward. The important function of such a matching process is to achieve not only success orientation for all, but equality of educational opportunity for all, within the firm parameters of a school ethos which espouses democratic, cultural pluralism in its values and actions. Variety, the old saying goes, is the spice of life. Thus, a multicultural curriculum which takes into account the cultural biography of the school and the pupils and aims for prejudice reduction needs to include:

- a diversity of content, materials and stimuli;
- the goal of an increased sense of involvement of pupils in the school culture;
- strategies aimed at supporting the self and ethnic image of the child;
- an acquaintance with the cultural experiences, values, beliefs and expectations of differing groups;
- the generation of a culturally receptive classroom and school atmosphere;
- the celebration of diversity in indirect as well as direct teaching, e.g. display, etc.;
- pedagogical strategies designed to boost pupils' locus of control;
- provision for a variety of achievements in different modes;
- the adoption of a wide range of stimuli: oral, verbal and visual;
- the inclusion of peer-group learning and co-operative group work;
- the use of multiple instructional methods, including experiential modes;
- the adoption of an iterative matching strategy for lesson planning and im- plementing and evaluating learning strategies;
- the identification of and with pupils' legitimate values and attitudes at the same time as teaching to correct for prejudice;

- the institution of continual discourse with parents and community;
- community-open appraisal and pupil assessment procedures.

It goes without saying, of course, that there can be no process of matching curricular and student facts without a healthy dialogue with the parents and the surrounding community. The development of multicultural education has to be seen as a holistic process in which all of the pieces of the jigsaw must be related to one another before an effective curriculum can be designed.

But are the teaching/learning strategies which have been briefly referred to as part of those 'iterative processes' beyond the scope of most teachers currently teaching in classrooms? This question leads naturally to evaluation for, it seems to me, self and collegial evaluation are indispensable to an effective iterative process for teaching/ learning strategy development and for the development of appropriate assessment, addressing both pluralist and prejudice reduction dimensions. For, as staff development is essential to the launching of multicultural education, so testing, examinations and assessment are symbiotic with the consideration of the multicultural curriculum, its aims, content and pedagogy.

To some extent, we need to come full circle, for we can only evaluate a multicultural curriculum to prepare for healthy cultural pluralism against such criteria as the social purposes, aims and societal values which were deployed earlier. Since the curriculum represents essential learning for all pupils, its success or failure cannot be judged against partial or sectoral special pleadings It cannot be the handmaid of industry, still less the slave of minority revolutionary aspirations. Ultimately, its success must be judged against the goals of multicultural education itself: social cohesion; cultural diversity and equality of educational opportunity.

PREJUDICE REDUCTION AND MULTICULTURAL EDUCATION

But now I want to focus more closely on issues concerned with prejudice reduction. Here it must be clear that early attempts at multicultural education did aim at the wrong target in this respect. For it is a truism that, for as long as the policies and strategies to eradicate racism in British society address black Britons, they are unlikely to alter or improve the racist attitudes of the majority of the population. At the very least, the Swann Report has placed that recognition on the agenda (Committee of Inquiry, 1985). The corollary of such recognition is that unless racism is accepted as a major explicator of the problems of victimised visible minorities, progress in adopting coherent and effective approaches to prejudice reduction in education and the broader society is likely to prove elusive.

Firstly, however, what do we mean by prejudice? In its literal sense, prejudice is the holding of a belief or opinion without adequate rational grounds or in the face of rational evidence to the contrary of that belief or opinion. Such prejudice may focus on persons or things. It may be for or against them. Thus, prejudice is not a priori a directly hostile or negative opinion — we may be prejudiced for as well as against. Moreover, we all have prejudices. The question thus arises of what kinds of prejudices have to be combated and when.

As teachers, we expect pupils in schools to make discriminations. These range from placing objects into sets, thus categorising them, to differentiating between discriminable stimuli and alternative good and bad behaviours. Children are not expected to categorise as identical phenomena for which there are rational grounds for discrimination. Thus, the task of educators and schools is to enable children to achieve the rational bases, information, techniques, views, attitudes and strategies which will enable them to categorise on the basis of rational evidence, while avoiding stereotypical representations, prejudiced opinions and discrimination, particularly — as far as this book is concerned — in the areas of race, social class, sex, creed and ethnicity. In other words, we expect children to be able to make some discriminations, while avoiding others. But which are which and how do we rationally judge between them?

Put briefly, it is those prejudices which offend against the moral basis of society and are likely to be inimical to its ethic and thus destroy it as a society if translated into overt attitudes and behaviour, which need to be countered. That need for corrective action is reinforced when a preconceived and stereotypical representation of a particular group or individual may cause us to act in what would be called a discriminatory manner towards that party.

There are, however, two problems with that formulation: firstly, far from combating stereotypes and prejudices, education in collusion with other agencies, such as the media, currently propagates and reinforces them. Indeed, social class and religious categorisation is fundamental to our very society in its organisation, its political structure and its education system. Secondly, no less in our present era of instrumental regulation than in past times of theological control of human behaviour, it is by no means impossible, even if difficult, to reach agreement on the basic ethics of a multicultural society. We would then be able to decide which prejudices to counter and why. Can education for national pride, or religious education, for example, be a source of prejudice against other ethnic groups?

Some theorists argue that it is only with fundamental changes in the broader society, its political structure and educational provision, that improvement is likely to be achieved in overcoming those prejudices which are self destructive and inimical to moral bases. And it is probably true that education can only *solve* educational problems. But it can contribute to the resolution of broader social problems, and has traditionally done so. So, the individual teacher and school do have an important role to play, and they daily have to make moral decisions which affect children's life chances. I have argued elsewhere two major ways in which the basis may be arrived at for moral behaviour in a multicultural society (Lynch, 1983, 1986). There are, no doubt, other ways. The crux is that the decision about what prejudice to tackle in schools is a moral one, insofar as it derives from what is considered to be good and bad, acceptable and unacceptable, positive and negative within a multicultural society.

One final point before I move on to the kinds of strategies which may encourage rational, non-prejudiced opinions and beliefs and may help to achieve attitudes and behaviour which do not negatively discriminate on the bases of race, sex, ethnic origins and creed. What a multicultural society is ultimately concerned with is 'good', acceptable behaviour — and it is the task of education to provide for the making of individual and group judgements to support that. To achieve that goal, education has to tackle the covert motivators of discriminatory behaviour by concentrating on what is rationally justifiable, acceptable behaviour within our society. Here, there are contrary views. Some argue that, if the behaviour is changed, the beliefs will also change. Others assert that the values and attitudes have to be changed so that behaviour will follow. To my mind, teaching for both goals is also tenable. But how? This is the theme of succeeding chapters: the pedagogical work which has attempted to address the task of prejudice reduction and the guiding principles which it may offer for the professional practice of teachers.

PREJUDICE AND ITS CORRELATES

But let us return, for the moment, to what prejudice is and how it relates generically to such specific forms as racism, sexism, classism and credism. It is important to make clear, here, that there are still very many unanswered questions in this field and any conceivable answer will be provisional and tentative. One thing is, however, certain, and that is that it is not mere perception of difference which constitutes prejudice, but the way in which those differences are explained, marshalled and utilised (Glock et al., 1975). This certainly seems to give the lie to those who say that discussion of difference in school accentuates prejudice and that teachers should, therefore, treat all children as the same i.e. as if there were no difference. There is a need, therefore, for teachers to make a forthright acknowledgement of difference and to include it within their teaching/learning strategies.

Having said that, however, teachers will need to regard such difference as part of the overall factual and conceptual development of the child, including both cognitive and affective domains. Learning will need to include how group differences come about and the size of those group differences, and the important distinction between relative and absolute differences will have to be made clear. Such processes will need to be seen as part of the overall biography of the child and its continuing conceptual development. For example, the tendency to overcategorise, i.e., assume that all persons in a given classificatory group are the same and manifest the same values and behaviours (Allport, 1979), will need to be countered by teachers as a normal part of their discriminatory skill development. Kohlberg adopts a similar argument when he states that prejudice in young children is primarily the active interpretation of physical and other crude differences between race and groups to which the child has inevitably been exposed and includes basic characteristics of the young child's thinking about social roles and groups (Kohlberg, 1974). He sees correction for such attitudes as necessarily a part of the moral and civic education of the child designed to achieve a higher stage of moral development, and of course cognitive sophistication.

This tendency to *overcategorise* is learned early by children and it highlights the need to adopt corrective strategies consistent with the age and development of the children from their first entry into formal schooling and as part of their overall conceptual sophistication (Clark, 1955). But I shall return to this theme in the next chapter. Overcategorisation leads, on the part of both children and adults, to a phenomenon which is at the base of prejudice, and which we call stereotyping. I have offered elsewhere a privisional formulation of stereotyping as: 'the classification of individuals and the attribution of characteritics to those individuals or to groups on the basis of prejudiced, irrational and non-factual conceptions and information.'

Stereotyping may provide the raw material for prejudiced attitudes and discriminatory behaviour and it may take many forms, both conscious and unconscious. The attribution of laziness or untrustworthiness to all members of a racial or ethnic group or the attribution of qualities of leadership or business acumen only to males are obvious examples. More subtly, however, so is the generalisation that certain racial or ethnic groups — or other nations — are poor because they deserve to be. A common 'stereotypical error' is to fail to take into account the oppression, violence and victimisation which visible minorities have to endure in explaining any 'underachievement' in both economic and educational spheres.

Prejudice, or its correlates, racism, sexism, credism and classism, is the subjective belief in the superiority of one's own grouping (or gender) over other people's. I have offered elsewhere a definition of prejudice as: 'a set of inflexible, institutional, personal and societal attitudes, values, behaviours and procedures which create or perpetuate privilege for one group of individuals and deprivation for another based on a cultural definition of groups and their members' (Lynch, 1986).

Discrimination occurs when these passive behaviours are translated into the active mode so that individuals are denied legitimate opportunity, reward or resource on the basis of another person's prejudiced attitudes. Such discrimination may be exercised verbally or non-verbally, personally or institutionally, consciously or unconsciously, intentionally or unintentionally, through decision or indecision, as much by expression as by silence. It may be reinforced by the use of particular vocabulary or conceptual structures, such as the semantic classification of race and the negative or positive loading of such words as 'black' and 'white' (Williams and Morland, 1976). It may be overt or covert and expressed as much through structure as through policy or practice. The aim is to place or maintain the 'oppressed' individual or group in a position or status of inferiority by means of subordinating categorisations such as ethnicity, skin colour, gender, creed and social class, so that negative outcomes arise. Such discrimination is a contradiction of a democratic society; it usurps basic human rights, undermines the culture of minorities, militates against the achievement of the goals of multicultural education by denying or attempting to deny, equality of opportunity or status to certain religious, racial, ethnic or social groups and it represents a human capital and potential economic loss. The important thing to note here is that the majority and its members exercise power, in this respect, over the minority in a relationship of dominance and submission and the majority, therefore, has a special responsibility for the abolition of such irrational values and behaviour.

So, looked at more broadly, prejudice is a social problem because it undermines social relations and democratic social order as well as wasting scarce resources. But it is a two-way influence. As prejudiced attitudes breed discrimination by individuals, groups and systems, so those very systems breed prejudice. As an early study on prejudice put it, 'they learn what they live' (Trager and Yarrow, 1952). So the social class structure itself mediates many prjudices, and it is likely that a component, perhaps even a major component, of such specific prejudice as racism or credism is related to the social class structure and roles and statuses, inherent within it. Information concerning these is 'imbibed' by children as part of their early enculturation and socialisation. What is certain is that racial prejudice can be aggravated by the social factor (Glock et al., 1975; Clore et al., 1978), and that racial prejudice can be confounded with class prejudice (Blalock, 1967). Thus, those already victimised economically are further oppressed by a prejudice which makes it unlikely that they will be able to overcome that economic disadvantage which could make them less victimised.

But there are other factors also involved in prejudice: the self-concept of the discriminator is one example, and here it is apparent that the healthier the self-concept of the individual, the less likely that person is to discriminate or be prejudiced against others. So it is not, as suggested in earlier writings, solely a matter of improving the self-concept of minority students, although that is an important educational goal. It is, however, interdependent with the goal of improving the self-concept of majority pupils so that they are not prejudiced, for that, in turn, has an effect on minority pupils and their achievements (Rubin, 1967). It is clear also that not all visible minorities face the same extent or kind of prejudice, nor does it have the same impact on all.

In a sensitive piece of writing, for example, Frideres (1975) reports the results of his research as indicating a ranking of ethnic groups by prejudice, a finding which is confirmed by a recent national survey in Britain (Williams, 1986). Frideres also found that other factors beyond 'racial' attributes account for the basis of prejudice and that the impact of these factors varied among minority groups. Religion, language and attitudes towards cultural maintenance were also seen to be factors comprising prejudice. Thus, social and microcultural as well as social status and broader macrocultural structures are 'mediators' of prejudice as these also need to be taken account of by teachers in their work (Ijaz, 1981). This is not of course to recommend a policy of 'blaming the victim', but rather to evoke insights into the reasons why people make irrational, prejudiced judgements about others and to seek to change that prejudice by pin-pointing the real causes. Clearly, this is necessary to correct for misinformation as it is a prerequisite to decisions about how to tackle prejudice.

One further point is necessary before I move on briefly to discuss a short list of tentative and provisional principles. As Merton (1976) has pointed out, it is quite possible for a person who is not him or herself prejudiced to be a discriminator. The circumambient values of the institution or society may exercise an influence which produces in the non-prejudiced, well-intentioned person false stereotypes, or even on occasions merely silence, either of which may enhance and facilitate the perpetration of discrimination. It is, therefore, important for strategies of prejudice reduction to bear in mind these major dimensions of prejudice: individual, structural and cultural (Bagley and Verma, 1979); and to incorporate this insight into the design of pedagogical initiatives and to correct for prejudice. After all, the structure may be an influence for good as well as for bad! Moreover, if the values of the school as a whole do not reflect a commitment to prejudice reduction, individual teachers are hardly likely to succeed.

Of course, such social factors may also be strongly correlated with the level of ability and cognitive sophistication of those who are prejudiced, and the amount of evidence or information which they have available or is made avaialable to them (Sussman, 1971; Glock et al., 1975), as well as the regularity, level and intensity of their interethnic contact with members of oppressed groups (Allport, 1979; Amir, 1976; Cook, 1970). In this latter respect, intergroup contact, it must be admitted that the evidence is contradictory and dependent on the fulfilment of additional criteria such as:

- the equality of status of those interacting;
- the support of influential and authoritative persons and institutions;
- continuing acquaintance on a personal rather than casual basis;
- the experience being positive, pleasant and rewarding;
- the interdependence of the activities;
- the availability of superordinate goals (Ijaz, 1981);
- the experience of positive interracial contact at an early age (Patchen, 1982).

This last matter recalls a point emphasised in the early work of Goodman, namely that superordinate goals create shared interests (Goodman, 1952). But more recent work conducted from the Johns Hopkins University over a five-year period in several hundred schools (Slavin and Madden, 1979; Slavin 1979, 1983), also indicates that co-operative group work, where individuals occupy equal roles, produces positive relationships, because such methods imply members of the group helping each other to achieve common goals and complete common tasks. Not only, however, does co-operative work improve interracial relationships, but is has the added bonus of increasing achievement as well. Such findings are also supportive of earlier propositions that prejudiced behaviour is influenced by the social situations in which a person is involved and the pattern of community practices and home attitudes (Raab and Lipset, 1963).

As Allport (1979) has envisaged them, attitudes comprise, both what we think and what we feel and there is certainly an opportunity for both the transmission of feeling-information and the reassurance of feeling-judgements through direct, purposeful and regular contact which is not available through normally used educational information-transmission techniques. Perhaps it is really commonsense, that where people work together in a satisfying atmosphere which is friendly and supportive of their efforts, friendships will blossom. A similar insight emerges from the work of Jeffcoate (1976, 1979a, 1979b), who was perhaps the first in the United Kingdom to set out a series of cognitive and affective objectives for a multicultural and multiracial curriculum. As his work has been amended by Cohen and Manion (1983) and Lynch (1986) it includes not only cognitive skills (it is important for cognitive knowledge to be transmitted in order to correct for misinformation), but it also includes affective attitudes, values and emotional sets. The important contribution here is the recognition that prejudice is composed of emotionality and emotional dimensions as well as cognitive ones, and that any education for prejudice reduction, if it is to be effective, has to include both dimensions.

But this process of cultural sharing has also been shown to be of importance for teachers and, reflectively, for the academic achievement of children. Pupils are found to benefit when their teachers have frequent contact with each other, co-operate in activities, assist one another's intellectual growth and share their ideas (United States Department of Education, 1986). This research, emphasising the importance of collegiality, when combined with the growing research on school ethos and its importance in making schools effective (Rutter et al., 1979; Brookover, 1979; Coleman, Hoffer and Kilgore, 1982; Crain, 1982), underlines once again the importance of the values, structure and activities of a school in enabling it to achieve its broader educational goals as well as its narrower curricular objectives. As such, both principles, *collegiality* and *ethos* to shorthand them, are mainstays of prejudice reduction, within the context of a coherent institutional policy for multicultural education; and that is the theme for chapter 4: whole school policies for prejudice reduction.

Before retrieving the theme of the importance of the school ambience in chapter 4, however, I want to take a look, in chapter 3, at what we know about prejudice acquisition. To conclude this chapter, I want to select a number of working principles which reflect and summarise the major points which I have made.

1. Tackling prejudice reduction in schools has to be seen as part of broader social measures, if it is to be maximally effective;
2. Prejudice reduction has to be seen as a normal part of the education of all children. It is an inevitable task for a school in a pluralist democracy and it needs to be planned into the life and work of the school;
3. Prejudice comprises both informational and emotional components. Strategies to correct for prejudice need also to include both cognitive and affective components;
4. Prejudice may take many forms: racism, sexism, classism, credism, etc.; and often specific 'prejudices' are intertwined in their causation and effect. Teachers need to be alert, in particular, to the mutually reinforcing effects of classism and racism;
5. The healthier the self-concept of the pupil, the less likely she or he is to be prejudiced;
6. Humane and sensitive discussion and explanation of difference is an essential component of education in a culturally pluralist society; such processes need to be seen as part of the overall development, cognitive and affective, conceptual and moral, of the child and treated as such;
7. The tendency to 'overcategorise' is not unusual in children or adults. It needs to be countered by the provision of increased informaton and interethnic contact and the achievement of improved rational sophistication and greater discriminatory skill development, as part of the moral and civic education of the learner;
8. The correction of misinformation and the provision of accurate information is a necessary but not sufficient component of prejudice reduction;
9. Schools must aim to improve pupil's moral problem-solving and decision-making capacity;
10. The pluralism of values of schools must aim to take into account the different socialisation and enculturation processes experienced by pupils;
11. The school aims must allow for mutual and multiple acculturation by pupils and teachers;
12. Teaching for self-concept enhancement is likely to benefit all pupils;
13. Collegiality of action and decision is essential in countering prejudice;
14. The racial climate of a school may adversely affect the achievement of minority children but not that of majority students;
15. A holistic policy, including the school ethos, implemented longitudinally throughout the school-life of the child is essential;
16. The institutional and systemic nature of prejudice has to be recognised and explored sensitively;

17. Schools will need to arrange for positive, friendly interethnic contacts on a basis of equality as part of their normal activities.

SUMMARY

In this chapter I have located prejudice reduction within the concept of multicultural education and placed them both firmly within the overall aims of schools. Then, I have indicated the relationship of specific forms of prejudice such as racism, sexism, credism and classism to the generic term prejudice, drawing attention to the intertwining of racial prejudice, social class prejudice and self-concept. Lastly I have listed a series of principles which arise from the literature discussed in this chapter.

ACTIVITIES

1. Consider the list of guiding principles at the end of this chapter. How far do you agree that they represent a reasonable outline agenda for teachers? To what extent do you already include such principles in your own teaching? Seek to amend, improve and extend them by reflecting on your own professional experience.
2. Consider the list of aims offered earlier in this chapter as overall goals for schools. Do you agree with them? Compare them with the goals of your school and consider to what extent they should be amended and amplified to take account of the need for schools to tackle prejudice reduction more effectively.
3. To what extent do you agree with the argument of this chapter that the acquisition of prejudice is inevitable within a pluralist society? Consider the criteria for identifying which prejudices it is most important to counter and give the moral reasons for your judgement. Try to think of specific examples of prejudiced behaviour and how you would tackle its eradication.
4. What are the implications for your grouping and teaching strategies of the list of criteria for interethnic contact assembled from the work of Ijaz and Patchen? Does your own experience support these criteria? Are there additional ones which you have felt to be necessary?

REFERENCES

Allport, G.W. (1979) *The Nature of Prejudice*. 25th Anniversary Edition. Reading MA: Addison Wesley.
Amir, Y. (1976) 'The role of intergroup contact in change of prejudice and ethnic relations', in Katz, P.A. (ed.) *Towards the Elimination of Racism*. New York: Pergamon Press.
Australian Curriculum Development Centre (1980) *A Core Curriculum for Australian Schools*. Canberra: CDC.
Bagley, C. and Verma, G.K. (1979) *Racial Prejudice, the Individual and Society*. Westmead, Farnborough: Saxon House.
Blalock, H. (1967) *Towards a Theory of Minority Group Relations*. New York: John Wiley & Sons.
Brookover, W.B. *et al.* (1979) *School Systems and Student Achievement: Schools Make a*

Difference. New York: Praeger.

Clark, K.B. (1955) *Prejudice and Your Child*. Boston: Beacon Press.

Clore, G.L., Bray, R.M., Itkin, S.M. and Murphy, P. (1978) 'Interracial attitudes and behaviours at a summer camp, *Journal of Personality and Social Psychology*. **36** (2) 107–116.

Cohen, L. and Manion, L. (1983) *Multicultural Classrooms*. London: Croom Helm.

Coleman, J.S., Hoffer, T., Kilgore, S. (1982) *High School Achievement*. New York: Basic Books

Cook, S.W. (1970) 'Motives in a conceptual analysis of attitude related behaviour', in Arnold, W.J. and Levine, D. (eds) *Nebraska Symposium on Maturation*. Lincoln: University of Nebraska Press.

Cook, S.W. (1972) 'Motives in a conceptual analysis of attitude related behaviour', in Brigham, J. and Weissbach, T. (eds) *Racial Attitudes in America: Analysis and Findings of Social Psychology*. New York: Harper & Row.

Committee of Inquiry into the Education of Children from Ethnic Minority Groups (1985) *Education for All*. (The Swann Report) London: HMSO (Cmnd. 9453)

Crain, R.L., Mahard, R.E., Narot, R.E. (1982) *Making Desegregation Work: How Schools Create Social Climates*. Cambridge, MA: Ballinger.

Department of Education and Science, Welsh Office (1980) *A Framework for the School Curriculum*. London: DES.

Department of Education and Science, Welsh Office (1981) *The School Curriculum*. London: HMSO.

Frideres, J.S. (1975) Prejudice towards minority groups: ethnicity or class? *Ethnicity*. **2** (1) 34–42.

Glock, Y.C., Wuthnow, R., Piliavin, J.A. and Spencer, M. (1975) *Adolescent Prejudices*. New York: Harper & Row.

Goodman, M.E. (1952) *Race Awareness in Young Children*. London: Collier Macmillan.

Her Majesty's Inspectorate (1980) *A View of the Curriculum*. London: HMSO.

Her Majesty's Inspectorate Department of Education and Science (1985) *The Curriculum from 5 to 16*. London: HMSO.

Ijaz, M.A. (1981) *Study of Ethnic Attitudes of Elementary School Children toward Blacks and East Indians*, ERIC Document ED 204 448.

Inner London Education Authority (1984) *Improving Secondary Schools*. London: ILEA.

Jeffcoate, R. (1976) Curriculum planning in multiracial education, *Educational Research*. **18** (3) 192–200.

Jeffcoate, R. (1979a) A multicultural curriculum: beyond the orthodoxy, *Trends in Education*. **4** 8–12.

Jeffcoate, R. (1979b) *Positive Image: Towards a Multicultural Curriculum*. London: Chameleon Books.

Kohlberg, L. (1974) *The Cognitive-Developmental Approach to Inter-Ethnic Attitudes*, ERIC Document ED 128 536.

Lynch, J. (1983) *The Multicultural Curriculum*. London: Batsford.

Lynch, J. (1986) *Multicultural Education: Principles and Practice*. London: Routledge.

Merton, R.K. (1976) 'Discrimination and the American creed', pp 189–216 in Merton, R.K. *Sociological Ambivalence and other Essays*. New York: The Free Press.

Patchen, M. (1982) *Black-White Contact in Schools: Its Social and Academic Effects*. West Lafayette, Indiana, Purdue University Press.

Raab, E., and Lipset, S.M. (1963) *Prejudice and Society* ERIC Document ED 001 985.

Rubin, I.M. (1967) Increased self-acceptance: a means of reducing prejudice, *Journal of Personality and Social Psychology*. **5** 233–238.

Rutter, M., Maughan, B., Mortimore, P. and Ouston, J. (1979) *Fifteen Thousand Hours: Secondary Schools and their Effects on Children*. London: Open Books.

The Schools Council (1981) *The Practical Curriculum*. London: Methuen Educational.

The Schools Council (1983) *Primary Practice*. London: Methuen Educational.

Scottish Education Department, Consultative Committee on the Curriculum (1977) *The Structure of the Curriculum in the Third and Fourth Years of the Scottish Secondary School*. Edinburgh: HMSO.

Secretary of State for Education and Science, Secretary of State for Wales (1977) Education in Schools: *A Consultative Document*. London: HMSO.

Secretary of State for Education and Science (1985) *Better Schools*. London: HMSO.

Slavin, R., and Madden, N.A. (1979) School practices that improve race relations, *American Educational Research Journal*. **16** (2) 169–180.

Slavin, R.E. (1979) Effects of biracial learning teams on cross-racial friendships, Journal of Educational Psychology. **71** (3) 381–387.

Slavin, R.E. (1983) *Co-operative Learning*. London and New York: Longman.

Sussman, E. (1971) *Prejudice as a Function of Intellectual Level and Cultural Information*, ERIC Document ED 048 421.

Trager, H.G. and Yarrow, M.R. (1952) *They Learn What They Live*. New York: Harper and Brothers.

United States Department of Education (1986) *What Works: Research about Teaching and Learning*. Washington, DC. United States Department of Education.

Walkling, P. (1980) The idea of a multicultural curriculum, *Journal of Philosophy of Education*. **14** (1) 87–95.

Williams, J.E. and Moreland, J.K. (1976) *Race, Color and the Young Child*. Chapel Hill: The University of North Carolina Press.

Williams, M. (1986) The Thatcher generation, *New Society*. 21 February.

Chapter 3

Prejudice Acquisition and Reduction

INTRODUCTION

In the previous chapter, I have sought to indicate the relationship between holistic policies for education in culturally diverse societies and the indispensable and continuing task of prejudice reduction which this necessarily involves for schools. I have offered some initial thoughts on the circumstances which breed and reinforce prejudice and on the interrelationship of racism and classism in particular. Following this I have indicated a series of provisional guiding principles which may help teachers to formulate their own overall approach to prejudice reduction as part of their normal professional work and under the umbrella of a holistic institutional policy, procedures and ethos.

In this chapter, arguing that in order for them to tackle prejudice reduction it is necessary for teachers to understand how prejudice is acquired, I want to give an overview of the literature on prejudice acquisition. I shall be mentioning the work of a number of writers, but, in particular, I want to formulate a more comprehensive 'map' covering four major domains: *environmental, social, cultural* and *personal*. Finally, I want to expand my previous references on how to modify and, if possible, extinguish prejudice, before concluding with a brief list of guiding principles for policy-makers and educators.

PREJUDICE ACQUISITION

There is a very extensive and growing literature on prejudice and discrimination stretching back over many years (Harding, Proshansky, Kutner and Chein, 1954; Harding, Kutner, Proshansky and Chein, 1969; Katz, 1976a; Bagley and Verma, 1979; Stephan, 1985). It is written from a number of disciplinary perspectives, including psychoanalytic, sociological, developmental and personality-oriented explanations. Thus, it is impossible for one brief chapter to cover all the literature in the field in detail. I have, therefore, needed to be eclectic in the material which I have chosen to review, in order to give both a longitudinal overview of its development and a latitudinal perspective on its contemporary extent. My criteria for selection have been twofold: I have sought to include reference to major 'classic' studies which express an important milestone or historical perspective; and, I have attempted to select material which is focused on, if not directly relevant to or informative of, the professional task of teachers in schools.

The term 'prejudice acquisition' arises from the early pre-war interest in intercultural education which was strengthened by the events of the Second World War and Nazi racism in particular. As mentioned in chapter 1, intercultural education became one of the major platforms of the Intergroup Education Movement in the early post-war era and continued to be a major interest in the United States throughout the desegregation years until the mid 1970s, when attention became more focused on structural causes of victimisation and oppression, before reviving somewhat in the mid 1980s (*Journal of Social Issues*, 1985).

There are three major orientations in the early work on prejudice. The one which may be labelled the 'neopsychoanalytic' was led by Adorno, with his work on the 'Authoritarian Personality' type, which appears to correlate highly with prejudice (Adorno et al., 1950). The second stream derives from social learning theory and relates to those parental upbringing practices which could make the young child prejudiced (Sears, Maccoby and Levin, 1957). Certain advocates of this theoretical orientation also emphasise the cultural influences in the acquisition of prejudice (Pettigrew, 1959). A third school sees social and cultural influences conjoined as causative of prejudiced attitudes, rather than personality or child-rearing practices alone, and this school has given rise to work more sensitive to the social structural causation of prejudice, including racial dominance and 'structural disadvantage' (Burkey, 1978). More recently, and in the context of a burgeoning literature in the field of intergroup relations from a social psychological perspective, the systematic study of relations between individuals as they are affected by group membership has received renewed attention (Stephan, 1985).

Much of the research and conceptual development work in this field has been conducted in the United States. It is, therefore, important that, while taking it into account, allowance is made for the fact that it may not be directly applicable to the United Kingdom. For example, the influential work of Allport (1954), which asserts that as soon as children learn to distinguish blacks from whites, they 'will undoubtedly reject' all blacks, has been challenged by recent work undertaken in the United Kingdom by Short (1981), who found that Allport's hypothesis could not be sustained. This does not mean that all such writing and research is inapplicable. What it does mean is that caution is needed in interpreting the fine detail of research and assuming that it is directly applicable to the United Kingdom.

But firstly, what do we mean by prejudice acquisition? As used in this book, prejudice acquisition is defined as: **the complex process of socialisation and enculturation, whereby an individual acquires the values, knowledge, attitudes and behaviour which motivate him/her to treat other individuals and groups differently and unequally on the basis of their racial, ethnic, credal, sex and cultural appurtenances or composition**.

So, inherent in the concept of prejudice as I am using it here, is a feeling of superiority and aversion, which has the potential to lead to unequal behaviour and therefore injustice and even violence towards persons or groups against whom that prejudice is focused. It follows, of course, that such prejudice is not only unjust to those to whom it is directed, but is also inimical to the basic ethic of a culturally pluralist society. And yet, as explained in the previous chapter, it may be the result of the cultural and social context in which the child has grown up (Clark, 1955). Europeans, in particular, should be aware that it may be necessary for certain Eurocentric attitudes to be extinguished if deeply embedded and racially antagonistic prejudices are to be conquered. This is not to attribute guilt; it is not a personal matter, but to understand the consequence of 'history become tradition', a particular case being the dominant position of many European cultures in slavery and colonialism.

Early workers in this field considered personality the most important factor in the formation of prejudice. The pioneering research here was conducted by Frenkel-Brunswick. In a detailed empirical study of a sample of some 1,500 children and their parents, she found significant differences in the personalities of prejudiced children (Frenkel-Brunswick, 1948). She and her associates also investigated the relationship between personality and prejudice in adults, concluding that some people have what they termed an *authoritarian personality*, needing to dominate and feel superior to other people in matters of racial, sexual, religious and political behaviour and beliefs (Adorno et al, 1950). Other early researchers followed similar lines of study (Allport and Kramer, 1946; Lindzey, 1950), but both the methods and results of the many studies have been subject to severe criticism, not least because of their reliance on a predominantly personality approach to the study of prejudice.

Blumer, (1966) challenges this approach and asserts that it is the social setting which is the main influence on behaviour, and that it is, therefore, norms and social settings which should be analysed not individual, personal attitudes. Both Saenger and Gilbert (1950) and Blalock (1956) found, in separate research, that discrimination and prejudice do not always coincide and may be affected by prevailing norms and economic factors. It should not be assumed, however, that merely placing individuals in situations with healthier norms and values will change them. As Pearlin (1954) indicates, the situation must be important to the individual. And, as Banks (1982) argues, individuals collectively influence group norms, and it is important to take into account both individual and social dimensions in attempting to understand and explain prejudice.

More recently, with a focus on the 'inner states' of the interacting individuals rather than exclusively on the situational variables, Stephan and Stephan (1985) have been concerned with the extent to which contact itself causes anxiety. Proposing a model encompassing the antecedents and consequences of intergroup anxiety, they hypothesise that it is created by three sets of factors: *prior intergroup relations*, for example, the amount and conditions of prior contact; *prior intergroup cognitions*, such as knowledge of the outgroup, existence of stereotypes, prejudice, expectations and perceptions of dissimilarity; and *situational factors*, such as the group composition, relative status, type of interdependence, extent of structure (Stephan and Stephan, 1985, p. 156). They argue that high levels of intergroup anxiety may, among other things, lead to augmented emotional reactions and polarise evaluations of outgroup members. Validating their proposition on data from Hispanic pupils, they find that high levels of intergroup anxiety are associated with low levels of contact with outgroup members, stereotyping of outgroup members and assumed dissimilarity from outgroup members.

So, unless contact is well prepared for and the necessary variables taken into account in structuring the situation, educators may well find that their efforts at using contact to reduce prejudice may have the opposite effect to that intended. I shall return to this point later in the chapter, for it has implications for the way in which prejudice reduction strategies may be planned and implemented.

There is little doubt that socialisation into one's own culture predisposes one to regard aspects of other cultures in a negative way. Some writers have argued, for example, that the very linguistic and evaluative repertoire of a culture may have this effect. Children are influenced by a pantechnicon of culture-messages at birth, from their parents, family, subculture and wider culture, either directly or vicariously (Clark, 1955). Williams and Moreland (1976), for example, point to the way that in certain cultures children may develop a predisposition to evaluate light things more positively than dark and they suggest that the general culture-symbols of the cultural ambience may involve the ethical designation of light and dark, white and black, as good and bad (Milner, 1983).

This confusion of colour and valuing, was also found in a study of 104 four -year-old nursery children by Goodman. She found evidence of racial awareness by the age of two to two and a half years and of incipient and firm attitudes in the later pre-school years. Among highly racially antagonistic children, she draws attention to their significant tendency to 'either/or', i.e. polarised thinking which involves strong feelings and sharp differentiations (Goodman, 1973). She also notes, as did Trager and Yarrow (1952), a reluctance on the part of parents to discuss or answer children's questions on race and prejudice. The important thing here is that such attitudes are not inherent, but are absorbed as part of an unconscious, subtle and often unintentional process of enculturation, predominantly but not exclusively in the early years of life. They represent a process of conforming to the cultural capital and social customs of a group — a process which may occur in the reverse direction i.e. extinguishing and changing as well — as part of a formal education. All the more important, then, that teachers realise the need to make such values sensitively explicit, to enable children to begin to feel respect for differences, from which they have previously felt a deeply subconscious uncomprehending aversion, whether of a sex, social class, credal or racial kind.

In the light of the very rich literature in the field and the disparate nature of many of the theories concerning how prejudice is acquired, a number of authors have attempted to sketch a map of the different approaches. Rose (1962), for example, has prepared an analysis of the theories available in the first two decades after the end of the Second World War, in which he identifies six major theoretical orientations:

1. the instinctive fear and dislike of others who are physically and culturally different;
2. antagonism evoked by competition between groups for employment and economic satisfaction;
3. conformity to society's traditions and norms as part of the usual process of social control;

4. the experience of a traumatic incident involving a member or members of a particular racial or cultural group;
5. frustration at the non-satisfaction of a particular need or needs leading to displaced aggression on a stigmatised group;
6. the projection onto others of motives which the individual holds but feels guilty about (Rose, 1962).

The problem with this list of theories is that some do not fit the facts, others do not explain the continuance of prejudice after it ceases to be functional and others fail to explain the emergence of prejudice convincingly. The central flaw in them is that they tend to underplay the structural aspect of prejudice, whereby the system of social stratification related to a market economy may develop a cultural momentum for the perpetuation of those prejudices which it has originated: an ideology of prejudice, including sexism, racism, credism and classism. This latter point is particularly important in the context of a number of criticisms of multicultural education, in general, and especially studies of racism for their 'gender-blindness'. Several recent Australian studies have drawn graphic attention to the fact that racism is neither gender nor class free (Bottomley and Lepervanche, 1984).

Vander Zanden (1963) in summarising a large number of studies which focused more heavily on the sociological foundations of race relations conjoins, as well as *personality factors*, including scapegoat theory, consideration of *sociocultural factors, economic power and status*, and *ideological factors*. In the first category, he points to the selective nature of perception. This may be distorted by previously acquired cultural definitions and learned categorisations, which may, in turn, make it difficult to accept alternative classifications and, when formulated as stereotypes, may cause antipathy, avertive behaviour and even violence. Vander Zanden also draws attention to the relationship between an individual's attitudes and his/her reference group and its social norms. This is an important consideration for teachers, who, widening the reference group for their professional activity, may also widen the criteria for their appraisal of their professional effectiveness. The point may also indicate the importance of a similar principle in devising teaching/learning strategies. It highlights, once again, the need for close relationships and involvement of parents and communities in the schooling of their children.

But, it is perhaps particularly in the appreciation of the interlocking nature of economic and ideological factors that Vander Zanden supports more modern conceptions of how prejudice is caused and perpetuated. In the former sphere, the importance of such factors as competition for scarce resources and the tendency of vested interest groups to defend their dominance over minorities by the use of prejudice and discrimination are highlighted. More recent research by Jackman and Muha (1984), using national survey data, has seemed to confirm the way in which dominant groups routinely develop new ideologies to legitimise and justify the status quo. One variant of this latter view is the neo-Marxist interpretation that racial prejudice has developed as a product of capitalism and nationalism. Associated with this development is the need for a core white supremacist ideology which may act as a fulcrum for accompanying group solidarity and a legitimator of its actions.

Simpson and Yinger (1965) offer a comprehensive theory of prejudice which includes many of the factors previously cited: personality, power structure and culture, on an interactive, mutually reinforcing basis. They emphasise the need for multifactor explanations of the complexity from which prejudice emerges and consider in detail many of the subcomponents within each of the above categories. While more recent work may cast doubt on the assumption that education makes people less vulnerable to appeals to intergroup negativism and generates increased commitment to democratic norms (Jackman and Muha, 1984), they draw attention to the way in which authoritarianism may decline with the rising intelligence and level of educational achievement of the individual. Accepting, in general, that there may be certain kinds of personality which are prejudice-prone, i.e., have inclinations and potentialities in that direction, they criticise the theory because it emphasises personality traits rather than process or interaction which can functionally interrelate the individual to the context of which she or he is a part (Simpson and Yinger, 1965, p. 77). They draw attention to the need to fit such a theory within the context of appropriate social settings and to take into account the fact that a people's relationship with those around them may strongly influence their attitudes and behaviour, as prevailing and countervailing associations of co-operation and accommodation or competition and conflict unite or separate individuals and groups.

This latter point leads to a greater appreciation of the role of prejudice in the battle to achieve status, power, prestige and economic rewards and opportunities in which racial and religious prejudice are used as economic weapons and instruments of social control. This second conglomeration of factors may be strengthened and reinforced by cultural factors such as the force of history and tradition which may be powerful contemporary informants of prejudice and generators of social norms and customs, so as to prevent accommodations i.e., new behaviours, which may be socially advantageous and profitable e.g., prejudice which is manifestly against the economic self-interest of the prejudiced individual or group.

Bearing in mind the complex, multidimensional nature of what it is that we are describing when we refer to prejudice, a number of authors have expressed dissatisfaction with the use of the word and its antonym tolerance. Jackman (1977), pointing to the three elements comprising an attitude (*cognitive, emotive* and *conative* or behaviour orientation), suggests that a prejudiced attitude, therefore, comprises: a set of negative generalised beliefs or stereotypes about a group; a feeling of dislike for that group; and a predisposition to behave in a negative way about a group, directly as well as vicariously. She argues that the use of the umbrella term 'prejudice' blurs the complexity involving beliefs and feelings along with action orientations which may vary considerably from one context to another. She usefully points out that recognition of these separate elements 'frees' the word tolerance — not as the mere attribute of someone who is not prejudiced but, as in the literature of political sociology, expressing the condition where an individual perceives difference which may be unattractive to that individual, but does not allow it to interfere with the general principles of civil rights. Thus the enjoyment of civil rights is independent of likes and dislikes.

More recently, Burkey, emphasising the socio-political structural dimension of ethnic relations, devotes attention to the dominance-submission relationship of race and ethnic groups, arguing that there are at least five major dimensions across which they may be envisaged in a complex society: stratification; segregation; cultural

Kind of society / Dimension	Monist state	Federation	Culturally pluralist democracy
Policy	Assimilation	Separation	Multiculturalism
Stratification	Caste Ethnicity	Social	Social
Geographical segregation	No	Yes	Internal
Cultural differentiation	No	Yes	Yes
Social distance	Yes	Yes	Yes
Economic competition	Yes	Yes	Yes
Political competition	No	No	Yes
Legitimation of prejudice	Yes	No	No
Status	Dominated	Equal	Dynamic

Figure 3.1 Interethnic relations in different national contexts

differentiation; social distance; competition and conflict (Burkey, 1978 p. 58). He emphasises the way in which political, economic and cultural dominance often go hand in hand. He also usefully underlines what is a missing dimension in other theories considered so far and which might be described as the environmental dimension, recognising that in the geographical dimension minority groups and races may be highly concentrated or dispersed in a society; they may be predominantly urban or rural or equally distributed, and if urbanised they may again be concentrated or dispersed. They may also be a distinctive, unique, individual group or they may be part of a cultural group which elsewhere may be dominant. He hypothesises the existence, across the five major dimensions introduced above, of three kinds of societies — empires, nations and pluralist societies.

Drawing on Burkey's three kinds of societies, but amending them, leads us to recognise that there are many different ways in which minority groups are treated in apparently pluralist societies. Some of these involve unequal status and overt discrimination. Others involve an attempt at a federal solution, while a third group is attempting to achieve a national covenant which recognises diversity as an asset and seeks to construct a political and economic arrangement which can accommodate it. This latter kind of society may involve social but not ethnic or racial stratification, segregated or concentrated patterns of settlement by choice, cultural independence and both social distance and contact as well as economic and political competition. Such a society is a democratic cultural pluralism, where prejudice on the basis of sex, religion, ethnicity, race or class is against the 'rules of the game' and threatens the continued existence of the overall covenant. The model, illustrated in figure 3.1, envisages three ideal societies and the kind of accommodation which might be implicit across eight major dimensions.

Thus it is recognised, nowadays, that a more comprehensive and dynamic theory of prejudice acquisition not only needs to comprehend the early work on personality and child-rearing practices, but also the social structural, cultural and environmental dimensions. This realisation is important for teachers because it implies that prejudice reduction strategies (to which we shall return shortly) must consider the school as an interrelated social system, thus necessitating holistic and comprehensive attention: both macro and micro approaches (Banks, 1982). Drawing on that point I have sought

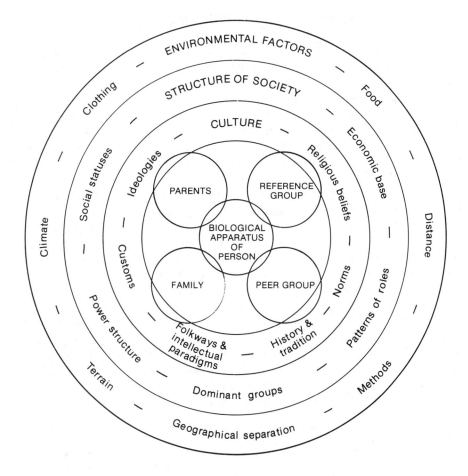

Figure 3.2 The dynamic process of prejudice acquisition

Note: Dynamic, multidimensional interaction is assumed between all levels and elements in the model.

in figure 3.2 to convey the complex interaction of factors causative of prejudice as a preparation for the next part of this chapter, which is concerned with prejudice reduction. The figure seeks to portray the complex interaction of four highly dynamic domains: *environment*; *social structure*; *culture* and *personality*. The latter derives from the subtle and complex relationship between the inherited biological apparatus of the child and an ever-widening circle of social, cultural and environmental influences, in the process of socialisation and enculturation through which sex roles, social status, religious and racial perceptions and predispositions first begin to be absorbed. In that connection, personality is also intended to encompass the factors referred to previously in the work of Stephan and Stephan (1985), concerning the way in which antecedent 'inner states' and anticipation of the consequences of intergroup contact may polarise evaluations of outgroup members.

PREJUDICE REDUCTION; GENERAL PRINCIPLES

As in the case of the literature on prejudice acquisition, the literature on prejudice reduction is extensive, complex and, in some respects, contradictory. In many cases, the samples are small, the experimental techniques not fully reliable and the results and interpretation ambiguous or opaque. In some cases, while the hope is pious, the evaluation is non-existent. In many cases, too, the literature is a fairly ancient vintage and, in some instances, assertions, or even experimental findings, have been refuted or partially amended by later work. There are few certainties in the field, except that unless the school educates to counter prejudice and discrimination, it is inevitably reinforcing those attitudes and behaviours. It cannot remain neutral. Notwithstanding the limitations, therefore, it is important to try to achieve an overview of what has been attempted in the field of prejudice reduction as a guide to one's own initiatives and as a spur to further ideas. The latter part of this chapter attempts to sieve the literature in the field for its wisdom, seeking to identify a series of principles which can inform the educational endeavour to reduce and, if possible, extinguish prejudice. I am particularly looking for general principles which may be derived from the literature for the work of teachers, although I would reiterate the need for these principles and any action to be seen as part of a broader assault on prejudice within society as a whole. It is also important to recall the point made earlier in this chapter, that, just as prejudice comprises *informational*, *emotive* and *behavioural* dimensions, so strategies for prejudice reduction will need to apprehend these three domains.

Firstly, however, what do we mean by prejudice reduction? Elsewhere I have offered a provisional working definition which I wish to use again, in slightly amended form in the context of this book (Lynch, 1986).

> Prejudice reduction is a deliberate and systematic process, which aims by means of coherent, rational, democratic and sustained educational and broader social strategies, policies and practices, at enabling individuals and groups to re-orient their values, attitudes, actions and behaviour, in such a way that predispositions to prejudice and discrimination are reduced, amended or eradicated.

A number of cumulative surveys of the literature have been made including those by Simpson and Yinger (1965), Katz (1976a), Balch and Paulsen (1979), Pate (1981),

Banks (1982), and Stephan (1985). Simpson and Yinger (1965) define two major orientations in prejudice reduction strategies, aimed respectively at changing the person and at changing the situation. Pointing out that different persons and different situations may necessitate different strategies, they retrieve Merton's (1949) classification of four ideal types of person, for whom differing attitude change strategies may be necessary:

- the unprejudiced non-discriminator;
- the unprejudiced discriminator;
- the prejudiced non-discriminator;
- the prejudiced discriminator.

Five kinds of approaches to changing persons are listed: *exhortation, propaganda, contact, education* and *personal therapy*, and it is pointed out that these are neither precise nor mutually exclusive categories (Simpson and Yinger, 1965, p. 498). Exhortation and anti-prejudice propaganda are regarded as having only a very minor and modest role in prejudice reduction, and attention is drawn to the contextual variables and necessary preconditions, if contact is to be effective. Warning against consideration of education as a 'cure all', they indicate that the eradication of some deeply rooted, functional prejudices may demand a high level of training. Personal and group therapy are seen as being more appropriate for those with overall personality inadequacies or instabilities. While they concern us less here, the strategies addressed to changing situations include the role of *legislation* and *administration, organisations, public agencies, public action* and *opposition* and *increased research*. They underline, throughout, the interactive and cumulative nature of the forces involved.

Commenting on intervention strategies, in a review of the literature, Balch and Paulsen (1979), state that only eight published studies of attempts to modify children's racial attitudes were available by 1965 and that the subsequent increase in such work indicated characteristics of shortsightedness and a piecemeal approach, with virtually no data available on the long-term effects. Balch and Paulsen classify two major fields of study: *curriculum* approaches and *reinforcement* approaches, this latter using positive reinforcement techniques and punishment. Summarising the curriculum approaches, they designate them as having been largely unsuccessful with the exception of two studies by Singh and Yancy (1974) and Katz and Zalk (1978), this latter including group interaction and vicarious identification techniques. A number of principles seem to emerge from their survey. These include that:

- single strategy, short-term interventions are inadequate for permanent changes;
- intervention has to be long-term and integrated into the continuous process of the school;
- curricula involving positive identification of various groups may be of assistance;
- attention needs to be paid to the stages of development of children involved;
- the validity and reliability of experimental measures must be carefully scrutinised.

Banks (1982), drawing on the work of Katz (1973), surveys the literature on both acquisition and reduction, classifying the latter into macro and micro approaches. He advocates the need for a holistic, multidimensional strategy by schools including all major variables.

In the United Kingdom, the work of Stenhouse in the early 1970s remains the most significant in its innovatory contribution to the development of approaches to improving race relations, successfully launched and evaluated. Reflecting on his work, he includes the following seven points, which I have paraphrased and rewritten for this chapter.

1. Direct teaching to correct for negative racial attitudes can result in positive gains;
2. Strategies compatible with the context and the skills of teachers who are involved are more likely to be successful;
3. The value of 'open-mindedness' is likely to transfer from discussion of one controversial issue into other areas;
4. The results of such gains are likely to be non-persistent without reinforcement;
5. Where the pedagogies involve 'appeal to the judgement of participants', they may result in regression in an undesired direction;
6. In the face of racism there is a need for collegiality of decision, and,
7. Only as part of broader social policies and interests, is it likely that tackling racism within the school will be successful.

These 'guiding principles' are not exactly as Stenhouse has formulated them, but, added to 'guiding principles' from the work of others, they begin brick-by-brick to construct a *pedagogy of multicultural education* which can come to grips with issues of prejudice reduction (Stenhouse, Verma and Wild, 1982).

A further publication by Sikes (1979) gives an account of an attempt to assess three strategies for teaching about race relations. The Humanities Project technique of the 'neutral chairman' has printed material available as evidence for critical appraisal along with improvised drama and existing and well-defined teaching techniques from the 16 participating schools. While the three 'groups' had slightly different aims, almost a thousand hours of classroom recordings were collected as were discussions of pupils assessing work without a teacher being present. Interviews and written comments were collected from teachers.

Other work in the United Kingdom has tended to remain uncontrolled in the sense of either comprising useful suggestions or implementations which have not been vigorously evaluated to provide *generalisability*. Klein, for example, outlines an indirect approach to race relations through the use of fiction as teaching material (Klein, 1982). In a more recent publication, she also alerts us to the continued importance of the material and books which are used and the need for criteria as well as continuing vigilance (Klein, 1986), an exhortation which is supported by work on both sides of the Atlantic (Zimet, 1976, 1983, Milner, 1979), indicating the positive movements in attitudes which may occur consequent on the use of appropriate text book material. Others such as Hicks (1976, 1981) also draw attention to the inherent bias in school books and have worked to draw the curriculum out of its traditional ethnocentricity by a 'world studies approach' (Hicks, 1981). Experimental gaming approaches are also reported by Page and Thomas (1984) including the use of the Cat and Mouse fantasy and the wearing of the purple arm-band.

While addressed to changing teachers' attitudes rather than those of children the work of Twitchin and Demuth (1985), also in the United Kingdom, draws our attention to the fact that combined group and filmic approaches may be helpful. Although their work has not been systematically evaluated, it does seem to evoke two further principles which might help to guide educational approaches to prejudice reduction, namely that any strategy for prejudice reduction must include the sensitive exploration of the feelings of institutional racism of both pupils and teachers; and, it must aim to achieve cognitive increments of understanding and knowledge of the phenomenon of institutional racism.

In the United States some of the early studies did appear to have positive results as a consequence of curricular initiatives. Trager and Yarrow (1952), for example, report that children exposed to a democratic curriculum expressed more positive racial attitudes and they suggest that if such attitudes are to be learned, they must be specifically taught and experienced. Confirmation of this postulate also seems to emerge from the work of Johnson (1966) who studied the effects of a programme of black history on racial attitudes and self-concepts. He found that, although the effects on the girls in the sample were not significant, substantial changes were recorded by the boys. In the case of Litchner and Johnson (1969), the effects of the introduction of multicultural readers on white pupils over a period of four months were studied and the development of more favourable attitudes to blacks was recorded. A shorter period replication study conducted later was, however, unsuccessful (Litchner, Johnson and Ryan, 1973).

Likewise, negative findings were reported by Walker (1971) who attempted to modify pre-schoolers' racial attitudes by the use of reading and co-operative work of a mutually satsfying kind. An 18 session black consciousness curriculum for black college students likewise reported negative results. Attempts at prejudice reduction involving the development of teaching techniques have yielded somewhat mixed results. Miller (1967), in the United Kingdom, reports that teaching to undermine prejudice had the opposite effect. Moreover, negative findings of a similar nature were reported by Tansik and Driscoll (1977) in the States, in work with supervisors at a military base, for whom attendance at a training course was made mandatory. That at least should serve as a warning of the possibility of negative changes in racial attitudes, to those who would make race awareness courses compulsory for all teachers.

But, clearly critical are the design of the experiment and the surrounding conditions, as well as the ability of the instruments used to measure change, and not all studies have had such a negative outcome. For example, in a complex and well-designed study, which has received commendation, Katz and Zalk (1978) examined the effects of four short-term intervention measures:

- increased positive racial contact;
- vicarious racial contact;
- reinforcement of the colour black;
- perceptual differentiation.

The perceptual differentiation and vicarious approaches were found to be more effective than the other two, and follow-ups, conducted four to six months later, found the younger children retaining most racial bias reduction.

This improvement in the attitudes of young children is also reflected in other studies. In one of the most extensive, conducted over a period of 30 school days, Singh and Yancy (1974) exposed 21 white subjects to life histories of famous American blacks and realistic fiction stories portraying blacks positively in multi-racial situations, filmstrips, films and activity boxes, art activities, multicultural readers and projects within English and Maths, in combination with an appropriate reward system. They report results indicating a significant reduction in racial prejudice. A similar piece of work by Best et al. (1975), involving 70 white children in two 45-minute seminars on the theme of colour and involving reading, art and games approaches with positive rewards, showed no significant difference.

The importance of reinforcement seems to be underlined by studies with other pre-school children using operant approaches (Edwards and Williams, 1970; McAdoo, 1970; Shanahan, 1972; Traynham, 1974; Best et al., 1975) which indicate that earlier tendencies to evaluate black more positively than white, and similar extrapolations to persons, can be easily modified.

One frequently proposed technique of prejudice reduction is intergroup contact. But caution is needed lest the assumption arise that such an approach will be beneficial regardless of the surrounding conditions and circumstances. Early research by Horowitz (1947), for example, indicates quite clearly the fallacy of such an assumption, concluding that social norms and adult models are powerful variables and that placing children together will not necessarily improve their attitudes. Early work by Watson (1947), Williams (1947) and Allport (1954 pp. 262–3) indicated some of the major variables which need to be considered if contact is to be used as an approach to prejudice reduction, including the frequency, duration and variety of contact, equal status and role of the parties, co-operative activity and designation of the group as important, typical, real and voluntary. This much abridged list vindicates the complexity of the variables that are involved in planning for contact approaches, if positive outcomes are to be achieved. More recently, Stephan and Brigham (1985) have identified four factors which emerge as core-conditions for contact to improve intergroup relations: equal status; co-operative interdependence, support by authority figures; and opportunities to interact with outgroup members as individuals.

Four major contemporary developments in intergroup contact work in the United States should be mentioned here because of their predominantly positive results and their relevance to the work of teachers as potential informants of alternative teacher/learning styles and pedagogical approaches: Jigsaw; STAD and TGT; Co-operative and Competitive Group Work; and pre-preparation and expectation training.

In the first (Aronson and Osherow, 1980; Aronson et al., 1978), the effects of organising so-called 'jigsaw-classrooms' were examined. These involved multiethnic groups of children in peer-group teaching with standard academic materials, in non-competitive situations, where the teacher acted as a facilitator and did no direct teaching. In general, the researchers found that when the group was ethnically balanced the techniques lead to increases in self-esteem, more positive attitudes towards school, increases in locus of control, enhanced role-taking skills, and an increase rather than a loss of academic achievement.

With regard to the second group, STAD (Student Teams Achievement Divisions) and TGT (Teams, Games and Tournaments), a group of investigators at the Johns Hopkins University developed and tested two co-operative learning techniques (De Vries and Slavin, 1978; De Vries, Edwards and Slavin, 1978; Slavin, 1977, 1979). In the first, pupils engaged in peer teaching in small multicultural groups and were tested in weekly quizzes. Their scores were compared with their previous performance or those of pupils of comparable attainment levels. Team scores were made available to all teams. In the second, the scoring system was based on academic tournaments between pupils of comparable attainment. Scores were then totalled within teams and pupils' success or failure was found to be correlated with cross-racial behaviour. Again there were no losses in academic achievement as a result of participation in these groups and some gains were reported.

In the same tradition, and drawing on similar research, a very interesting study is reported from Israel. That experiment compared the effects of three different teaching methods on the pupils' academic learning, co-operative behaviour and attitudes towards peers of their own and another ethnic group (Sharan et al., 1985). The three methods were: co-operative group investigation; student-teams-achievement division; and traditional whole-class instruction. The research design drew on the work of Slavin (1983) in the field of co-operative group work; that of Allport (1954) with regard to contact theory; and that of Tajfel (1981; Tajfel and Turner, 1979), with regard to the theory of intergroup relations. It is one of very few studies to offer a comparison of co-operative learning methods and traditional whole-class instruction, and the only one so far to seek to assess the effects of the group investigation method on interethnic behaviour and attitudes. The results showed that the co-operative learning methods fostered more co-operative behaviour within and between groups and was more beneficial to their relationships, ethnic attitudes and learning progress than whole-class instruction.

In the third group of studies (Johnson and Johnson, 1975; Johnson, Johnson and Scott, 1978), there was competition between co-operative groups, and it was found that more favourable interethnic attitudes developed. In a fourth group of studies, 'priming' techniques such as pre-preparation and expectation-training were used in an attempt to overcome domination of blacks by whites in mixed group situations (Cohen, 1980). Again, there were no negative results and most studies reported a mixture of positive and no results or positive results. As Stephan points out, while emphasising the importance of positive outcomes and of the competence of the group members, the results of such studies are clear: co-operation in multiethnic groups improves intergroup relations (Stephan, 1985).

Later work by Banks (1982) also indicated the significance of the attitudes and predispositions of the teacher, and research by Rist (1970), the United States Commission on Human Rights (1973) and Gay (1974) underlines the way in which teachers often interact more positively with white middle-class pupils rather than minority or lower-class pupils. There are also indications of language and dialect bias on the part of some teachers (Saville-Troike, 1981), and Purnell (1978) argues the way in which many negative assumptions about blacks are reflected in current language, materials and tests. A useful categorisation of different types of racially offensive language to be found in books has been suggested by Milner (1975). This classification includes: outright hostile racist descriptions; racial stereotypes; ethnocentric view-points and lastly, 'silence' i.e., the total omission of ethnic minorities. In the United States, Moore (1976) has sought to classify the ways in which the English language reflects and promotes racism through black/white colour symbolism, terms reflecting obvious bigotry and ethnocentrism. He also provides a lesson plan and specific classroom activities for assisting pupils to use less biased and less racist language. All of this, of course, merely seems to underline the importance of the teachers' own attitudes, the need for critical self-appraisal and professional improvement and conscious effort to eliminate racist language and behaviour by discouraging the use of negative language and by helping pupils to adopt more flexible language, sensitive to and reflecting cultural diversity.

A study reported by Sussman (1971), including both minority and majority children, both high achieving and low achieving pupils, exposed to a two-week training programme, including historical and cultural information about several minority groups, found that the programme had a positive effect on attitudes of both majority and minority children. The relationship between prejudice, intelligence and education has been much discussed, and, following on the work of Glock et al. (1975), a number of writers have argued for educational programmes to aim at higher levels of intellectual functioning and social and moral perspective taking (Gay, 1982), if they are to be maximally effective. Work by Hall and Frederikson, (1979) in the field of sex role stereotyping indicates that men with college-level training stereotype less than those without, although, as mentioned earlier, more recent work has seemed to challenge the facile assumption that those who achieve higher levels of education will *per se* be less involved in prejudiced social behaviour.

Whilst is is not without its critics for its alleged chauvinism, ethnocentrism and determinism, Kohlberg's theory of moral reasoning — an extension of Piaget's views on the stages of intellectual development — envisages a stagewise development of the concept of 'fairness' or justice which may have considerable importance for developments in prejudice reduction in schools. Kohlberg argues that progression through his six stages, which are progressively complex, is linked to achieving cognitive sophistication and that it is constant across cultures (Kohlberg, 1969, 1971). Appropriate strategies may stimulate and accelerate moral stage development. The work is, thus, of theoretical and practical importance to teachers in its explanation of the relationship between the amount of prejudice and moral stage development (Davidson, 1971, 1977). Arbuthnot and Faust describe a moral education format, based on the Kohlbergian cognitive-development model of moral reasoning, which can facilitate increased maturity of moral reasoning. They describe their method as having four major advantages:

- it is consistent and based on scientific theory which can be used in a variety of settings;
- it is sensitive to differing abilities;
- it can promote moral growth by focusing on conflicts and dilemmas and encouraging higher-level thought;
- it is consistent with and apace of theoretically-based empirical research as it develops (Arbuthnot and Faust, 1981).

Materials have also been produced to match the theory and develop an appropriate pedagogy (Lockwood and Harris, 1985) and an extensive review of the literature on moral and values education has been produced by Oser (1986). I shall be amplifying my reference to this tradition of research and development in chapter 5 and attempting to clarify its classroom applications in chapter 6.

An enterprising series of related approaches has been attempted by Kehoe using 'principle testing' and evaluating its possible interaction with level of moral development (Kehoe and Rogers 1978). Principle testing discussions are a procedure adopted in values education. Kehoe draws on the work of Coombs and Meux (1971) in this respect and on the work of Festinger (1957) with regard to dissonance theory, whereby the demonstration of inconsistency in the application of the same principle towards two groups will produce dissatisfaction with the behaviour or belief and consequently a change in attitude. One major technique of principle testing is role simulation, where participants are expected to assume the role of a person being discriminated against. In one study (Kehoe and Rogers 1978), investigating the relative effectiveness of principle testing, three groups frequently discriminated against, women, the handicapped and East Indians, were considered in a junior high-school classroom. While the results were equivocal, more positive attitudes towards the handicapped were recorded and Kehoe comments that, as Kohlberg suggests, it may be that only those at the higher levels of moral development may be able to value others as equal to themselves. Thus, implementing the principle of 'reversability', i.e. empathising with the role and predicament of others, and acceptance of mutuality of ethical relationships, — accepting that what applies to others applies equally to oneself — may also be interdependent with level of moral development. Kehoe has continued his interest in this field through the development of social studies materials for schools.

Some educators, arguing the early impressionability and rapid learning of young children, have sought to develop pre-school strategies, activities and experiences (Sciara and Cunningham, 1982). Others have sought to teach to achieve change through drama (Nixon, 1980), through films including realistic enactments of a social situation involving prejudice (Goldberg, 1956) and by initiating children into discourse (Jeffcoate, 1979). Yet others have tried through values clarification (Dunbar, 1980), through focusing on the diversity of human beings (Kattmann, 1975) and through the use of the simulation game 'Starpower' in the development of more positive attitudes towards blacks and women (Chapman, 1974). Human relations work with teachers has been used (Blackburn 1980), and teachers have been assisted to study and improve their own practice (Adelman et al., 1984). Children's literature and the comparative study of events such as the Revolutionary War from two contrasting points over slavery (Taxel 1982) have been used to the same ends. Through exposure to a coherent and structured body of information in the form of a resource unit guide to methods of teaching about race and ethnocentrism (Leviatin 1971), through text analysis, including tone and usage of language (Redling 1977), through the evocation of empathy with victims of discrimination (Kehoe and Sakata 1979) and by presenting case histories involving prejudice to those holding the same prejudice (Katz, Sarnoff and McClintock 1956) attempts have been made to reduce and eradicate prejudice. A project to teach through folk culture, including dance, music and crafts and role playing (Ijaz and Ijaz 1981), is reported to have resulted in significantly improved racial attitudes. The researchers comment on the association, in some cases, between parents' occupational status and the children's racial attitudes. A very early comparative study of interest is reported by Hayes and Conklin (1953) in which the results of interethnic contact, normal instruction and vicarious reading, acting and listening approaches, supported the latter as being more effective in changing attitudes.

Banks (1982), has suggested that institutional reform needs to address the whole school and all of its major components, including norms, power relationships, verbal interactions, culture, curriculum, teaching/learning strategies, extra-curricular activities and attitudes towards language. He argues that the latent or hidden values may have a more cogent impact on students even than the overt curriculum, pointing to the way in which the negative values of the larger society are often reinforced and perpetuated by the school. Katz (1978), highlights the need to regard racial prejudice as a white problem and to produce strategies to focus on the majority — a dimension of prejudice reduction which had been influential in the United Kingdom and is the basis of many race awareness training (RAT) programmes (Twitchin and Demuth, 1985).

In his work Banks (1981; 1984), identifies and clarifies underlying principles which must be addressed if education for prejudice reduction is to be successfully implemented. These include the following:

- holistic strategies which include the total school environment;
- permeation of the purposes, values and attitudes of multiculturalism into every facet of the school's functioning, including examinations;
- measures that are comprehensive in scope and sequence;
- multi-disciplinary approaches and multi-directional purposes;
- mutual and multiple acculturation of pupil and teacher by each other in a process of cultural reciprocity;
- positive multiethnic interactions with significant others;
- staff composition reflective of ethnic pluralism;
- learning styles including systematic reinforcement;
- pedagogical strategies addressing decision-making and social-actioning capacities and competences;
- curricula strengthening the intercultural competence of pupils;
- potent involvement of, and use of, local community resources, including languages.

It goes without saying that an overall holistic strategy will include more than assessment strategies for pupils. The evaluation of programmes, teachers and institutions, the strategy as a whole, has to be seen within the context of the development of not only community and national, but also global, multicultural competences. We also need to add to these the principle inherent within the series of BBC programmes addressing issues of racism (Twitchin and Demuth, 1985) that, at the core of any effective strategy of multicultural education, there has to be a commitment to staff development which starts where teachers are now and with their current attitudes and knowledge.

In spite of the disparate, unconnected and normally non-continuous nature of the work reviewed in this chapter, important principles emerge from it. These are not firm conclusions, but provisional 'guiding lights' in a field where there is much rhetoric but still all too little illumination. Such work, it seems to me, affords useful bench-marks to institutions and schools who themselves are embarking on the long and difficult road of planning, implementing and evaluating the strategies of prejudice reduction which arise from the cultural biography of their own institution, community and societal context.

The upshot of this brief excursion into the writing concerned with prejudice acquisition and reduction can be no more than a series of tentative and provisional reflections, identifying possible guiding principles for the establishment of policies of multicultural education by teachers in schools. I would summarise these briefly as follows:

- Staff development, starting from where teachers are now and including their study of their own practice, is an indispensable starter;
- Teachers need to consider what we know about prejudice as a base to extend their frame of reference for their professional judgements;
- Inclusive, comprehensive, systematic, continuous and holistic school approaches are likely to be most effective;
- Multidimensional and interdisciplinary pedagogical approaches are necessary, including interconnected and coherent phases of reinforcement, addressing, wherever possible, higher levels of mental functioning;
- Pedagogical initiatives need to be reflective of the cultural, racial and linguistic biography of the school and society;
- Strategies need to be true to the underlying ethical principles which may be derived either from philosophical speculation or from international agreements and covenants and national legislation;
- Within a democratic society the initiatives must rest on democratic principles of non-coercion and persuasion, backed up by agreed instrumental regulations;
- Prejudice reduction must address both cognitive and affective dimensions, if it is to come to terms with the intellectual and emotional dimensions of prejudice and influence behaviour;
- Positive ethnic interactions with 'significant others' as part of a process of multiple and mutual acculturation of both staff and pupils, will need to be on a co-operative, equal, voluntary and satisfying basis;
- By conceptual and political coalitions prejudice reduction must become an integral part of the curriculum rather than a 'tissue-rejected' graft;
- Holistic strategies must involve all aspects of the school's functioning, including its assessment and evaluation approaches;
- Social actioning within a democratic society will be part of basic education and development of prejudice reduction;
- Prejudice reduction will need to take account of the economic, community and social context, but it cannot be delayed until they change;
- The community has to be recognised as something broader than local or national and, thus, issues of human and civil rights beyond the borders of the nation state, including international agreements, covenants and conventions, offer clarification

and definition of basic ethical principles essential to effective and fair judgements and decisions.

Clearly, it follows from what I have said that manifestations of racial, credal, sex or class discrimination and other prejudiced behaviour on the part of pupils and/or teachers should be seen as disciplinary offences and treated accordingly on the basis of an explicit policy and delivery statement. It is important that all teachers recognise that prejudiced behaviour cannot be tolerated in a multicultural school, for it is incompatible with the ethics of that institution and its society.

I shall be dealing with that issue in the next chapter. For, while the difficulties of transferring statements and policies into actions should not be underestimated (see, for example, Troyna and Ball, 1985), as part of its overall strategy, each school will need to draw up a policy and delivery document. This should include guidelines for teachers on how to react to manifestations of racism and prejudice in their own schools and classrooms. The delivery will need to be collegially supported and organically implemented and evaluated, and that represents an enormous task for institution-based INSET. None of us can claim that we are adequately prepared for the complexity of the task of implementing education in a manner which will achieve prejudice reduction and hopefully eradication; and without a whole school policy and strategy no significant change can be expected. It is that issue of appropriate whole-school strategies which forms the theme of chapter 4.

SUMMARY

In this chapter I have given an overview of the main items in the literature concerning how prejudice is acquired and have drawn them together into a model, which shows four interactive and mutually reinforcing domains: personal, social, cultural and environmental. I have offered a diagrammatic representation of that interaction (figure 3.2). In the second part of the chapter, I have surveyed the literature of prejudice reduction and have devised a series of guiding principles for the work of educators and policy makers.

ACTIVITIES

1. What do you consider to be the main strengths and weaknesses of the literature on prejudice acquisition, as presented in this chapter? Consider the model proposed at the end of the first section, critically appraise it and seek to construct your own model aimed at helping you devise new criteria for your own personal practice.
2. What are the implications of the research on the usefulness of interethnic contact for your own institution? Draw up a series of guidelines for making such contact maximally effective. How would you monitor such contacts, for example, in grouping practices in the classrom, to make sure that they are having positive outcomes?
3. Scrutinise the list of principles proposed at the end of chapter 3. How helpful may they be to you in the actual practice of your professional work? Amend, expand

and amplify the principles into a policy document for distribution and discussion by colleagues at a staff meeting.
4. How far do you think that different strategies for prejudice reduction are needed for children from different cultural backgrounds? How would you actually implement such a strategy, bearing in mind the cultural biography of the institution where you work?

REFERENCES

Adelman, C. et al. (1984) *A Fair Hearing for All: Relationships between Teaching and Racial Equality*. Early Reading: Bulmershe College of Higher Education, Bulmershe Research Publication No. 2.

Adorno, T.W. et al. (1950) *The Authoritarian Personality*. New York: Harper & Row.

Allport, G.W. (1954) *The Nature of Prejudice*. New York: Addison Wesley.

Allport, G.W. (1979) *The Nature of Prejudice*. Reading, MA: Addison Wesley (25th Anniversary Edition).

Allport, G.W. and Kramer, B.M. (1946) Some roots of prejudice, *The Journal of Psychology*. **22**, 9–39.

Arbuthnot, J.B. and Faust, D. (1981) *Teaching Moral Reasoning; Theory and Practice*. New York: Harper & Row Publishers.

Aronson, E. and Osherow, N. (1980) 'Co-operation, prosocial behaviour and academic performance: experiments in the desegregated classroom', in Bickman, L. (ed.) *Applied Social Psychology Annual*. Beverley Hills, CA: Sage.

Aronson, E., Stephan, C., Sikes, J., Blaney, N. and Snapp, M. (1978) *The Jigsaw Classroom*. Beverley Hills, California: Sage.

Bagley, C. and Verma, G.K. (1979) *Racial Prejudice, the Individual and Society*. Westmead, Farnborough: Saxon House.

Balch, P. and Paulsen, K. (1979) 'Strategies for the Modification and Prevention of Racial Prejudice: A Review'. Paper presented at the Annual Meeting of the Western Psychological Association, San Diego, California, April 5–8.

Banks, J.A. (1981) *Multicultural Education: Theory and Practice*. Boston: Allyn & Bacon.

Banks, J.A. (1982) 'Reducing prejudice in students: theory, research and strategies', A Paper presented at the Kamloops Spring Institute for Teacher Education, Faculty of Education, Simon Fraser University, Burnaby, British Columbia, February 3.

Banks, J.A. (1984) *Teaching Strategies for Ethnic Studies*. Boston: Allyn & Bacon.

Best, D.L., Smith, S.C., Graves, D.L. and Williams, J.E. (1975) The modification of racial bias in pre-school children, *Journal of Experimental Child Psychology*. **20**, 193–205.

Bettleheim, B. and Janowitz, M. (1950) *Dynamics of Prejudice*. New York: Harper.

Blackburn, G. (1980) 'An examination of the effects of human relations on the attitudes of certificated in-service teachers in Minnesota', University of Washington, Seattle; PhD thesis.

Blalock, H.M. (1956) Economic discrimination and Negro increase, *American Sociological Review*, **21**, 584–8.

Bottomley, G. and Lepervanche, M.M. (eds) (1984) *Ethnicity, Class and Gender in Australia*, Sidney: Allen and Unwin.

Blumer, H. (1966) 'United States of America', in UNESCO, *Research on Racial Relations*. Paris: UNESCO.

Burkey, R.M. (1978) *Ethnic and Racial Groups: The Dynamics of Dominance*. Menlo Park, CA: Cumming Publishing Company.

Chapman, T.H. (1974) 'Simulation game effects on attitudes regarding racism and sexism', Maryland University, Cultural Study Centre, *Research Report*. **8** (74).

Clark, K.B. (1955) *Prejudice and Your Child* 2nd edn. Boston: Beacon Press.

Cohen, E.G. (1980) 'A multi-ability approach to the integrated classroom', Paper presented at the American Psychological Association, Montreal, Canada. Quoted in Stephan (1985).

Coombs, J.R. and Meux, M. (1971) 'Teaching strategies for value analysis', in Metcalf, L.E. (ed.) *Values Education*. Washington DC: National Council for the Social Studies.

Davidson, F. (1971) *Respect for Persons and Ethnic Prejudice in Childhood*. Harvard MA: Centre for Moral Education and Research.

Davidson, F.B.H. (1977) 'Respect for persons and ethnic prejudice in childhood: a cognitive developmental description', in Tumin, M.M. and Plotch, W. (eds) *Pluralism in a Democratic Society*. New York: Praeger.

De Vries, D.L., Edwards, K.J. and Slavin, R.E. (1978) Biracial learning teams and race relations in the classroom: four field experiments using Teams–Games–Tournaments, *Journal of Educational Psychology*. **70**, 356–62.

De Vries, D.L. and Slavin, R.E. (1978) Teams–Games–Tournament (TGT): A review of ten classroom experiments, *Journal of Research and Development Education*. **12**, 28–38.

Dunbar, L.H. (1980) 'The utilization of values clarification in multicultural education to reduce prejudicial attitudes of eight grade students', Northern Arizona University, EdD dissertation.

Rosards, C.D. and Williams, J.E. (1970) Generalization between evaluative words associated with racial figures in pre-school children, *Journal of Experimental Research in Personality*. **4**, 144–55.

Festinger, L. (1957) *A Theory of Cognitive Dissonance*. Palo Alto: Stanford University Press.

Frenkel-Brunswick, E. (1948) A study of prejudice in children, *Human Relations*. **1**, 295–306.

Gabelko, N.H. and Michaelis, J.U. (1981) *Reducing Adolescent Prejudice: A Handbook*. New York: Teachers College Press.

Gay, G. (1974) Differential dyadic interactions of black and white teachers with black and white pupils in recently desegregated social studies classrooms: a function of teacher and pupil ethnicity, Washington, DC: National Institute of Education.

Gay, G. (1982) Developmental prerequisites for multicultural education in the social studies, in Rosenzweig, L.W. *Developmental Perspectives in the Social Studies*. Washington, DC: National Council for the Social Studies (Bulletin 66).

Glock, Y.C., Wuthnow, R., Piliavin, J.A. and Spencer, M. (1975) *Adolescent Prejudice*. New York: Harper & Row.

Goldberg, A.L. (1956) The effects of two types of sound motion pictures on the attitudes of adults towards minorities, *Journal of Educational Sociology*. **29**, 386–91.

Goodman, M.E. (1973) *Race Awareness in Young Children*. New York: Collier Books.

Hall, J.L. and Frederikson, W.A. (1979) Sex role stereotyping: a function of age and education as measured by a perceptual–projective device, *Sex Roles*. **5**(1), 77–84.

Harding, J.H., Proshansky, B., Kutner, N. and Chein, I. (1954) 'Prejudice and ethnic relations', in Lindzey, G. (ed.) *The Handbook of Social Psychology* Vol. II. Reading MA: Addison Wesley.

Harding, J.H., Kutner, N., Proshansky, B. and Chein, I. (1969) 'Prejudice and ethnic relations', in Lindzey, G. and Aronson, E. (eds) *The Handbook of Social Psychology* 2nd edn Vol V. Reading MA: Addison Wesley.

Hayes, M.L. and Conklin, M.E. (1953) Intergroup attitudes and experimental change, *Journal of Experimental Education*. **22**, 19–36.

Hicks, D. (1976) *Teaching in Multicultural Schools*. London: Methuen.

Hicks, D. (1981) 'Bias in school books: messages from the ethnocentric curriculum', in James, A. and Jeffcoate, R. (eds) *The School in the Multicultural Society*. London: Harper & Row.

Horowitz, E.L. (1947) 'Development of attitudes towards Negroes', in Newcomb, T.M. and Hartley, E.L. (eds) *Readings in Social Psychology*. New York: Herny Holt.

Ijaz, M.A. and Ijaz, I.H. (1981) A cultural programme for changing racial attitudes, *History and Social Science Teacher*. **17**(1), 17–20.

Jackman, M.R. (1977) Prejudice, tolerance and attitudes towards ethnic groups, *Social Science Research*. **6**, 145–169.

Jackman, M.R. and Muha, M. (1984) Education and intergroup attitudes: moral enlightenment, superficial democratic commitment or ideological refinement, *American Sociological Review*. **49** (6), 751–769.

Johnson, D.W. (1966) Freedman school effectiveness: changes in attitudes of Negro children, *The Journal of Applied Behavioural Science*. **2**, 325–330.

Johnson, D.W. and Johnson, R. (1975) *Learning Together and Alone: Co-operation, Competition and Individualization*. Englewood Cliffs, NJ: Prentice Hall.

Johnson, D.W., Johnson, R. and Scott, L. (1978) The effects of co-operative and individualistic instruction on student attitudes and achievement, *Journal of Social Psychology* **104**, 207–216.

Jeffcoate, R. (1979) *Positive Image: Towards a Multicultural Curriculum*. London: Writers and Readers Co-operative for Chameleon.

Journal of Social Issues (1985) **41**(3).

Kattmann, U. (1979) The attitudes of 11 year old pupils toward people of other races, *Studies in Educational Evaluation*. **5**(3), 243–52.

Katz, D., Sarnoff, I. and McClintock, C. (1956) Ego-defense and attitude change, *Human Relations*. **9**, 27–45.

Katz, J.H. (1978) *White Awareness: Handbook for Anti-Racism Training*. Norman: University of Oklahoma Press.

Katz, P.A. (ed.) (1976a) *Towards the Elimination of Racism*. New York: Pergamon.

Katz, P.A. (1976b) 'Attitude change in children: can the twig be straightened?', in Katz, P.A. (ed.) op. cit., 213–241.

Katz, P.A. and Zalk, S.R. (1978) Modification of children's racial attitudes, *Developmental Psychology*. **14**, 447–61.

Kehoe, J.W. and Rogers, W.T. (1978) The effects of principle testing discussions on student attitudes towards selected groups subjected to discrimination, *Canadian Journal of Education*. **3**(4), 73–80.

Kehoe, J.W. and Sakata, C.L. (1979) Achieving empathy for victims of discrimination, *History and Social Science Teacher*. **14**(3), 195–202.

Klein, G. (1982) *Resources for Multicultural Education: An Introduction*. London: Longman/ Schools Council.

Klein, G. (1986) *Reading into Racism*. London: Routledge.

Kohlberg, L. (1969) 'Stage and sequence: the cognitive development approach to socialization', in Goslin, D.A. (ed.) *Handbook of Socialization Theory and Research*. Chicago: Rand McNally.

Kohlberg, L. (1971) 'From is to ought: how to commit the naturalistic fallacy and get away with it in the study of moral development', in Mischel, T. (ed.) *Cognitive Development and Epistemology*. New York: Academic Press.

Leviatin, V. (1971) *Resource Unit on Race, Prejudice and Discrimination*. New York: Anti Defamation League of B'nai B'rith.

Lindzey, G. (1950) Differences between high and low in prejudice and their implications for a theory of prejudice, *Personality*. **19**, 16–40.

Litchner, J.H. and Johnson, D.W. (1969) Changes in attitudes towards Negroes of white elementary school students after use of multiethnic readers, *Journal of Educational Psychology*. **60**, 148–152.

Litchner, J.H., Johnson, D.W. and Ryan, F.L. (1973) Use of pictures of multiethnic interaction to change attitudes of white elementary students towards blacks, *Psychological Reports*. **33**, 367–72.

Lockwood, A.L. and Harris, D.E. (1985) *Reasoning with Democratic Values*. New York: The Teachers College Press, Columbia University. Vols. 1 and 2: 1607–1876; 1877 to the present.

Lynch, J. (1986) *Multicultural Education: Principles and Practice*. London:Routledge and Kegan Paul.

McAdoo, J. (1970) 'An explanatory study of racial attitude change in black pre-school children using different treatments', University of Michigan, PhD dissertation.

Merton, R.K. (1949) 'Discrimination and the American creed', in McIver, R.M. (ed.) *Discrimination and National Welfare*. New York: Harper and Row. (Institute for Religious and Social Studies).

Miller, H.J. (1969) The effectiveness of teaching techniques for reducing colour prejudice, *Liberal Education*, **16**, 25–31.

Miller, H.J. (1967) 'A study of the effectiveness of a variety of teaching techniques for reducing colour prejudice in a male student sample aged 15–21', London: University of London, MA Thesis.

Milner, D. (1975) *Children and Race*. London: Penguin.

Milner, D. (1979) 'Does multicultural education work?', in Open University, *Ethnic Minorities and Education*. (Unit 14 Curriculum Issues for Schools) Milton Keynes: Open University Press.

Milner, D. (1981) 'Racial Prejudice', in Turner, J. and Giles, H. (eds) *Intergroup Behaviour*. Oxford: Basil Blackwell.

Milner, D. (1983) *Children and Race: Ten Years On*. London: Ward Lock Educational.

Moore, R.B. (1976) *Racism in the English Language*. New York: Council on Interracial Books for Children.

Nixon, J. (1980) Teaching about race relations, *Secondary School Theatre Journal*. **19**(3), 16–18.

Oser, F.K. (1986) 'Moral education and values education: the discourse perspective', in Wittrock, M.C. (ed.) *Handbook of Research on Teaching* 3rd edn. New York: Collier Macmillan.

Page, A. and Thomas, K. (1984) *Multicultural Education and the All-White School*. Nottingham: University of Nottingham, School of Education.

Pate, G.S. (1981) Research on prejudice reduction, *Educational Leadership*. January, pp. 288–91.

Pearlin, L.I. (1954) Shifting group attachments and attitudes towards Negroes, *Social Forces*. **33**, 41–47.

Pettigrew, T.F. (1959) Regional differences in anti-Negro prejudice, *Journal of Abnormal and Social Psychology*. **59**, 28–36.

Purnell, R.B. (1978) Teaching them to curse: a study of certain types of inherent racial bias in language pedagogy and practice, Denver CO: Paper presented at the Annual Meeting of The Conference College Composition and Communication, March 30–April 1.

Raab, E. and Lipset, S.M. (1963) *Prejudice and Society*. New York: Anti Defamation League of B'nai B'rith. ERIC document ED 001985.

Redling, J. (1977) Landeskunde im Englischunterricht der Sekundarstufe 1, *Praxis des Neusprachlichen Unterrichts*. **24**(21), 125–31.

Rist, R.C. (1970) Student social class and teacher expectations: the self-fulfilling prophesy in ghetto education, *Harvard Educational Review*. **40**, 411–51.

Rose, A.M. (1962) 'The causes of prejudice', in Barron, M.L. (ed.) *American Cultural Minorities: A Textbook of Readings in Intergroup Relations*. New York: Alfred A. Knopf.

Saenger, G. and Gilbert, E. (1950) Customer reaction to integration of Negro sales personnel, *International Journal of Opinion and Attitudes Research*. **4**, 57–76.

Saville-Troike, M. (1981) 'Language diversity in multiethnic education', in Banks, J.A. (ed.) *Education in the 1980s: Multi-ethnic Education*. Washington DC: National Education Association.

Sciara, F.J. and Cunningham, D. (1982) 'Racial prejudice in young children: a case for multicultural education'. Paper presented at the Annual Conference of the Indiana Association for the Education of Young Children, Indianapolis: 1 October.

Sears, R.R., Maccoby, E.E. and Levin, H. (1957) *Patterns of Child Rearing*. Evanston: ILL: Row, Paterson.

Shanahan, J.K. (1972) 'The effects of modifying black-white concept attitudes of black and white first grade subjects upon two measures of racial attitude', Seattle: University of Washington, PhD Dissertation.

Sharan S. *et al.*, (1985) 'Co-operative learning effects on ethnic relations and achievement in Israeli junior high-school classrooms', in R.E. Slavin *et al.*, *Learning to Co-operate: Co-operating to Learn*. New York: Plenum Press.

Short, G.A. (1981) Racial attitudes among caucasian children: an empirical study of Allport's total rejection hypothesis, *Educational Studies*. **7**(3), 197–204.

Sikes, P. (ed.) (1979) *Teaching About Race Relations: Teaching and Action Research*. Norwich: CARE, University of East Anglia.

Simpson, G.E. and Yinger, M.J. (1965) *Racial and Cultural Minorities*. New York: Harper and Row.

Singh, J.M. and Yancy, A.V. (1974) Racial attitudes in white first grade children, *The Journal of Educational Research*. **67**, 370–2.

Slavin, R.E. (1977) How student learning teams can integrate the desegregated classroom, *Integrated Education*. **15**, 56–58.

Slavin, R.E. (1979) *Student Team Learning as a Total Instructional Programme: Effects on Achievement and Attitudes*. Baltimore: Centre for Social Organization of Schools, Johns Hopkins University.

Slavin, R.E. (1983) *Co-operative Learning*. New York: Longman.

Stenhouse, L., Verma, G. and Wild, R. (eds) (1982) *Teaching about Race Relations: Problems and Effects*. London: Routledge and Kegan Paul.

Stephan, W.G. (1985) 'Intergroup Relations', pp. 599–658, in Lindzey, G. and Aronson, E. *The Handbook of Social Psychology*. New York: Random House.

Stephan, W.G. and Brigham, J.C. (1985) Intergroup contact: introduction, *Journal of Social Issues*. **41**(3), 1–8.

Stephan, W.G. and Stephan, C.W. (1985) Intergroup anxiety, *Journal of Social Issues*. **41**(3), 157–75.

Sussman, E. (1971) 'Prejudice as a function of intellectual level and cultural information', address prepared for the American Educational Research Association Meeting, New York, February 5.

Tajfel, H. (1981) 'Social stereotypes and social groups, in J. Turner and H. Giles (eds) *Intergroup Behaviour*. Chicago: University of Chicago Press.

Tajfel, H. and Turner, J. (1979) 'An integrative theory of intergroup conflict', in Austin, W. and Worchel, S. (eds) *The Social Psychology of Intergroup Relations*. Monterey, CA: Brooks-Cole.

Tansik, D.A. and Driscoll, J.D. (1977) 'Temporal persistence of attitudes induced through required training', *Group and Organisation Studies*. **2**(3), 310–21.

Taxel, J. (1982) *Sensitizing Students to the Selective Tradition in Children's Literature*. Paper presented at the Annual Meeting of the American Educational Research Association, New York, March, 1982. ERIC document ED 213 647 S00 13929.

Trager, H.G. and Yarrow, M.R. (1952) *They Learn What They Live*. New York: Harper & Row.

Traynham, R.A. (1974) 'The effects of modifying colour meaning concepts on racial concept attitudes in five and eight year old children', University of Arkansas, MA thesis.

Troyna, B. and Ball, W. (1985) *Views from the Chalkface: School Responses to an LEA's Policy on Multiracial Education*. Coventry: University of Warwick.

Twitchen, J. and Demuth, S. (1985) *Multicultural Education* 2nd edn. London: British Broadcasting Corporation.

United States Commission on Human Rights (1973) *Teacher and Students: Differences in Teacher Interaction with Mexico American and Anglo Students*. Washington, DC: United States Government Printing Office.

Vander Zanden, J.W. (1963) *American Minority Relations*. New York: The Ronald Press.

Walker, P. (1971) 'The effects of hearing selected children's stories that portray blacks in a favourable manner on the racial attitudes of groups of black and white kindergarten children', University of Kentucky: PhD dissertation.

Watson, G. (1947) *Action for Unity*. New York: Harper and Row.

Williams, J.E. and Morland, J.K. (1976) *Race, Colour and the Young Child*. Chapel Hill: The University of North Carolina Press.

Williams, R.M. (1947) *The Reduction of Intergroup Tensions: A Survey of Research on Ethnic, Racial and Religious Group Tensions*. New York: Social Science Research Council (Bulletin 57).

Zimet, S. (1976) *Print and Prejudice*. New York: Hodder and Stoughton.

Zimet, S. (1983) Teaching children to detect social bias in books, *Reading Teacher*, **36**, 418–21.

Chapter 4

Whole-School Policies for Combating Prejudice

INTRODUCTION

In the last chapter, I attempted to give a cameo of the extensive and complex literature on prejudice acquisition and reduction, and I proposed a model which seeks to encompass the complex mechanisms whereby prejudice is acquired. On the basis of a selected literature survey of prejudice reduction strategies, I also suggested a provisional list of guiding principles for the development of overall policies of prejudice reduction.

In this chapter, I want to focus those principles more closely on the school as a social system, attempting to define what an effective school might be in the field of prejudice reduction. I shall be emphasising the importance of a holistic approach, sensitive to the needs and cultural biography of each school and the way in which the ethos, norms and structure of schools communicate a powerful message about their real intentions and values. I want to stress that good school policy and practice in this field may also contribute to heightened academic achievement and to give some examples of whole-school policies. Finally, I want to offer some institutional guidelines and provisional criteria for prejudice reduction.

EFFECTIVE SCHOOLS

There is now an interesting convergence of official and non-official writing and the results of research on both sides of the Atlantic indicate what may be involved in an effective school. This convergence is all the more remarkable if one considers the different administrations and organisational structures involved as well as the differing objectives and styles of approach.

In the United States the work of Brookover et al. (1979) and Coleman, Heffer and Kilore (1982), drawing on the need to recommit the nation's schools to the pursuit of excellence, has been particularly influential. While not strong on cultural diversity, the report of the National Commission on Excellence, *A Nation at Risk* (1983), drew on a back-to-the-basics, conservative ideology but provided momentum for more detailed discussion and criticism of educational provision and the effectiveness of schools. Drawing on extensive practical and research work over a period of years, the so-called Effective Schools Movement called attention to the fact that well-organised schools can make a difference to the educational achievement of children from disadvantaged communities. One outcome of that movement was a sourcebook (Kyle, 1985) which drew together the voluminous research in the field and clearly identified five factors characteristic of effective schools:

- a school climate conducive to learning;
- teacher's expectations that all students can achieve;
- an emphasis on basic skills instruction and high time-on-task for learners;
- a system of clear instructional objectives for the monitoring and evaluation of learning;
- a head teacher who creates incentives for learning, sets school goals, maintains discipline, observes classrooms and is a strong leader.

The sourcebook provides an extensive review of key ideas and concepts and lists 39 effective schools projects in 20 different states, active in late 1984.

More recently, an official publication of the Department of Education stated unequivocally;

> The most important characteristics of effective schools are strong institutional leadership, a safe and orderly climate, school-wide emphasis on basic skills, higher teacher expectations for student achievement, and continuous assessment of pupil progress. (United States Department of Education, 1986)

The publication further emphasises the importance of clear, consistent and fair decisions by the head teacher, collegiality among teachers in support of pupil achievement, and agreement among teachers, pupils and parents on the goals, methods and content of schooling. A core of this effectiveness is seen as deriving from the school climate, or learning environment, which the teachers, pupils, parents and community members work to develop. Fullan (1983), drawing on research on educational change and linking it with research on school effectiveness by Purkey and Smith (1983) and Edmonds (1979; 1982), identified the major characteristics possessed by effective schools; both organisational and processual as:

Organisational
- strong instructional leadership;
- emphasis on curriculum and instruction;
- clear goals;
- high expectations;
- effective monitoring of performance;
- continuing staff development;
- involvement and support of parents.

Processual
- a value system directing the school towards its strategic goals;

- intense interaction and communication among everyone in the school;
- collaborative planning and implementation of improvements;
- a feel for the change and improvement process on the part of school teachers.

In an ethnographic study of six high schools selected because they were perceived by the school inhabitants as being good and challenging the narrow definition of school effectiveness as instructional effectiveness, Lightfoot (1981) picks up the two major themes of the research cited above, when she writes:

> The people most responsible for defining the school's vision and articulating the ideological stance are the principals and headmasters. . . . Their personal image is inextricably linked to the public persona of the institution. . . . Good high schools provide safe and regulated environments for building student–teacher relationships. Rules and behavioural modes are the most explicit and visible symbols of order and structure.
> (Lightfoot, 1983, pp. 323 and 350)

Moreover, she also comments on the way in which an explicit ideological vision and a clear articulation of the goals of education coalesce as ideology, order and authority to support the evolution of a coherent but changing institution that supports human interaction and growth.

Such considerations as strong and consistent leadership, a coherent ideological commitment and espousal of an ordered and disciplined environment seem to me to be at the heart of a good and effective school determined on prejudice reduction in the context of multicultural education. I shall return to these themes later as part of my proposals for monitoring the strength of attachment to the ideal of prejudice reduction by the school.

Earlier research by Crain, Mehard and Narat (1982) was based on work in 200 desegregated secondary schools and involving some 10,000 students and upwards of 2,000 teachers and administrators, funded by the Federal Government. It indicated quite clearly, according to the investigators, that good schools have an overall positive ambience or social climate. Such good schools were 'effective' in reducing student alienation and misbehaviour and raising student self-esteem. They encouraged inter-racial friendships, helped the integration of teaching for racial equality into the curriculum, and promoted greater involvement of parents. The researchers found, moreover, that teacher attitude and behaviour was an important factor in influencing pupil attitudes and behaviour and that teachers' racial attitudes affected the achievement of black students with predictive validity. They comment that while the achievement of white children may not be affected by the racial climate of the school, that of blacks, and especially black males, is strongly affected by that climate. In related work over a number of years, Slavin (Slavin and Madden, 1979; Slavin, 1983), looked into the effects of co-operative group methods on race relations. From their work they are led to comment that the very fact of organising co-operative work groups on a mixed ethnic basis is a powerful communicator of institutional norms. It generates a number of outcomes such as increased self-esteem, low school anxiety, interethnic friendships, a high sense of personal efficacy – and high academic performance.

In a research project conducted in Florida middle schools, under the auspices of the Anti-Defamation League of B'nai B'rith, an attempt was made to link the research on school climate and whole-school policies and strategies for prejudice reduction. Although at the time of writing those results are not yet available, the outcomes appear to have been positive and encouraging, endorsing the importance of school ethos in achieving prejudice reduction goals. One particular feature of this project appears to have been the emphasis on parent involvement. As the Principal of one of the participating schools is quoted as saying, 'a lot of their prejudices are of the cottage industry variety, they bring them from home' (Gaiter, 1985).

Official publications in the United Kingdom too have emphasised the crucial role of the school head teacher and the importance of the ethos of the school. In an informal and small-scale survey of ten secondary schools, undertaken to test out the feasibility of generalisable factors which contribute to success in secondary education, members of Her Majesty's Inspectorate found that, for all their differences, the ten good schools had certain commonalities: 'What they all have in common is effective leadership and a 'climate' that is conducive to growth' (HMI, 1977, p.36). The report concludes that the schools see themselves as places designed for learning, with explicit philosophies which are explained to parents and pupils and with an acceptance of shared values as the foundation of their corporate life. Sometimes teachers may tire of all the work involved in discussing, agreeing and writing up specific aims for their professional activities in school. The report, though, underlines the need for participation, teamwork, consultation and for specific educational aims, both social and intellectual, as a major aspect of these good schools. Such aims and rationales form the theme of this chapter on whole-school policies for prejudice reduction.

Independent research, too, has underlined these and similar factors as being the foundations of an effective school. The work of Rutter et al. (1979), for example, places the ambience of the school as the most potent factor in its success, underlining, also, the need for high teacher expectations and attention to the detail of an ordered environment. This study involved a comparison of 12 secondary schools in the Inner London Education Authority and included data on academic attainment, attendance, behaviour and delinquency. Although all served areas of social disadvantage, schools were found to have varying influences on their pupils. Some schools had a clearcut positive effect, while others actually had a negative effect. Interestingly, the researchers discovered that in those schools where teachers engaged in collegial planning, were punctual and well-prepared, children's behaviour, attendance and achievement were better. Participation in the running of the school by pupils also resulted in positive behavioural and academic outcomes. They comment that the cumulative effect of such factors as a particular ethos, set of values, attitudes and behaviour becomes characteristic of a school and is more influential than any other individual factor.

All together, the force of the research and writing quoted above is such as to persuade us that a good school can have both a school ethos, committed to good human relations and the attenuation of prejudice, as well as effective academic attainment. Indeed, the effort to improve school ethos and promote better attitudes will probably have the by-product effect of improving achievement as well. So the argument of this chapter is certainly not that academic performance must take a back seat to prejudice reduction, but rather that the one actually facilitates the other. Moreover, as good schools espouse both intellectual and social aims, a high standard in one cannot be seen as a compensation for a low standard in the other. Quite the reverse, where high standards in the two are seen as the goal, they become mutually reinforcing.

Moreover, a recent recommendation of the Committee of Ministers of the Council of Europe (Council of Europe, 1985), on teaching and learning about human rights in schools addresses specifically the issue of the climate of the school. It states:

> 4.1 Democracy is best learned in a democratic setting where participation is encouraged, where views can be expressed openly and discussed, where there is fairness and justice. An appropriate climate is, therefore, an essential complement to effective learning about human rights.
> 4.2 Schools should encourage participation in their activities by parents and other members of the community . . .
> 4.3 Schools should attempt to be positive towards all their pupils . . .
> (Council of Europe, 1985, p.3)

Multicultural educators have tended to pay scant regard to such research and writing at home or abroad, preferring to adopt *ad hoc* and disparate initiatives towards isolated and usually non-prestigious aspects of the school curriculum or devoting enthusiasm and energy to criticising teachers and schools for their manifest limitations and inadequacies in failing to achieve social or even political revolution. The result has been an absence of holistic and coherent proposals for school policies for multicultural education and an almost total neglect of aspects such as prejudice reduction.

Multicultural education has thus been an easy prey to any number of accusations. Not only has it been held guilty of neglecting prejudice and discrimination, but also of ignoring issues of power, politics and access to resources, of blaming the victims, disguising the way in which minority groups are oppressed and victimised and acting as a palliative to a deterministically prejudiced and racist social system and economic–political order. Yet, as Banks (1981) cogently argues, any effective policy for multicultural education must address the whole school as a social system with values and objectives, a hidden and expressed curriculum, organisation and procedures, assessment and disciplinary procedures and a relationship with its ecosystem. So, what might an effective multicultural school which is committed to a policy of prejudice reduction look like?

In a powerful advocacy of the need for macro approaches to prejudice reduction, Banks argues that, because the school is an interrelated social system, it is insufficient to focus on isolated aspects of it. What is needed, he suggests, is institutional reform of the whole school, including institutional norms, power relationships, communication, culture, curriculum, language policy, assessment and extra curricular activities (Banks, 1985). He points to the way in which hidden values have a more cogent impact on pupils' attitudes than the formal programme of studies, and he subdivides the total school environment into 11 major components: school policy and politics, school culture and hidden curriculum, learning styles, languages and dialects, community participation, counselling, assessment and testing procedures, instructional materials, formal curriculum, teaching styles and strategies, school attitudes, perceptions, beliefs and actions (Banks, 1981, p.22). He argues that, while initial school reform may focus on any one of these variables, changes must take place in each of them to create and sustain an effective, multiethnic educational environment.

Gollnick and Chinn (1986) affirm that the climate of a multicultural school is central to the development and delivery of an effective multicultural education. They focus on such items as the function of displays and bulletin boards, the composition of games teams, the staffing composition (including teaching and non-teaching members and the balance and roles of males and females), pupil involvement in school governance, assemblies, extra-curricular activities and participation in subjects within the curriculum including both sexes and all cultural groups (Gollnick and Chinn, 1986, pp. 276–279).

The school climate tends to comprise intangible factors which are multifaceted and difficult to identify, let alone to include in a policy statement, except after rigorous reflexive scrutiny. Kehoe has produced a manual for enhancing the multicultural climate of schools, including several proforma, semantic differentials, interview schedule and open-ended questionnaire approaches (Kehoe, 1984a, pp. 9–19). He draws particular attention to those aspects of a school's existence which are taken for granted and may deny equality of educational opportunity to all pupils, such as long-embedded regulations and unexamined practices. He cites, for example, mixed physical education classes and school dances or even, in some cases, mixed field trips. Because norms and expectations surrounding such practices are often implicit, Kehoe argues, teachers may not be aware that such practices may be inconsistent with — or even offensive to — the culture of some minorities.

Some schools have attempted to seize the intangible and to incorporate within their overall policy statement references to the ethos and atmosphere of the school. One such is the policy statement agreed by the staff at North Westminster Community School, in London, which states that the ethos and atmosphere of the school should show the respect which is the entitlement of all persons entering the school, and that school rules and regulations should be sensitive to, and show respect for, diverse cultural practices such as religion, diet and dress. It also makes suggestions for dealing immediately with racist graffiti and for discouraging their re-appearance by 'alternatives' such as displays of pupils' work, notices, etc. (North Westminster Community School, 1983).

One of the few school policy statements which takes as its point of departure the broad definition of prejudice adopted in this book, is the one produced by Wyke Manor School in Bradford. The major platform for that statement is the racist, sexist and classist nature of British society, and it contrasts this with the commitment on the part of all members of the school to equal opportunity in education for all pupils, regardless of race, sex, colour, religion or class. It accepts that the above contrast and commitment necessarily involves making an effort to eradicate evil prejudices (Wyke Manor School, 1984).

More narrowly conceived in its definition of prejudice but none the less emphatic in its opposition to racism is the statement by Quintin Kynaston School in London. Here it is the *demonstration* of the school's commitment to equal regard and value for all students that is stated emphatically. Racism, being diametrically opposed to that principle is unacceptable and must therefore be positively countered through the vigilance of the staff, through direct teaching and through explicit procedures for dealing with unacceptable behaviour such as racism (Quintin Kynaston School, 1983).

Of course, if such a holistic school policy is embedded in a policy and delivery document by the local education authority it is immeasurably assisted. Such is the case in Bradford where Administrative Memoranda have been issued which guide head teachers, staff and committees in the preparation of their own institutional policy and practice. Setting out particular aims for education in that area the first of two major memoranda states as its intent:

1. To seek ways of preparing all children and young people for life in a multicultural society.
2. To counter racism and racist attitudes, and the inequalities and discrimination which result from them.
3. To build and develop the strengths of cultural and linguistic diversity.
4. To respond sensitively to the special needs of minority groups.

(City of Bradford Metropolitan Council, 1982)

This memorandum deals with areas of school life such as school and community, and parental rights. Included are such matters as access to information, school assemblies, religious education, religious festivals, prayers for Muslim pupils. Further, cultural issues such as school uniform, jewellery, physical education, meals and the recording of names are included along with an instruction that the memorandum and its contents should be discussed regularly with staff. This collegial aspect of the policy is very important if the implementation is to be effective and consistent for all across the whole life of the school. A further memorandum then focuses more closely, practically and helpfully on racialist behaviour in schools and how it may be dealt with. In this way teachers recognise and know how to respond consistently and immediately to such behaviour, while aiding and supporting the victim and dealing with the impact on the school community. Racialist behaviour is defined as: 'any hostile or offensive act or expression by a person of one racial group against the person of another racial group, or any incitement to commit such an act, where there is an indication that the motivation is racial dislike or hatred' (City of Bradford Metropolitan Council, 1983). This definition is needed to facilitate the introduction of effective disciplinary action which is seen to be evenhanded. Another important recognition in this document is the realisation that such racialist behaviour has an impact on the school community as a whole; that unchecked it could be mistakenly believed to be part of the hidden curriculum or ethos of the school.

Teachers' unions also have an important role in helping to establish the ambience of a school and in supporting the institutional commitment to prejudice reduction. In the United Kingdom, the National Union of Teachers was an early leader in the field with the publication in 1981 of *Combatting Racism in Schools* (National Union of Teachers, 1981) which was subsequently revised in 1983. That same union has also issued an account of its race awareness training programme (National Union of Teachers, 1983). Another union which has also grasped the centrality of the problem of racism is the Assistant Masters and Mistresses Association (AMMA, 1983). In Canada, the British Columbia Teachers Federation states explicitly that it:

condemns any expression of racial, religious or ethnic bias by any of its members or employees . . . and is committed to developing and publicizing . . . procedures to be followed by members and employees in dealing with racial, religious or ethnic incidents. These procedures must preserve the dignity and integrity of the victims.
(British Columbia Teachers Federation, 1984a)

The federation has, however, not only adopted policies emphasising a commitment to education which fosters the growth and development of every pupil, regardless of sex, age, race, religion or socio-economic status, it has also appointed a 'Committee against Racism' with the following objectives:

> urging local school boards of trustees, through the development of clearly stated policies, to take a firm stand against racism in the school system;
> identifying institutionalized racism and working for its elimination from the school system;
> developing a belief in a program of equal opportunity for all students and teachers;
> assisting local school boards to improve the quality of teaching materials which deal with ethno-cultural minorities;
> working for pre-service and in-service training for teachers who must work in ethnically-diverse classrooms;
> sensitizing all teachers to the challenges and needs of a plural society working for a truly multicultural school system
> (British Columbia Teachers Federation, 1984b)

That same Federation has launched an extensive series of professional development activities on both anti-racism and anti-sexism and is encouraging school boards to include these dimensions in their contracts.

Thus, while I shall be dealing with the issue of professional development in chapter 8, it is important to place on record that teachers' associations can and do contribute, through their professional and syndical activities, to the establishment and growth of an appropriate ethos in individual schools, by making clear the norms and behaviour which they expect of their members and by supporting them with ideas, information, material and above all new and extended criteria by which they can judge their own professional practice.

We are now nearer to a position in which to answer the question posed earlier in this chapter about what a school prejudice reduction policy might look like. Indeed, we have a number of starting points which indicate the need for both implementation and evaluation policies to address the following:

1. The governance of the school, including the Board of Governors, issues of parental and community involvement and, as appropriate to age, pupil participation directly or through parallel structures.
2. The issue of an explicit policy statement and delivery document which state unequivocally the school's commitment against prejudice and for prejudice reduction and how they are to be implemented, together with an explicit disciplinary code, indicating how prejudiced behaviour will be dealt with.
3. The composition, appointment, promotion and development of staff, both teaching and administrative/ancillary.
4. Communications both oral and non-oral, verbal and non-verbal, such as bulletin boards, displays and exhibitions, library instructions, directions, etc.
5. Materials acquisition and evaluation including print and non-print and library resources.
6. Language policy, including issues of standard English, English as a second language, home language and dialect and their use across the spectrum of the school's activities including translations and interpreting for parent–teacher meetings.
7. School rules and regulations concerning issues such as behaviour, dress, jewellery, religious education and other curriculum subjects such as swimming,

physical education, dance, craft design technology, where issues of racism, credism or sexism are likely to arise.

8. Extra-curricular activities including arrangements for parent–teacher meetings, membership of clubs, teams, etc.

9. Staff development including cognitive, affective and behavioural components on a collegial and supportive basis.

10. Curricula and teaching/learning strategies which seek to take account of cultural and cognitive diversity as well as aiming for prejudice reduction.

11. Examination, assessment and testing policies that are attentive to the school's policy as in 1., together with a policy of maximum openness with regard to school records, their interpretation and transmission including the involvement of parents.

12. Institutionalised structures and procedures for the ongoing evaluation of the policy and its practical implications.

I now propose to take each of these areas, in turn, and to raise a series of questions about them, completing each section with an initial checklist of questions which may assist teachers in beginning that essential process of review of what exists, before policy can be developed for new directions in multicultural education for prejudice reduction.

GOVERNANCE OF THE SCHOOL

I have deliberately used the word governance rather than merely referring to the Board of Governors, in order to draw attention to the fact that this section concerns not only issues of the ethnic and gender mix on the Board of Governors but also the involvement of parents and the wider community, and the ways in which staff and students govern themselves. For, it is inconceivable that democratic values, such as

Checklist 4.1 *Initial questions about governance*

	Yes	No	Don't know
The Board of Governors			
Does the composition of the Board of Governors reflect the racial and cultural make-up of the surrounding community?			
Does the school have a coherent, comprehensive race relations and sex equality policy?			
Are new policies always formulated in accordance with the principles of that race relations and sex equality policy?			
Has the Board effective mechanisms for ensuring the accountability of staff in implementing the prejudice reduction policy?			
Does the Board have effective mechanisms for ensuring that parents and pupils (according to age) from all racial/ethnic and socio-economic groups have meaningful and potent participation in decision making?			
Does the Board of Governors address social issues such as employment, law, housing, and other matters as they relate to schools, racism, sexism, credism and social class?			

respect for persons, may be educated for within an authoritarian structure. Moreover, this area overlaps with others such as language and communications policies and the activities and policies of professional associations. Most of all it conjoins with the crucial role of the head teacher in exercising authority and leadership, inspiration and vision without stifling the fragile plants of democracy and dialogue, which are so crucial to the effective school committed to multicultural education and prejudice reduction. There are no guidelines for success for the head teacher, and the difficulty of the dilemma is accentuated by the power of his/her position, which if used may assist only in frustrating his/her goals and breaking the coherent ideology, order and authority which Lightfoot (1983) sees as so essential to a 'good school'.

As a starter checklist 4.1 suggests a number of questions which teachers might like to raise about the present and future appropriate governance of their school.

POLICY STATEMENT

A policy statement is a necessary but not a sufficient first step in establishing a school climate. It is, in a sense, a public nailing of the school colours to the multicultural mast. In addition, however, such a statement needs to be firmly linked to what is called a delivery document viz., a description of the means whereby the institution intends to implement the policy and to monitor its effectiveness. Part of the delivery document will need to make clear to pupils and teachers, parents and community the disciplinary consequences and sanctions which are available to the school should the policy be infringed. In any case, this 'disciplinary code' will need to make clear the consequences at different levels of gravity and the way in which the victims' self-esteem is to be restored and the impact on the community repaired. As vigour, consistency and immediacy of response are so important, all staff, pupils and parents will need to be issued with a copy of the statement, delivery document and disciplinary code. Ideally, the policy should include a coherent philosophical section linking it to the overall aims of the school, a section dealing with the school's commitment to cultural diversity and a section on the school's approach to prejudice reduction. It should include reference to issues such as naming pupils, religious customs and festivals, dress and jewellery. Information should be given to parents and their rights in such matters as school assemblies, religious education, their children's school records, asserted. They should have access to the school and to teachers for discussion and consultation. Absence for religious observance and diet should be accepted and the fact that the activities of extremist political organisations committed to racism are not compatible with the school ethos directly stated along with information about special curricular areas. A section on conflict resolution will also be necessary and, as stated above, if there is to be a coherent, ordered community a statement of disciplinary procedures and sanctions is also necessary.

A series of questions such as those set out in checklist 4.2 may suggest starting points from which such a document could be considered although the importance of parental and community involvement in arriving at a final document cannot be overestimated if the document is to carry conviction and muster support from all. Even so, parents and teachers must realize that procedures for consultation — perhaps even conciliation — are a necessary part of the delivery of such a policy.

Checklist 4.2 *Questions concerning policy statements*

	Yes	No	Don't know
Does your school have a coherent/explicit policy statement on multicultural education as part of the overall goals of the school?			
Does the policy statement address issues of prejudice, such as racism, sexism, credism and classism?			
Is it circulated to all pupils, staff, parents and key community organisations?			
Did parents, pupils and the community collaborate in drawing it up?			
Does it include explicit guidance to parents on their rights in such matters as dress, records, religious education, etc?			
Has it been approved by the Board of Governors?			
Does it have an attached delivery document?			
Does it include a 'disciplinary code' indicating the consequences for various kinds of non-permissible behaviour?			
Is it regularly revised by staff, parents and the community?			
Does it include procedures for the evaluation of the policy and its effectiveness?			

STAFF COMPOSITION

The structure and composition of the staff speak volumes about the real policy of the school as well as providing a kind of cultural capital for the implementation of the school's curriculum. If there are no bilingual staff, or staff from visible minorities, among both the teaching and ancillary staff, that situation beams powerful messages about the real as opposed to the declared policy of the institution. Clearly, schools cannot dismiss staff in order to change the ethnic composition overnight, but part-time and new appointments must aim to reflect more accurately the racial and ethnic mix of the school's community and there should be a balance of the sexes in different grades. Of course there is no one-to-one correspondence between the ethnic mix of society and that of individual schools. Staff development and appraisal will also need to include criteria for evaluation which address issues of justice for all regardless of race, class, sex or religion.

An initial checklist of issues might include some of the items listed in checklist 4.3 but it must be clear that schools will formulate their approach differently, although all should be committed to certain fundamental items such as justice. No one, though, can tell a school exactly how to develop its policy, although I know lots of people like to think that they can!

COMMUNICATIONS

As a number of sources mentioned previously have stated, communications, verbal, oral and non-verbal, are clearly an important medium through which the school makes manifest its support for multicultural education and prejudice reduction. While such 'static' items as displays, exhibitions, friezes, notice and bulletin boards, library instructions, directions to pupils, staff and visitors, etc. are of central importance, they

Checklist 4.3 *Questions concerning staffing*

	Yes	No	Don't know
Is the staff reflective of the racial and ethnic mix of the community?			
Is there a section appropriately staffed to ensure that race relations and sex equality policy and practices are carried out institution-wide?			
Do personnel practices — appointments, promotion, training, job classifications, ensure that the composition of staff aims to reflect the ethnic composition of the community?			
Do the appointment and promotion of all staff take into account teachers' commitment to multicultural education and prejudice reduction as well as technical competence?			
Are staff who are actively countering racism, sexism, classism and credism recognised, rewarded and supported through resources in the form of training, materials, positive feedback?			
Are heads of departments, and the head teacher held accountable for ensuring that implementation is consistent with, and promotes the tenets of national and local race relations and sex equality policy?			
Are the head teacher, all heads of department in the school and all staff, clear as to their roles in carrying out race relations policy, and are they held accountable for doing so?			
Is there regular in-service training for all staff, including the head teacher and department heads, which deepens their understanding of prejudice reduction practices, and their role in ensuring policy?			
Do mechanisms and procedures exist so that head teachers and heads of departments feel comfortable in seeking assistance in developing policies and programmes in their schools to counter racism?			
Are head teachers and teachers evaluated for their skills in multicultural education for prejudice reduction and given real recognition as part of teacher appraisal?			
Do the staff enlist the participation of all pupils and parents in implementing policy and developing new practices which challenge racism, sexism and other undesirable prejudices and discrimination?			

are only a part of the overall setting for the ambience of the school. Non-verbal communicators such as lowering the eyes or different hand signals (snapping of fingers, crossing fingers) have different meanings or weightings in those cultures where they exist. Kehoe (1984b) gives a series of critical incidents which he uses as cross-cultural communicators to illustrate the way in which such matters may be a source of major misunderstanding because of teachers' lack of skill in intercultural communication. Teachers need to be aware of the scope for misunderstanding.

The way in which the school writes to parents, what it expects of them in return and the access which it grants to children's records are additional items. If children's records are written in lay language and marking scales are explained, parents are more likely to feel involved and to be able to participate in important decisions about their children. Commitment is, however, also expressed through other forms of communication — choice of music for assemblies, the language available, whether translation and interpretations are sought for parents who may have difficulty with English, seating arrangements for parents' meetings and in school and classroom: all of these are powerful communicators of the ethos of a school. Lastly, how staff relate to each other in front of pupils and with pupils, inside and outside the classroom indicates whether prejudice reduction is likely to permeate into the hidden curriculum of peer group influences. Checklist 4.4 attempts to pose a few fundamental questions about this influential area which is so difficult to define.

Checklist 4.4 *Questions concerning communication*

	Yes	No	Don't know
Are there clear guidelines on permissible means and modes of communication in the school?			
Are there clear procedures for monitoring the content of notice and bulletin boards?			
Are clear directions issued with regard to action to be taken in the case of racist and sexist graffiti?			
Does the content of displays, exhibitions and friezes reflect the cultural diversity of the school and its catchment area?			
Are home languages used in the school and for parents meetings, for signs, directions, translation, letters, etc?			
Are communications media such as those above used as a means of challenging prejudice and correcting for misinformation?			
Do seating patterns at parents' meetings encourage communication, equality and respect?			
Are criteria for decisions such as placement, subject choice and career choice open for discussion with parents?			
Are communications with parents and particularly reports, vetted to see that they communicate effectively and adhere to the school policy?			
Is encouragement given to children and parents to loan artefacts from community cultures for display and exhibition in the school?			
Do staff exercise great caution in interpreting and transmitting information about pupils?			
Are teachers aware of the differing meaning and weighting of non-verbal cues in some cultures, e.g., looking someone in the eye, 'hand signals', etc?			
Is there a person or committee vested with responsibility for monitoring and developing school policy in this area?			

MATERIALS ACQUISITION AND EVALUATION

There are a number of excellent lists of criteria for assessing the extent to which materials and resources used in and by the school are appropriate to multicultural education and the reduction of prejudice. Ultimately, however, each school will need to make its own decisions on the content of its own cultural make-up and policy. It goes without saying, for example, that such resources must seek to reflect the racial and cultural diversity of the United Kingdom and to give a balanced and fair representation of other cultures. As an adjunct to this, the school itself needs to establish clear guidelines for evaluating the accuracy, authenticity and fairness of the treatment of ethnic minorities in texts, learning materials and resources, and to identify material for weeding out which is in any way biased. But this is a continual process, not just because of the advent of new materials, but also because new information, insights and understandings are continually becoming available. The early 'exotic' phase of multicultural education, for example, is now realised to have been a mistake and a generator of superficial stereotypes and it is now appreciated that the diversity within cultures is an important balancing momentum to excessive emphasis on difference. Moreover, material reflecting the roles and contributions of all to the United Kingdom and indeed the world, provides useful — indeed essential — role models for both black and white children and children of both sexes. Checklist 4.5 raises some initial starting points for items which might be included in this aspect of a school's policy and practice.

Checklist 4.5 *Questions concerning resources*

	Yes	No	Don't know
Are there policies and procedures (and a committee?) to review materials for bias in all areas of the curriculum as well as administrative and examinations material?			
Are the groups responsible, representative of the school professionals, parents (including minority and feminist groups), and pupils (age permitting)?			
Do the tasks of such groups include: establishing clear guidelines for evaluating the accuracy, authenticity treatment and portrayal of non-white and ethnic minorities in texts and other learning materials? identifying materials which are deemed racist/sexist for weeding out, or for use to assist in detecting bias; reviewing all instructional materials, library resources, etc; recommending and circulating recommendations on approved materials; reviewing criteria as new information and new understandings become available?			
Are there clear procedures to ensure that committee recommendations are discussed and acted upon?			
Do the school library, the media department and the careers guidance and counselling section provide materials which reflect the racial and cultural diversity of the United Kingdom and both sexes in a variety of vocational occupations?			
Does information about the cultural experiences and histories of all permeate all curriculum materials, texts and resources?			
Can teachers regularly supplement classroom materials with a variety of resources which are multi-ethnic and multi-racial?			
Do materials avoid superficial or 'exotic' aspects of culture, and explore values, belief systems, history, and daily lives of peoples as well as issues of life chances and access to rewards and resources in society?			
Do they depict the diversity *within* cultures?			
Do they explore the roles, and contributions of all people to the United Kingdom and the factors which shaped those roles?			
Do they deal openly and frankly with the issues of oppression in our history and our present at home and overseas?			
Do they encourage frank and open discussion of racial conflict in the larger society, the community and the school?			
Do they present minority values as well as dominant values in society, and challenge students to examine the basis of those values?			
Are materials available in minority languages as appropriate to the linguistic backgrounds of pupils?			
Is there a library policy with regard to such material?			

LANGUAGE POLICY

The area of language is one of the areas where different schools, even those in close geographical proximity, may quite legitimately have different policies, according to the linguistic profile of the community within the catchment area and the children attending the school. This profile may vary across time and the need is, therefore, for a careful and persistent scrutiny and close continuing dialogue with parents, community groups and organisations, and supplementary schools. Bearing in mind that you cannot exercise respect for persons unless you respect their culture and language, schools should seek, as a matter of fundamental principle and policy, to involve children in the use of their own languages to a degree consistent with the expected mastery of English as the common language of British society. This will certainly involve the use of home language as part of the normal curriculum insofar as numbers permit. This, in turn, will have implications for resource allocation and library provision and policy as well as staffing policy. In addition, and particularly in the case of languages with only small representation in the school, the opportunity may be taken to arrange clubs or working groups or to provide material, available from such places as embassies, which will acknowledge the importance of their wonderful gift of bilingualism. Perhaps they could interpret for their parents on parents' evenings or translate communications to be sent home.

There is, however, another side to the language policy for the school where a number of pupils may not speak English at home and may, in some cases, enter school late. It is very important that, consistent with the special needs of these children, they are integrated as fully and quickly as possible into the normal school life and programme of activities and are not seen as pariahs. The grouping and timetabling of

Checklist 4.6 *Questions concerning a school's language*

	Yes	No	Don't know
Is there a regularly updated record of the home languages spoken by pupils?			
Does the school have a policy on bilingualism?			
Are there clubs centred around the languages of the school?			
Is there a case for bilingual instruction in the school? In which languages, subject areas and levels?			
Does the school have staff who are fluent in the languages represented in the school?			
Is the opportunity of parents' meetings utilised for community languages? Is translation available when required?			
Is any correspondence conducted with parents in community languages?			
Does the school encourage children to learn, understand and respect each other's languages?			
Is there special provision for students of home languages other than English?			
Is such provision as integrated as possible into the normal working of the school?			
Is there a committee or group of staff with special responsibility for minority language policy and procedures and for evaluating the school's performance in this respect?			

their curriculum will be eloquently expressive of the extent of the school's real commitment to the multiracial and multilingual nature of British society. Great care needs to be taken, therefore, to measure the policy in this area against the overall policy lest an unintended and subconscious linguistic apartheid should soak into the very fabric of the school's life.

Checklist 4.6 suggests a few initial questions which may enable schools to begin to formulate and evaluate their language policy, although it is clear that not every school will have a linguistic diversity in its pupil body and, where it exists, it will vary considerably.

SCHOOL RULES AND REGULATIONS

From the research introduced in this chapter, the importance of an ordered and well-regulated environment will be eminently clear. Such school rules will need to be agreed and negotiated with the community and parents if they are to carry conviction in such matters as dress, wearing of specialist clothing for physical education and swimming, procedures for changing and showering, etc. In many schools the existence of such rules has been seen to add a positive dimension to the life of the school and in particular, to avoid the withdrawal of pupils from particular parts of the curriculum. Under the 1980 Education Act the rights of parents to information about the school so that they may express informed preferences is guaranteed. Over and above this, however, the school needs to share with all parents and pupils, what is and what is not acceptable behaviour and what the consequences of unacceptable behaviour will be.

It goes without saying that a central component of the school's rules and regulations must address prejudice reduction with firm and consistent procedures and policies. Regardless of where they occur such expressions of racist behaviour as direct physical prejudice, racially offensive graffiti in whatever form on walls or elsewhere, the circulation of racist literature, the wearing of badges or other insignia or manifestations of extremist groups or the use of slogans or vocabulary known to be associated

Checklist 4.7 *Questions concerning a school's rules and regulations*

	Yes	No	Don't know
Is there a set of rules and regulations including details of action in the case of prejudiced behaviour such as racism, sexism, credism and classism?			
Have the rules and regulations been agreed with parents and pupils?			
Are they distributed to all pupils, staff and parents?			
Do they include specific details on how to deal with incidents involving racism, sexism, credism and classism?			
Are they discussed and regularly reappraised at staff meetings?			
Do they envisage the involvement of the parents of offenders?			
Is there a laid-down procedure for reporting and recording such incidents? including details of the kind of incident, the children involved, the action taken and the sanctions imposed?			
Is there a particular member of staff or staff group with particular responsibility for monitoring policy in this area reporting back to staff, keeping records and initiating a regular review?			

with them — all of these must be covered. The regulations will also need to include an admonition to staff and pupils that racist, sexist and credist behaviour is totally unacceptable, that it must never be 'allowed to pass' and it must always be reported to the person or persons designated as responsible.

Checklist 4.7 attempts to set a certain limited number of questions which may be raised by teachers seeking to agree a disciplinary code and procedure in this respect. It must be emphasised that such regulations should be comprehensible and written in a lay manner.

EXTRA-CURRICULAR ACTIVITIES

Great sensitivity and circumspection, as well as close consultation with parents, is needed in the area of extra-curricular activities, if harmful misunderstandings are to be avoided and the maximal involvement of all pupils facilitated. Often a process of discourse can overcome parent's fear and misgivings about the involvement of their children — daughters especially, with all round benefit. There can, of course, be no question of compulsion, and a good school will realise when it can negotiate no further but must respect the wishes of the parents. There are, however, many instances where parents have agreed to swimming, for example, provided that certain safeguards are observed, such as single sex swimming, covering of the body during showering or wearing of special clothing such as churidar-pyjama. Parents need to be acquainted with their rights but it should not be asumed that all parents of a particular religious or ethnic group will make the same demands or have the same requirements. It hardly needs saying, of course, that the same stipulations apply to items of clothing and food, including the provision of ritually slaughtered meat separately cooked from other food and particularly foods containing pork.

Conversely, it is self-evident that no pupil must be automatically excluded from extracurricular activities because of assumed objection, associated stereotypically with a particular ethnic group. All parents have a right to information and to be consulted and this must be made clear to them before their children enter school in writing as part of the school handbook in original or translated form. The same need for sensitivity applies to such areas as home-visiting and parent–teacher meetings. It must not be assumed, particularly in the case of male teachers, that teachers will be welcome to visit pupils' homes and any such access must be diligently and carefully negotiated beforehand. Also with regard to parents' evenings, of fundamental importance is the way in which they are 'set up', including timing, seating arrangements and functions, that is to say whether they are to be preponderantly social and recreational or professional. Often different ethnic parents groups are willing to organize an evening 'event' and such an event which may include cooking, dancing, exhibitions, displays and talks can be a useful 'ice breaker' for all concerned.

Checklist 4.8 poses a few initial questions about this important supportive area, but it should be emphasised that the education of children needs to be a real partnership across all the activities of the school. Moreover, the very fact of organising a particular activity or club communicates fluently the school's commitment to its own cultural diversity. In some schools, for example, where there are Muslim children, a room is set aside for prayer: an eloquent testimony to anti-credism in practice.

Checklist 4.8 *Questions concerning extra-curricular activities*

	Yes	No	Don't know
Is there a school policy on extra-curricular activities which takes into account cultural diversity?			
Does it encourage parent involvement in decisions?			
Is it circulated to all parents prior to their children coming to the school?			
Does it encourage support for special needs in the form of clothing, etc?			
Are there clubs and activities reflective of the school's cultural and linguistic diversity?			
Are parents involved in arranging extra-curricular activities such as language clubs, religious associations, music groups, etc?			
Are community activities welcomed into the school?			
Are there recreational parents' meetings?			
Do school teams have a balanced representation of different ethnic groups?			
Do the school meals reflect the cultural mix of the school?			
Do the extra-curricular activities include arrangements for student government?			
Are parents from all racial and ethnic groups encouraged to participate in school programmes?			

STAFF DEVELOPMENT

At the core of an effective multicultural school committed to prejudice reduction is the staff and its expertise. No member of staff and no group of staff can continue to maintain professional effectiveness without continually updating competence and knowledge. Some of the activities associated with in-service development will be conducted on an individual basis, some on a small group basis and even on a whole-staff basis. Regardless, however, of the grouping, each school will need to have an explicit policy with regard to staff development which will need to be continually appraised and each member of staff should have a profile of staff development which is discussed with him/her at least once a year. The aim should be to facilitate and help staff to reflect on their own professional practice to identify their needs and jointly to agree a programme of action.

Calling to mind what was said earlier in the book about the three dimensions of prejudice — cognitive, affective and behavioural — the policy and profile will need to address all three. A major thrust of any such activities must be to enable staff working sensitively and collegially to appraise the extent of their own ethnicity encapsulation by race, creed, gender and class, so that, at best, in a non-threatening way, they may begin to identify any biases or prejudices in themselves and their work. Part of that staff development, of necessity, will be in their trying to acquaint themselves with the cultural biography of their school and its pupils, and especially of the pupils whom they teach. Needless to say they will need to achieve greater professional expertise in recognising and dealing sensitively with incidents of prejudice and discrimination in their pupils. Some of this work can be done as part of the regular discussion of the overall multicultural policy of the institution, some on a paired or grouped intervisiting basis, some by study groups, but certain of it may need to be achieved by attendance at specialised courses. In this latter case, institutional needs will require harmonising with individual aspirations and a system of 'broadcasting the benefits' will need to be instituted.

Checklist 4.9 seeks to cover some of the areas for inclusion in an institutional policy while once again drawing attention to the fact that the fine detail of such a policy will naturally vary from school to school, as does the cultural biography of each school, its staff composition and the more precise needs of all its pupils.

Checklist 4.9 *Questions concerning an outline for staff development*

	Yes	No	Don't know
Is there an institutional staff development policy addressing needs arising from the cultural diversity of the school and a commitment to prejudice reduction?			
Are there collegial and individual staff development activities?			
Are staff encouraged to intervisit?			
Are different manifestations of racism in classroom materials and the media discussed by staff?			
Do staff counter statements which are racial or culturally biased from both students and colleagues?			
Do staff concern themselves with real problems in intergroup relations problems with immediate relevance to the lives of their students?			
Are teachers given recognition, support, encouragement, training, and resources to attend in-service workshops, courses or activities on multi-cultural/multi-racial education?			
Do staff search for ways to overcome their own cultural captivity and that of their students and to recognise and discuss racial, gender and ethnic questions?			
Do staff recognise racial and cultural biases in themselves and in students, and attempt to overcome them individually and collegially?			
Do staff read books and articles to increase their understanding of and sensitivity to particular aspirations, needs, problems, and frustrations of the different minority groups represented in the school?			
Is there a regular procedure for monitoring staff development and enabling staff to indicate their needs?			
Does staff development include activities addressing informational, emotional and behavioural needs?			

CURRICULA AND TEACHING/LEARNING STRATEGIES

At the heart of a school's efforts to educate children is the curriculum and the way in which that curriculum is delivered: the teaching/learning strategies. In this book, these two areas are considered separately and in detail (chapters 4 and 5). As an introduction to what I have to say there, I want to review here some of the issues against which teachers may wish to check their schools. Some are more obvious, such as whether the curriculum as a whole reflects the cultural diversity of the school and aims to educate young people away from prejudice and towards rational and moral decision-making and behaviour. These two principles should lead to detailed criteria and policies about such issues as minority languages, religious education and humanities, but they will also influence the overall shape of the curriculum and individual subject components as well as how that curriculum is taught and learned. Materials and other resources will, as stated earlier, need to be scrutinised for bias and the balance of subject offerings regularly reviewed to make sure that they are not ethnocentric. The vocabulary and exemplars will also need to be attentive to a pluralism of culture and 'greatness'.

Checklist 4.10 attempts to indicate some of the questions which might be posed about the curriculum and pedagogies. Once again, however, attention must be drawn to the pluralism of pluralisms which constitutes society and its schools and the unique needs of each school and its clientele within the content of more generally identifiable principles and issues.

Checklist 4.10 *Questions concerning curriculum and teaching methods*

	Yes	No	Don't know
Does the curriculum, as a whole and in its component parts reflect the cultural diversity of society and the school catchment area?			
Do the teaching methods take account of the ethnic background of children?			
Are the community and parents involved in the delivery of some parts of the curriculum?			
Does the curriculum develop in students a sense of social responsibility for facing and overcoming racism?			
Are pupils trained to detect both overt and subtle manifestations of racism and other prejudice in the curriculum and their larger environment?			
Does the classroom reflect a diversity of legitimate values, styles and viewpoints, even when these run counter to teachers' own preferences and views?			
Are students encouraged to learn, to understand and to respect each other's language, dialect and culture and to communicate in language and ways which show respect, openness and honesty?			
Do teachers recognise a variety of cognitive learning styles among children, and develop teaching strategies which complement them?			
Do teachers use a variety of independent and co-operative approaches to learning and varying motivations and rewards strategies?			
Is a means provided by which students can relate their ordinary everyday lives and issues to the classroom and curriculum?			

EXAMINATIONS, ASSESSMENT AND TESTING

There is now ample evidence of the way in which teachers' attitudes and expectations can fundamentally influence the learning and achievement of all students. It is, therefore, important that methods of judging pupils' progress express high expectations for all students and that the form, pattern and content of all assessment are strictly fair, free from bias and compatible with society's cultural diversity. Great and particular care will need to be exercised with the use of so-called 'objective tests' which may have been validated on only one ethnic group, and materials developed with only one cultural group or gender should be regarded with suspicion (Lynch, 1983).

It is not only the assessment which plays a crucial role in making justice manifest for all children though. It is also the interpretation, communication and recording of these results. Teachers should never forget that they are responsible for children's life chances and that they need to exercise great care when making academic or behavioural judgements about children. This is particularly so where subject or career choice, grouping or referral, or welfare or social work reports are to be completed, this latter perhaps as part of judicial proceedings. Judgements need to be checked, if at all possible, against those of other colleagues.

Finally the policy and practice in this area need to be firmly keyed into the school's overall curriculum policy for multicultural education and prejudice reduction and regularly monitored for gender, racial and other imbalances. Assessment should comprise a broad spectrum of different approaches in order to try to provide a just basis for the appraisal of all pupils, and judgements should be regarded as open to challenge and, if necessary, amendment (see Lynch, 1986). There should be clear and promulgated procedures for the involvement of parents and, if necessary, appeal.

Checklist 4.11 *Questions concerning assessment policy*

	Yes	No	Don't know
Is there an explicit assessment policy keyed into the overall multicultural curriculum policy of the school?			
Do assessment procedures reflect a belief in the ability of all students to learn, and is this manifest in teachers' expectations, patterns of assessment, options available and chosen, training of staff and their practices with parents and pupils?			
Do teachers recognise legitimate differences in values, social skills, and language which exist in children, and do they assess children accordingly?			
Are staff trained to recognise the bias of culture, gender and class in standardised tests?			
Do staff exercise extreme caution in interpreting the results of tests utilising a wide variety of observations and other practices?			
Are there clear and effective mechanisms to involve parents in procedures, criteria and options placements, in the language of the home?			
Are there clear, unambiguous and effective mechanisms to inform parents of the results of their children's assessment grades from the time of their first years in school? (In the language of the home?)			
Do clear procedures exist for parents to appeal against decisions and are they well publicised in the necessary languages?			
Is there continual evaluation of which cultural/racial groups are concentrated in which curricular 'tracks' to ensure that there is no distortion or imbalance?			
Do staff seek corroboration of their judgements collegially and from parents and the community?			
Do all examination papers seek to achieve a balanced representation of ethnic and gender diversities?			

STRUCTURES AND PROCEDURES FOR EVALUATION

No policy or practice can remain both totally static and totally healthy. If, therefore, the school is to continue to keep abreast of new information and ideas, as well as of the changing needs and composition of its pupils, there needs to be a built-in review procedure to keep those policies and practices active and effective. Different schools will achieve this in different ways. Some will have, as a part of their formal structure, a group or committee of governors, staff and parents. Others may prefer to deal with it less formally as part of normal staff meetings or parent–teacher meetings. There are many other ways manifest in the literature, as in the case of the Vancouver School Board where schools report annually to the Board. The important thing is that the mechanism functions effectively and regularly and has terms of reference which include the whole spectrum of the school's activities.

Concerning the forms of evaluation it will need to include the other areas enunciated in this chapter, including their interaction with each other. Moreover, and insofar as the ethos of a school also comprises intangible elements, it will need to include feedback about how pupils, parents and teachers feel about the institution and the progress of its policy for multicultural education and prejudice reduction. In that sense, it will need to include data from these three sources (and the wider community) of a factual, attitudinal and behavioural kind.

All of this is certainly a big task for teachers, in addition to their existing duties, and it will imply some specialisation of training, responsibility and function, at the same time as the responsibility of all members of the community for the policy and practice of the school is firmly maintained. Checklist 4.12 attempts to pull together some of the evaluation issues which might be included in an institutionalised policy which is resilient, flexible and responsive to new information, ideas and techniques. Once again, I should emphasise that the list is a starter list and should automatically be regarded as susceptible to further development and amendment in the context of the school, its location, composition and needs. Thus far in this chapter I have identified

Checklist 4.12 *Questions concerning the evaluation of a school's multicultural education policy*

	Yes	No	Don't know
Are there clear and consistent policies and procedures for evaluating the school's effectiveness in implementing its multicultural policy for prejudice reduction?			
Is there representation from parents and pupils in that process?			
Does the evaluation policy address the major areas identified in this chapter, individually and in their composite effect on the school and its ethos?			
Are data collected for that purpose from parents, pupils, teachers and the wider community?			
Are the evaluation policy and procedures themselves subject to a regular review?			
Are the results of the evaluations available to all groups comprising the school?			
Are efforts made to include all groups in discussion of such evaluations?			
Are there mechanisms for including the results of evaluation, after consultation, into the normal life of the school as necessary?			
Is a senior member of staff with appropriate training responsible for this?			
Does the evaluation include information about behaviour, opinions and facts?			

12 major areas of a school's multicultural education policy and practice as aimed at prejudice reduction. It should be emphasised that different institutions will tackle the problem, see the issues and categorise their policy in different ways. So, the checklists are intended, not as final products, but to suggest areas where action may be appropriate.

SUMMARY

Drawing together the strands of this chapter and preparing the way for my next chapter, which is concerned with curriculum, I want briefly to recapitulate the points which I have made and draw them together with the help of a diagram. I have introduced some of the major work on school effectiveness, pointing to the way the research indicates the crucial importance of school ethos. While recognizing the rather ephemeral-sounding nature of that word, I have tried to break it down into 12 major areas for policy and action in pursuit of a school's multicultural and prejudice reduction initiatives. I argue that a good and effective school is a good and effective school in the field of multicultural education and prejudice reduction, if it has the will to be so and plans its implementation. Its plan should take into account the often intangible components of ethos, but should include the need for an ordered, well-disciplined environment where all facets of the school's planned life express the commitment to multicultural education and prejudice reduction. In figure 4.1, I have tried to express that equation in diagrammatic form and to include the 12 areas identified in this chapter.

The figure tries to convey the idea that the entire school community should be included in the process of formulating a policy and delivery document (the first of the 12 areas dealt with in this chapter), which will then be expressed in the institutional structure and values across the other areas indicated. This process should help the construction of a well-regulated and culturally 'comfortable' ambience in the school which enhances all pupils' sense of personal worth and the interaction between all cultural groups on a sensitive and just basis. The school ethos flows from the thorough application of the policy to all school practices and attitudes and leads to an 'effective' school (defined here as one which values high achievement and a sense of personal worth for all pupils, regardless of race, sex, creed or class). This process, in turn, leads to a feeling of justice for all pupils and that, in due succession, feeds back into a heightened school ethos. The process, once commenced, can thus be self-reinforcing while, at the same time, mechanisms for continual review ensure that it does not become self-serving or a gloss to a different reality. The declared values and institutional structures, practices and attitudes are thus brought into congruence.

ACTIVITIES

1. Consider the research on effective schools introduced at the beginning of this chapter. Trace some of the material back to the sources, for example, *Ten Good Schools* or *Fifteen Thousand Hours*, examine them and draw up your own description of the characteristics of an effective school, committed to prejudice reduction.

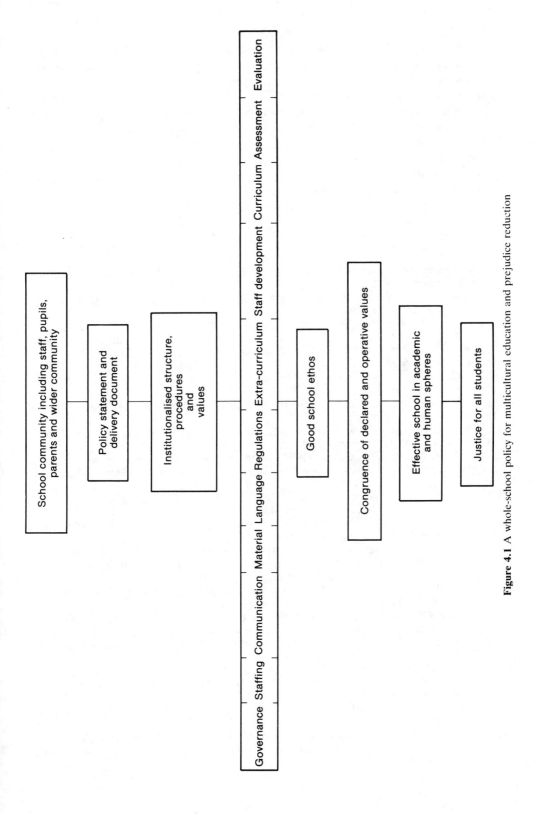

Figure 4.1 A whole-school policy for multicultural education and prejudice reduction

2. Review the 12 areas proposed for action in the development of an effective multicultural school committed to prejudice reduction. Amend and amplify the list to suit your own professional institution and enter the specific items which would need to be considered in each category.
3. Look again at figure 4.1. Try to draw up, in the form of a proposal for a staff meeting, a similar flow chart and then prioritise the areas for action, making specific proposals for implementation.
4. Do you think that it is possible to bring the declared and operative values of an institution into full congruence, as implied in figure 4.1? Are academic achievement and justice for all attainable? Amend the figure in the light of your consideration and suggest what 'justice for all pupils' might be in practice.

REFERENCES

Assistant Masters and Mistresses Association (1983) *Our Multicultural Society: The Educational Response*. London: AMMA.

Banks, J.A. (ed.) (1981) *Education in the 80s: Multiethnic Education*. Washington DC: National Education Association.

Banks, J.A. (1981) *Multiethnic Education: Theory and Practice*. Newton MA: Allyn & Bacon.

Banks, J.A. (1985) 'Reducing prejudice in students: theory, research and strategies', in Moodley, K. (ed.) *Race Relations and Multicultural Education*. Vancouver, BC: Center for the Study of Curriculum and Instruction, University of British Columbia.

British Columbia Teachers Federation (1984a) *A Message from the Committee against Racism*. Vancouver BC: BCTF.

British Columbia Teachers Federation (1984b) *Policies and Priorities for 1984*. Vancouver BC: BCTF.

Brookover, W.B. et al., (1979) *School Systems and Student Achievement: Schools Make a Difference*. New York: Praeger.

City of Bradford Metropolitan Council (1982) 'Education for a multicultural society: provision for pupils of ethnic minority communities' Local Administrative Memorandum 2/82 Bradford.

City of Bradford Metropolitan Council (1983) 'Racialist behaviour in schools', Local Administrative Memorandum 6/83 Bradford.

Coleman, J.S., Heffer, T. and Kilore, S. (1982) *High School Achievement: Public, Catholic and Private Schools Compared*. New York: Basic Books.

Council of Europe, Committee of Ministers (1985) Recommendation of the Committee of Ministers to Member States on Teacher and Learning about Human Rights in Schools. Strasburg: Council of Europe. (Recommendation No.R.(85)7).

Crain, R.L., Mehard, R.E. and Narat, R.E. (1982) *Making Desegregation Work: How Schools Create Social Climates*. Cambridge MA: Bellinger Publishing.

Edwards, R. (1979) Effective schools for the urban poor, *Educational Leadership*. **37**(1).

Edmonds, R. (1982) Programs of school improvement, *Educational Leadership*. **40**(3).

Fullan, M. (1983) *Change Processes and Strategies at the Local Level*. Washington DC: National Institute of Education. (A paper prepared for the NIE).

Gaiter, D.J.(1985) A tale of two schools and cultural relations, *Miami Herald*. June 13.

Gollnick, D.M. and Chinn, P.C. (1986) *Multicultural Education in a Pluralist Society*. Columbus, OH: Charles E. Merrill.

Her Majesty's Inspectors of Schools (1977) *Ten Good Schools: A Secondary School Inquiry*. London: HMSO.

Kehoe, J.W. (1984a) *A Handbook for Enhancing the Multicultural Climate of the School*. Vancouver, BC: Western Education Development Group, Faculty of Education, University of British Columbia.

Kehoe, J.W. (1984b) *Multicultural Canada: Considerations for Schools, Teachers and Curriculum*. Vancouver BC: University of British Columbia, Faculty of Education. (Public Issues in Canada Project).

Kyle, R.A. (ed.) (1985) *Reaching for Excellence: An Effective School Source Book*. Washington DC: United States Government Printing Office.

Lightfoot, S.L. (1983) *The Good High School*. (Portraits of Character and Culture) New York: Basic Books.

Lynch, J. (1983) 'Curriculum and assessment' in Craft, M., *Education and Cultural Pluralism*. Brighton: Falmer.

Lynch, J. (1986) *Multicultural Education: Principles and Practice*. London: Routledge and Kegan Paul.

National Commission on Excellence in Education (1983) *A Nation at Risk*. Washington DC: United States Department of Education.

National Union of Teachers (1981) *Combatting Racism in Schools*. London: NUT.

National Union of Teachers (1983) *Race Awareness Workshop Report*. London: NUT.

North Westminster Community School (1983) 'Policy statement', in Minority Rights Group, *Teaching about Prejudice*. (Report No 59) London: MRG.

Purkey, S.C. and Smith, M.S. (1983) Effective schools: a review, *Elementary School Journal*. **83**(4) 427–52.

Quintin Kynaston School (1983) 'Quintin Kynaston policy on racist behaviour', in University of London Institute of Education, 'Racist society: geography curriculum', Paper for a Conference on 29 March. London.

Rutter, M., Maughan, B., Mortimore, P. and Ouston, J. (1979) *Fifteen Thousand Hours: Secondary Schools and Their Effects on Children*. London: Open Books.

Simpson, G.E. and Yinger, M.J. (1965) *Racial and Cultural Minorities*. New York: Harper.

Slavin, R. (1983) *Co-operative Learning*. London and New York: Longman Publishing.

Slavin, R. and Madden, N.A. (1979) School practices that improve race relations, *American Educational Research Journal*. **16**(2) 169–80.

United States Department of Education (1986) *What Works: Research about Teaching and Learning*. Washington DC: United States Department of Education.

Vancouver School Board (1982) *Race Relations Policy*. Vancouver BC: VSB.

Vancouver School Board (1983) *Guidelines for Implementation of VSB Race Relations Policy*. Vancouver BC: VSB.

Wyke Manor School (1984) *Statement and Guidelines*. Bradford Metropolitan District, Local Education Committee.

Chapter 5

A Curriculum Strategy for Prejudice Reduction

INTRODUCTION

In the previous chapter, I attempted to identify the dynamic and influential factors in effective schools and to link effectiveness with success in the field of prejudice reduction. I drew attention to the central importance of a climate conducive to both social and intellectual growth: a multicultural school ethos. I then introduced a 12 part model of the necessary components of a whole-school policy which can encourage good practice including initiatives for prejudice reduction. Each of these components was the subject of closer focus and in each case an initial checklist was suggested, which could begin to draw attention to some of the major issues. Finally, a diagrammatic representation of the model was introduced (figure 4.1) which emphasises the need for schools to take account of all major components in drawing their declared and operative values into closer harmony and thus achieving greater justice for all pupils, regardless of race, sex, creed and class.

In this chapter, and returning to the fact that prejudice comprises informational, emotional and behavioural dimensions, I will indicate the ways in which the curriculum of each school must reflect its overall commitment to multicultural education and prejudice reduction. I will emphasise the symbiotic nature of all components in the policy, while at the same time particularly addressing curricular issues. I do not intend to repeat my previous work on the multicultural curriculum, but rather to provide a flexible model illustrative of the way in which a curriculum may respond to the imperatives implicit in a commitment to prejudice reduction. The chapter prepares the groundwork for chapter 6, which is concerned with pedagogies for prejudice reduction and it concludes with a set of curricular guidelines for educators. It begins by endeavouring to draw together a clear definition of a multicultural curriculum and its components which is dynamic and yet culturally responsive and attentive to the work of prejudice reduction.

THE MULTICULTURAL CURRICULUM

It is important to understand to begin with that a school curriculum — the learning activities and content planned for the pupils to experience in schools and delivered by teachers either directly or vicariously — is a portion of the total accumulation of human experience and scholarship, selected for transmission to the young as part of the formal process of education. It includes cognitions and intellectual operations, feelings and dispositions and such psychomotor areas as perception and movement. Curricula are usually categorised according to disciplines or occupational groupings, selected and organised with regard to ideological yardsticks emanating from the wider social, cultural and political context. Thus, major value changes in the broader society may be expected to result in curriculum change.

Neither the relationship between the curriculum as planned and the curriculum as learned, however, nor that between societal value change and curriculum change is automatic and linear. On the contrary, both operations are parts of a complex, multidimensional, interactive process and are subject to 'negotiation', whether formally or informally, consciously or subconsciously, at an individual or group level. Pupils modify what they are intended to learn through their own cognitive processes to fit in with their previous learning biography, including enculturation and socialisation; and, in a similar process, education systems and schools do likewise in processing the implications of value, knowledge and perception changes in the wider society for their planned programmes of learning.

In this latter process, ideology, i.e., clusters of values and beliefs held by individuals and groups, and the power to wield ideology in a socially influential and effective way are important determinants of the curricular outcomes of societal value changes. The curriculum is thus a politically — or at least ideologically — influenced selection of the wider macro-culture. Within pluralist democracies, this process includes the diversity of microcultures which make up a culturally diverse society, although it will be apparent that the ideological power of minorities is usually less than that of majorities and also subject to evasion and marginalisation strategies on the part of that majority. Thus, as Musgrave (1979) points out, knowledge (and its representation in the curriculum) is selected, organised and stratified in ways deeply dependent on the power structure. That is why a prerequisite of a truly multicultural curriculum is a commitment on the part of majorities to share power with minorities. The validity of any curriculum is thus determined by factors of time and space, culture and ideology, concepts of teaching and learning, and it is limited over time, space and cultures. The fact of its limited validity means that it has to be subject to continual renegotiation and that it is a selection arising from that negotiation. In a democratic society with a pluralism of legitimate cultures that selection has to carry the consent of all legitimate cultural groups. In addition, however, the selection must have the potential to address three major areas of commitment: social justice; provision for common values and continuity; and support for the existence of legitimate diversity.

The reason for this tripartite commitment will be fairly clear: the need for a democratic society to provide for its continued existence and against disintegration and anarchy; the need to support the existence of legitimate diversity both as a human right and as a sharpening stone to peaceful change and progress; and the need to afford justice to all citizens as a civil right and as a source of mutuality and reciprocity for citizens in dealing with each other.

Within this overall commitment of a multicultural curriculum to commonality, to diversity and to justice, a central core, addressing all three aims, must be a duty for the attenuation and eradication of socially harmful prejudice and discrimination. This is so for two major reasons: the pre-school and out-of-school socialisation of children in a culturally diverse society, includes, as I have argued in previous chapters, the absorption of prejudiced attitudes into their cultural biography. Secondly, unaddressed prejudice is reinforced by schools, and it conflicts with all three major aims for a multicultural curriculum identified above. Schools cannot remain neutral and, thus, neither can their curricula. But what would be the components, priorities, strategies and criteria of a curriculum centrally concentrated on prejudice reduction?

COMPONENTS OF THE PREJUDICE REDUCTION CURRICULUM

In the voluminous literature on curriculum, many attempts have been made to identify the components of a curriculum. Perhaps the most influential and enduring has been the schema developed by Tyler (1949) involving purposes, learning experiences, organisation and evaluation. Such components are, of course, seen to be interactive and interdependent. In a culturally diverse and technological society, the limited validity/life of a curriculum is further constrained by the rapidity of change taking place simultaneously at a number of different levels and in a number of different sectors of that society. It is thus important for apprehension of curriculum to focus closely on that process of rapid change, if it is to be reflective of that dynamism. I propose, therefore, adopting Tyler's component categorisation, in the light of subsequent work (Goodlad, 1979) to identify the commonplace components of a multicultural curriculum dedicated to prejudice reduction as:

- an ideological rationale about society;
- a learner and learning rationale;
- expressed and implicit aims;
- a planned selection and categorisation of subject matter and experiences;
- logistics including resources, materials, space, time, environments and community;
- planned modes of transaction, including methodologies, learning environments;
- evaluation strategies, including assessment approaches.

I want to emphasise that while a curriculum, according to this seven-part model, is planned, it includes unexamined, sometimes mindless, assumptions and practices and it will be differently processed by different children and will result in differential learning, expressed in the form of performance. That process of interaction is the subject of chapter 6. For the moment, I want to use the seven-part description of a multicultural curriculum, committed centrally to prejudice reduction, and to illustrate the priorities in each area.

IDEOLOGICAL RATIONALE

Here I want to identify a number of major arguments, without thereby implying that there are not others, which support the rationale for the schools' responsibility for prejudice reduction. As I have argued elsewhere (Lynch, 1983), a multicultural curriculum derives from the *nature of the society* in which it is located. That society espouses democratic values, such as justice and equality for all citizens and includes legal sanctions against discrimination on the basis of race or sex. Just as it is also a technological society and certain implications for the curriculum flow from that dimension of the ideological rationale, so also implications flow from the fact that a just, democratic, culturally diverse society cannot tolerate prejudice and discrimination. The school, as the major formal cultural transmission agency, has the responsibility of managing and implementing society's commitment to justice and against prejudice and discrimination. There are also a number of other elements within this overall commitment, however. One might describe them as arguments for such a commitment on the part of the school.

Thus, for example, pupils and teachers will wish their legitimate culture to be respected and supported, and it is logical that they should afford others the same respect. This argument we might label *mutuality* or *reciprocity*. It is an important part of the rationale, for there are those who argue that reversibility is an indispensible aspect of full moral maturity. (Kohlberg, 1979). By that is meant the ability to 'place oneself in the shoes of the other person', to imagine a reversal of roles and, thereby to empathise with the other. Thirdly, within the rationale for prejudice reduction, one could argue that *human rights*, as defined in major international agreements, outlaw discrimination and abhor prejudice and that citizenship of a state which is signatory to these instruments commits one to observing them. This argument one might shorthand as *international morality*.

Fourthly, one could argue that to discriminate on the basis of race, sex, class or creed is destructive of society. If everyone did that, society would break down, fragment and lose its cohesion, with disastrous consequences for all individuals and groups. Moreover, in addition to the social consequences, one could argue that it is illogical to be prejudiced against individuals for their race, creed, sex or class because human beings have no control over their 'placement' in these categories at birth. It is illogical and unjust to blame and disadvantage someone for matters over which they have no control. One might label this the *cultural logic* argument.

The final argument is a pragmatic one and rests on the need within democratic societies to work for *consensus by persuasion*. It is unlikely that open arguments for discrimination would achieve consent and they would, therefore, involve a coercion of minorities by the majorities which is itself anathema to the ethical base of a multicultural society and the values which that majority declares that it espouses. All of these arguments imply, as Wilson, Williams and Sugerman, (1967) have indicated, accepting others on an equal footing to ourselves. They also, incidentally, provide the basis for the closer identification of the moral foundation and commitment of a multicultural curriculum, committed to prejudice reduction, which is so essential in the human relationships involved in delivering such a commitment. That morality implies that the curriculum delivers the competence, as part of its strategy of prejudice reduction, to enable pupils to reflect upon the principles which guide their actions (Peters, 1981). That process of reflection, again, involves a commitment to rationality as a major aim of the curriculum and that, in turn, implies a process of negotiation with communities so that shared meaning may provide a foundation for that negotiation. Otherwise the negotiation will be unequal and the outcome unjust,

Level Focus	Society	Community
Criteria	e.g. technological	e.g. multilingual
Substance	e.g. technology	e.g. mother tongue

Figure 5.1 Discourse to achieve a curricular rationale for prejudice reduction

yielding the rationality only of the majority and dominant group. So, within the ideological rationale for a curriculum, core-dedicated to prejudice reduction, there has to be a means of integrating the narrower school community as well as the broader society into the process of discourse.

This commitment to school-community discourse is important on ethical and rational grounds, but it is also important for functional reasons related to the concept of curriculum as a selection from the circumambient culture. Selection implies criteria and criteria to be acceptable have to be negotiated. Each school will be involved in a different process of negotiation, each 'selection' will probably be slightly different, reflecting not only the criteria and demands of the wider society, but also of the narrower community. In slightly simplified form, I have tried to illustrate this imperative in figure 5.1. Discourse or negotiation take place to define both criteria and substance at both societal and institutional levels. Thus, as part of the overall rationale of our society is that it is technological, we can expect that dimension to be represented in the school curriculum. Concomitantly, as the local community is multilingual (this is chosen as an example, because clearly not all schools are multilingual) it is reasonable to assume that mother tongue provision will be negotiated with the local community.

A similar process of negotiation may be expected to apply to prejudice reduction. Thus, a societal imperative would be that negotiation and discourse concerning the school's approaches to prejudice reduction should take place. The community imperative would then dictate the form, focus and substance of its exact implementation. In a denominational school the rationale may focus more closely on the religious tenets of that group and divine prohibition. In a lay school, the rationale may swing more to arguments based on lay rationality, such as those advanced above. The conflict between religious certainty and schools serving a multifaith society is a crucial and difficult area for such negotiation.

Let me recapitulate what I have said in this section. A curriculum which addresses prejudice reduction derives its rationale from six major sources: the nature of a *multicultural society and its basic ethic; mutuality* or reciprocity; international human rights instruments, prohibiting discrimination and representing a kind of *global morality; social disintegration; illogicality and irrationality;* and *consensus.*

LEARNER AND LEARNING RATIONALE

Because much of chapter 6 is devoted to this aspect of the prejudice reduction curriculum, I propose to do no more than outline the issues underlying the learner and learning rationale in this section, leaving their illustration and exemplification to the next chapter. Here, I want to identify some of the promising middle-range theories which may, with caution, be integrated into a school's prejudice reduction rationale, insofar as that applies to the area of the learner.

The reader will no doubt be aware, even just at the level of folklore, of the self-fulfilling prophecy (Rosenthal and Jacobson, 1968): pupils live up to — or down to — teachers' expectations of them. There may, though, be less knowledge of theories concerned with what I am going to call the 'culturally-determined learning styles' of many minority children. The difference in learning styles may relate to cognitive modes, internalisation–externalisation, reward perception, attention-giving, verbal and non-verbal behaviour and the pupil's ability to 'get the floor' (Philips, 1983) and thus be integrated into the continuing dialogue of the classroom. Such differences in values, perceptions and behaviours lead to conflict and misunderstanding on the part of both pupils and teachers and may become part of the teacher's self-fulfilling prophecy for at least some minority pupils. Equally importantly, if not made explicit, these same value and behaviour differences between teachers and minority pupils may be the source of stereotype reinforcement, prejudiced attitudes and personal and institutionalised discrimination.

If, as a result of the recognition that society is multicultural, ethnic minority groups have a right to maintain attachments and identifications with their first cultures, and if schools are attempting to recognise and develop these as part of their policy of multicultural education and prejudice reduction, such has to be reflected in the learner rationale — the teaching/learning strategies derived from teachers' perceptions of how learning takes place. In this process, account will need to be taken of Ogbu's argument that 'the extra-scholastic opportunity structure in society' influences the dominant group's perceptions of minority children, surrounding them in a caste-like status. These perceptions then deeply influence the way in which minority children are educated for their future place in society (Ogbu, 1978). Ogbu suggests that caste-like minorities internalise their stigmatisation and that members of the dominant group — including teachers — find their low expectations confirmed and reinforced. Thus, many children from those groups are locked into a vicious cycle of poverty, low status, underachievement and social and educational isolation and alienation.

So what are the elements of the learner rationale that may underpin a curricular policy for prejudice reduction? The first principle, it seems to me, is to extend the ethic of respect for persons and their unique biography into the realm of learning. Thus, teachers should bear in mind that not only is each learner unique, but that each teacher is too, and that the values, perceptions, attitudes and knowledge of some teachers will engage more easily with those of some pupils than others, and vice versa. They will influence the way teachers teach and pupils learn from that teaching. Thus, learning to learn from teaching is an important aspect of a pupils' curriculum. The shared meaningfulness between a teacher's teaching and a pupil's perception of that teaching and, therefore, ability to learn from it, is not, however, set for all time. For, it can be increased by well-established, good teaching techniques, such as multiple cueing, exemplification using overlapping approaches, shaping the ratio of new to old information, rehearsing and practising associations as a game, variable sequencing, different approaches to reward reinforcement: all techniques aimed at making the 'active site' in the pupil's cultural biography more receptive to the teaching style of the teacher.

Put another way, a good teacher will seek a variety of means to motivate the learner to activate his/her prior learning as a means to achieving new learning. Of course, the process is reciprocal and it would be expected that, through a process of mutual acculturation (Banks, 1981), the teacher would also become more sensitive and receptive to a pupil's cultural biography and its effects on learning. Most importantly, there are factors other than ability which determine attention, responsiveness, participation, reaction to praise and eventual learning. There is also sometimes a gap between learning and the manifestation of learning in performance, depending on the 'mode of performance' chosen by the teacher: i.e., the way in which the pupil is expected to show what he or she has learned.

A graphic illustration of this is to be found in the work of United States authors. They show that the preferred instructional strategies in American schools are inconsistent with the cognitive styles and cultural characteristics of some minority children (Kleinfeld, 1975), and that ethnicity influences the way that pupils process and interpret information in ways which have deep implications for teaching/learning strategies (Stodolsky and Lesser, 1975). Because of the differing values, behavioural patterns, cognitive styles, expectations, etc., of minority children — and particularly poorer minority children — teaching them all alike pedagogically is probably the surest way of denying them access to equality of educational opportunity (Ramirez and Castaneda, 1974). More recently ethnographic research by Philips, working with Native Americans on a reservation, showed fundamental differences in the structuring of attention and the regulation of talk between Indian pupils and their white teachers. This results in frequent miscommunication and reinforces the general uncertainty of the pupil's experience. These and other differences, such as dialect, rules for discourse and cultural knowledge, lead the teacher to define the pupil's behaviour as inappropriate and unacceptable (Philips, 1983). Philips emphasises that, whereas earlier work may have attributed such mismatches to discrimination (United States Commission, 1973), even where the teacher is well-intentioned, the results are similar, since the pupil's efforts at communication are misconstrued by the teacher, because they are incomprehensible. Yet, by dint of the teacher's authority, it is the pupil who is defined as inadequate (Philips, 1983, p. 129).

Research by Clark (1983) also highlights the fact that social class may not be the most important factor to influence the acquisition of behaviour which is well oriented to success. In a study of poor black children who succeed or fail in school, he found a complex relationship between family socialisation, school achievement and social class, with important differences between successful and failing children, all of whom were members of poor families. A number of other research studies have also documented the cultural styles of poor children from ethnic minority groups in the United States, and the way in which the behaviour and values of such pupils differ from their middle-class peers and teachers (White, 1984). Such differences become manifest in both verbal and non-verbal communication and may lead to conflicts and misunderstandings between pupils and pupils and teachers and pupils.

Vasquez (1979) draws our attention to the issue of locus of control. By this is meant the extent to which pupils believe that they can influence their own success or failure, on the one hand, and the extent to which they believe that it is determined by factors beyond their control on the other. He points to the fact that there is no consistent correlation between IQ and locus of control, but most motivational techniques used by teachers are more compatible with 'internal' than with 'external' pupils. He sees such knowledge as indispensable to educators and he proposes strategies which may improve the pupils' perception of their control over their own destiny and educational achievements. Where children differ along social class and cultural dimensions, different and varying motivational and reinforcement techniques are necessary if the teacher is to give all children equality of opportunity.

Of direct relevance to the learner and learning rationale is the theory of moral development, evolved by Kohlberg and substantially based on Piaget's theory of cognitive development. According to this theory, the ability to reason morally develops sequentially in a hierarchy of stages, which comprise three levels: the preconventional, the conventional and the postconventional. At the preconventional level the child responds to rules and labels interpreted in concrete terms such as the physical or hedonistic consequences of action for him or herself and the physical power of those who set the rules. At this level, there are two stages: the *egocentric punishment and obedience* stage, where physical consequences determine the decision with regard to an action's morality; and, the *individualistic–concrete–instrumental* stage, where morality is decided according to the instrumental satisfaction of one's own — and sometimes other's — interests and needs.

At the conventional level, conformity with the expectations of one's own family, group or nation is seen as moral. At this level, there are two stages: the *interpersonal conformity* stage, where good is judged by whether the action pleases others and is thus approved by them, and where mutual, interpersonal expectations and relationships are potent determinants of morality as is interpersonal conformity, and, the *law and order* stage, where morality is seen as doing one's duty and respecting authority and thus contributing to the group, society or the institution. The postconventional level, also comprises two stages: the *social contract* stage, where the individual is aware that people hold a variety of values and views that are relative, and there is concern for rules and due process to achieve consensus. Stage 6, the final stage and the second of the two postconventional stages is concerned with *universal ethical principles*, where right is defined by a decision of conscience taken by reference to such universal principles of justice, as the equality of human rights and respect for the dignity of human beings as individual persons (Kohlberg, 1973).

The rationale for learning will need to be tapered, because, if correct, Kohlberg's developmental theory of the structure of moral progression is age-related and sequential (although neither directly nor without the potential for acceleration) (Kohlberg, 1969, Nisan and Kohlberg, 1978). Very young children tend to reason at the lower stages and as they grow up they tend to reason morally at the higher stages. According to Kohlberg, pupils cannot understand moral reasoning more than one stage higher than their own, and conversely, teaching below their level of moral development will not encourage their moral growth. While the sequence of stages may be universal, the levels and content of reasoning are strongly influenced by cultural differences and the degree of modernisation in the culture concerned. Teachers must, therefore, be careful to match their expectations of moral development and behaviour and teaching to the pupils' level of development and culture, while, at the same time, shaping their learning rationale in such a way as to stimulate the growth of rational thinking and moral behaviour by involving pupils in such activities as reasoning and discussing dilemmas at one stage beyond their own.

Banks (1981, 1986) also proposes a similar stage development model which recognises that many pupils will enter school having had little or no experience of other ethnic groups. This Banks terms 'cultural psychological captivity' — the pupil is automatically internalising negative societal beliefs about cultural and ethnic groups. The scale progresses through six stages to the point where pupils have reflective and positive ethnic, national and global indentification. While Banks' model is focussed on the internal identity of minority children, it is also valuable in drawing our attention to the external dimension for all children i.e., how children perceive other children's cultures.

To recapitulate the components of a learning rationale for prejudice reduction, one might say that it should start from a recognition of the unique cultural biography of each child and involve the construction of a kind of pluralist 'learnothon' to take account of that cognitive diversity. The strategy will need to be tapered to take account of the fact that certain minority children will probably need more help with learning from teaching than other children at the commencement of their formal schooling. It must take into account that there is more than one 'right' way to learn and teachers must, therefore, be diffident of leaping from performance to conclusions about ability. They should be willing and able to take into account the fact that pupils process what is being taught through their cultural biography, seeking where it may tie in with the accumulated cultural information in their permanent memory.

The process will be influenced by the cultural receptiveness of the classroom and school, the pupil's culture and locus of control, the way in which the pupil registers attention, gains turns to speak and communicates, and the system of motivation and reward to which the child has been accustomed and is then faced in school. Teachers must be able to understand that the process of learning from teaching is long and complex, and that the pupils' cultural biographies determine the way in which they perceive the information to be learned and influence their attention. Weinstein and Mayer (1986) have indicated the state of the art in terms of the deliberate teaching of learning strategies and they have proposed a list and description of some of the major categories of learning strategy. Only when the new material has locked onto material in the permanent memory of the pupil will a cognitive product follow that may, in turn, manifest itself in pupil performance. This the teacher receives as feedback and will base professional judgements upon it. I have tried to illustrate this process in figure 5.2.

With more specific regard to prejudice, the school will need to take into account from the outset that many children will enter school with prejudiced attitudes. These attitudes may continue to be reinforced by peer groups, community and society throughout the formal education of the children. To counteract this the school must make clear where it stands and attempt to build into its learning rationale the need for children to learn, in a diversity of ways, new and corrected information, new and changed affective predispositions and new or amended behaviours. Skilfully man- aged, these ends can be achieved as part of the overall curriculum delivery, provided that the children's cultural framework is understood and individual and varying modes of cognition are taken into account. There is little doubt that it is the responsibility of

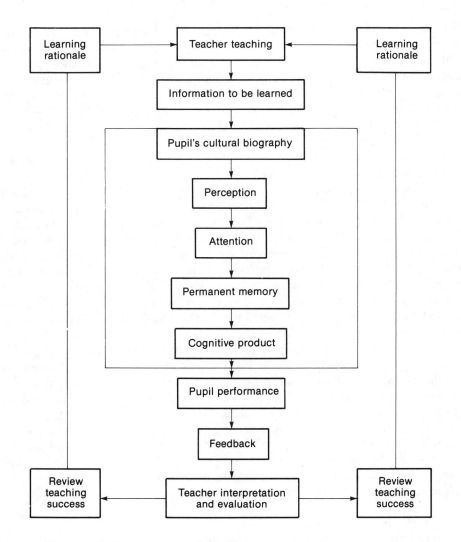

Figure 5.2 Learning process and learner cultural biography

the school to enable pupils to function effectively in alternative social settings and relationships to those into which they have been socialised. But the research continues to be sparse in this area. It is, however, conclusive enough for us to be able to take it into cautious account in our learning rationale, as part of the overall commitment of a school to prejudice reduction. That has been the function of this section.

EXPRESSED AND IMPLICIT AIMS

The reader will recall that we are centrally concerned, in this chapter, with prejudice reduction. To some extent, therefore, it is necessary to take as read the fact that the school has its all-encompassing multicultural aims (Lynch, 1983, 1986), against which it may test the validity of its global educational aims for the school. Within that context, we are concerned here exclusively with the identification of a set of what we might term paradigmatic 'prejudice reduction' aims for the school, although these latter may overlap and repeat some aspects of the multicultural education aims for all children. Moreover, the prejudice reduction aims will of necessity incorporate elements from the two preceding curricular components dealt with already in this chapter: societal and learning rationales. Thus, they derive from both the way in which we read society and the way in which we read the nature of learning.

I should like, now, to return briefly to what I said in chapter 2 about the aims of education and their relationship to prejudice reduction. There I argued that a multicultural curriculum derives its master aims from the nature of a democratic, multicultural society with its espoused commitment to respect for persons and their legitimate cultures. Within that context, I argued that a set of broad institutional aims should address such items as qualities of human feeling; judgemental rationality; skills, knowledge and abilities appropriate to a multicultural society; intercultural competence; the acquisition of moral bases for behaviour; a commitment to combat prejudice and discrimination; and a critical appreciation of oneself and others. Clearly all of the aims address prejudice reduction in some measure or another, but I have extracted those which are more specifically applicable to the prejudice reduction aspect of a multicultural curriculum.

The fact, as previously stated, that a pluralist society generates prejudiced attitudes as part of the generally experienced extra-scholastic process of socialisation and enculturation, along with the need shown in the first two sections of this chapter for both societal and learning rationales, provide the components for a more specific set of prejudice reduction aims, which address the three major aspects of prejudice: cognitive; affective; and, conative or behavioural. With these established we are then in a position to construct a set of working aims which schools would embrace for their pupils, organised across these three areas as a preparation for decisions about a theory of instruction, content and evaluation to govern our teaching.

To achieve prejudice reduction, schools should aim on behalf of their pupils:

1. *Cognitive aims*
    to facilitate the highest possible intellectual and rational development of all pupils;
    to provide accurate, up-to-date information and understanding concerning the cultural composition of society;
    to make pupils fully acquainted with the school's policy and commitment against prejudice and discrimination;
    to correct misinformation and bias;
    to counter the use of factual knowledge as a basis for prejudice;
    to sustain and extend information and understanding about the values, beliefs and achievements of all legitimate cultural groups in society;
    to enable the recognition of prejudice and discrimination, and their social and personal effects;
    to provide the intellectual skills to counter prejudice;
    to support the development of the knowledge necessary for greater moral maturity;

to initiate pupils into the common values and culture of a democratic society;

to provide pupils with firm and detailed guidelines on acceptable and non-acceptable values, attitudes and behaviour in the school context;

to enable pupils to discriminate between acceptable and non-acceptable discriminations;

to acquaint pupils with the structural aspects of prejudice and discrimination.

2. *Affective aims*

to expect and encourage the highest academic and moral standards of all pupils and staff;

to enable pupils to feel comfortable with their own identity and culture;

to facilitate the ability to interrelate with those from other cultures;

to appreciate the unique value of each human being;

to develop a moral commitment, based on rationality, against prejudice and discrimination;

to encourage appreciation of the personal and social damage done by prejudice and discrimination;

to develop mutuality and reversibility in moral decisions.

3. *Conative (behavioural) aims*

to nurture and encourage non-prejudiced verbal and non-verbal behaviour and discourage and eradicate prejudicial discrimination of word or deed;

to facilitate respectful, creative interaction between all pupils and staff;

to provide a transferable 'moral' framework for non-prejudiced, non-discriminatory behaviour in school;

to develop 'mutuality and reversibility in action' in all pupils;

to support pupils' development of both moral autonomy and social responsibility;

to encourage critical–reflexive perception, analysis and interpretation of social situations for any prejudice and discrimination;

to encourage the development of a repertoire of response strategies to cope with individual and group manifestations of prejudice.

It will be evident that the above aims are intended both to be set at the side of the overall aims of the school as a kind of evaluative paradigm *and* to be subject to exact working definition only after discussion and negotiation with pupils, parents, teachers and the wider community. They may also need amplification because, as expressed, they address the aims espoused by the school for its pupils. Schools, of course, also have aims for their staff, including teachers, and those are interdependent with the aims for pupils. Thus, the successful achievement of these latter goals is dependent on the formulation and successful achievement of the former, staff development goals. Clearly there will be overlap and commonality between the two, but there will also be additional components which will directly address only the specific needs of the teachers.

For example, schools will need to foster cognitive, affective and conative development in their staff in areas such as precise knowledge and accurate information about the macroculture and the school's microcultures. They will need to support staff in the odyssey of growth of self-critical awareness about their own values, attitudes and actions. Above all, schools will need to facilitate the staff in their learning of how to study and improve their professional practice and to make it more fully reflect the schools' commitment to social justice and educational equity, as defined by Graham; that is, with a focus, not only on input variables such as curriculum, access and resources, and output variables such as achievement and other results but also on the educational process in between (Graham, 1980). At the heart of that commitment to justice and equality is a school's and a teacher's commitment to, and competence in, prejudice reduction. But I shall be dealing with the staff development aspect of a school's responsibilities more fully in chapter 8.

CONTENT AND EXPERIENCES

Thus far in this chapter, I have considered the societal and learning rationales that may underlie a prejudice reduction policy and the overall aims of that policy. In this section, I seek to draw out the implications of these three areas into the most explicit part of a school's curriculum: namely that content and those experiences which are planned by the school for the pupils to learn. In doing this, we ask the question, 'what are those areas of content and planned experience which are indispensable to a school's commitment to prejudice reduction, bearing in mind that the school espouses cognitive, affective and behavioural objectives?' Linked with that question is, of course, another concerning the kind of assessment procedures to which the content and learning experiences are subjected.

I would like now to recall to the reader the areas of knowledge introduced in chapter 2 as specified by Her Majesty's Inspectorate (HMI, 1985): aesthetic and creative, human and social, linguistic and literary; mathematical; moral; physical; scientific and technological; and spiritual. Emphasising that each one of these may serve the prejudice reduction curriculum throughout the life of the child, I want to organise consideration of the content under four major headings. I shall label these in a shorthand as: *knowledge of self*; *knowledge of society*; *knowledge of the environment*; and *knowledge of knowledge*. With regard to the learning experiences also introduced in chapter 2, and recalling the admonitions of a number of writers and researchers quoted thus far in this book on the need to aim for cognitive sophistication and high levels of intellectual functioning if improved moral judgement is to be achieved, each of the ten learning processes quoted there must also be marshalled to achieve prejudice reduction and eradication.

With regard to *knowledge of self*, children need to know, and have a positive orientation to, their own culture as a basis for a healthy self-image. This should include facts about their own history and the geographical location of their precursor community, as well as pride and competence in their mother tongue. They should have an appreciation of the unique value of each individual, an ability to learn from others and an awareness of their own prejudices and biases — but without guilt or shame. They should be taught how to feel comfortable with diversity and to encounter different cultures and a sense of 'strangeness' without feeling threatened. They should understand the concept of mutuality and be encouraged to 'climb the ladder' of moral autonomy combined with social responsibility, including a knowledge of their own view on the common values of British society. Among these will be a commitment to understand and come to terms with competing value-claims and to resolve such claims by persuasion and negotiation. At the core of this is the achievement of ever higher levels of rationality as a means of formulating their own moral value positions, to govern their attitudes and behaviour.

So, although the response to the question posed above will naturally depend on the age and background of the child, none the less the school has to come to terms with the way in which a pluralist society continually produces prejudice and thus the need is for a longitudinal policy which continues throughout the school life of the child. As the study by Grant and Sleeter shows, the knowledge of cultural diversity which pupils bring with them to school is not inconsiderable and will include both 'pluses' and 'minuses'. The authors point out that discussions of race, including physical appearance, to which symbolic meaning was attributed, were referenced to criteria such as those used to evaluate members of the opposite sex. They comment that all pupils had some perceptions and beliefs about diversity that helped them make sense of each other. (Grant and Sleeter, 1986, p. 27). The prejudice reduction curriculum must, thus, encompass content addressing *knowledge of society*. There are certain 'constants', that all stages of schooling must provide for in the field of knowledge of society. These are the provision of accurate information about other groups, an understanding of the invidious effects of prejudice, moral development, the correction of misinformation, and the promotion of growth of a feeling of human empathy and increasing comfort with different cultures. Some of these can be achieved directly, others will demand vicarious experience, some will be short term, others will continue throughout the life of the child. Some may involve parents and the community, some are 'delivered' by the children themselves and their very pluralism (Grant and Sleeter, 1986).

Some areas of content and experience do, however, derive automatically from the subject of the previous section of this chapter, and indeed from chapter 4, and they apply to the whole curriculum throughout the school life of the child. For example, the curriculum must seek, together with the assessment methods, to reflect the school's cultural diversity in the knowledge contained in the syllabus. That reflection will have two major dimensions: the local community and the national community. With regard to the materials and content of the latter, much is already provided from textbooks, tradition and examination syllabuses, although much needs to be changed there too. Each school will, however, have a different local community and the 'map' of that community may change rapidly. Thus, teachers will need to prepare such materials for themselves, individually and collegially.

An important part of that reflection of cultural diversity will also need to be knowledge of the rules of society and of the school *vis-à-vis* prejudice, what is encouraged and supported and what is prohibited. In this respect issues of prejudice and discrimination, what they are, how they work and the effects they have is a further area of content indispensable to the prejudice reduction curriculum. Allied with both of the these areas are gaming exercises which will enable pupils to develop their ability to empathise with and understand members of other communities. These exercises vary from dressing up as, and playing the part of, children from other countries in infant schools, to more mature students learning the music and dance of others wearing their traditional dress and role-playing conflict situations. Such activities have a functional and important purpose in the prejudice reduction curriculum and must not be dismissed as 'tokenist'.

While it may have been denigrated by some writers, knowledge of the lifestyles of other children can provide an important challenge and corrective to the stereotypical representations which often underpin prejudice. Nor is there any reason why, especially with older pupils, issues of the life chances for children from other groups should not also be included. In some schools too, the language of certain groups may, with benefit to all, be a part of the formal curriculum.

In the area of *knowledge of environment*, pupils need to be acquainted not only with issues such as the geographical distribution of communities, the impact of housing policies on education and life chances and the imbalance in usage of natural resources nationally and internationally, but also to understand their own growing moral responsibility in a global context as well as a local and national one. Twinning with a school in a developing country is often a useful way of extending the affective commitment of children to respect for other persons and to empathy with their lot. They should also have available factual, accurate and up-to-date information concerning the life of people abroad, their values, customs and beliefs and an appreciation of the interdependence of people around the globe. One aspect of this interdependence which should be emphasised is the reasons why immigration has taken place.

Concerning *knowledge of knowledge*, pupils need to be able to recognise knowledge as flexible and changing and not as fixed. They need to know how to think out new approaches to language usage and to the organisation of knowledge and to realise that not all cultures organise their knowledge in the same way and that knowledge is not for possession but for application and use. Within this context of the provisional and often uncertain state of knowledge it may be easier for them to live with the value divergence inherent within a culturally pluralist society rather than to seek facile and superficial consensus. Above all, they need to use their knowledge to develop a wide array of skills of inquiry, combined with expertise in speculating, social modelling, creating, interrelating and social actioning. They should also be aware of the way in which knowledge and language are used to discriminate against certain cultural groups, and be able to appraise evidence contained in generalisations for its validity. They need the intellectual response strategies to enable them to deal, in a rational way, with arguments which support prejudice and discrimination and to counter them.

In the field of *learning experiences*, there are three particular aspects of the list proposed in chapter 2 which need specific attention. These are: the need for activities which provide the rational basis for appropriate classification and discrimination; the nurturing of acceptable personal and social attitudes and moral values; and the development of social skills such as co-operating, taking responsibility for oneself and others and competing fairly. Each of the areas of experience should be seen as relating to the knowledge domains referred to above via six major components: dispositions and values; competences, skills and abilities, factual information, learning and thinking techniques, interpersonal relations and practical competences.

As will be clear from the work of a number of diverse contributors to the field, including Banks (1981) and Kohlberg (1973, 1979), factual information alone is insufficient. Pupils have to be engaged in learning activities and experiences which aim to increase the level of their thinking and motivate them to proceed to a higher level of intellectual functioning. If we look at this issue from an alternative point of view, in terms of Bloom's cognitive domain, that means more than providing pupils with the facts of cultural diversity and prejudice in Britain today. Rather, that should provide the initiative to move them through comprehension, application, analysis, synthesis to evaluation where they may develop the ability to judge the worth, value or merit of their own behaviour and attitudes as well as those of others. Perhaps at this level they may also be in a position to achieve a set of consistent, reflective moral values to guide individual, group and societal judgements and actions. For this, as Banks points out (1985) a classroom atmosphere is necessary where pupils may be free to derive their own democratic values reflectively and to internalise them. For this, didactic methods are inadequate and attempts at forced value injection doomed to failure. I have tried to portray this process of aiming at reflectivity as a means of prejudice reduction diagrammatically in figure 5.3, using the cognitive domain of the Bloom Taxonomy. The message for teachers is that appeal to the judgement of pupils is necessary if they are to progress morally and that the appeal should aim at as high a level of intellectual functioning as the children are capable of so as to motivate and stimulate their moral progression and ability to make autonomous moral decisions and act accordingly even when the 'authority' is no longer present.

To summarise this section briefly, the knowledge essential to the prejudice reduction curriculum has been seen as relating to *self, society, environment* and *knowledge*. Attention has been drawn to the fact that such knowledge may comprise dispositions and values, competences, skills and abilities, factual information, interpersonal and personal competences and practical skills. Further, each of these may be mediated by *learning experiences*, including the ten areas referred to in chapter 2 and particularly the areas of classifying and discriminating; processing values; and social interacting. Referring to the work of Kohlberg, Bloom and Banks, I have drawn attention to the need to 'stretch' pupils by motivating them to think at increasingly higher levels of cognitive thinking and facilitating their moral development by appeals to their judgement in a democratic classroom atmosphere where they may reflectively derive their own values from the dilemmas and problems that may be tackled there though rational discourse.

Figure 5.4 gives a simplified overview of the parameters of content and learning experiences which may contribute to the prejudice reduction curriculum, seeking to express them in diagrammatic form.

LOGISTICS

There are a number of aspects of the logistics of a school which have received very considerable attention with regard to their bias. School textbooks and teaching materials, while still far from being bias-free, have been subject to increasing scrutiny since the foundation of such organisations as the Council on Interracial Books for Children in 1966. Checklists are available from a number of sources including schools and education authorities, and guides have been published to assist teachers in identifying biased or racist material or information that is inaccurate or demeaning of women, minority groups and particular denominations (Klein, 1986). Few, if any, of

Evaluation
e.g. ability to judge the worth, merit or value of aims and methods of prejudice reduction in school and society
Building on:
synthesis
and
analysis
and
application
and
comprehension
and
knowledge

Synthesis
e.g. ability to use material from several sources to produce a coherent and rational case against racism
Building on:
analysis
and
application
and
comprehension
and
knowledge

Analysis
e.g. ability to identify the component parts of institutional racism and their interconnections
Building on:
application
and
comprehension
and
knowledge

Application
e.g. ability to apply the knowledge about *and* understanding of prejudice to the school situation
Building on:
comprehension
and
knowledge

Comprehension
e.g. understanding of how racial discrimination works
Building on:
knowledge

Knowledge
e.g. ability to recall the facts of cultural diversity and of information concerning racial prejudice

Figure 5.3 A cumulative model of prejudice reduction approaches to knowledge. Adapted from Bloom B.S. (1956) *Taxonomy of Educational Objectives: Handbook 1: Cognitive Domain*. New York: David McKay.

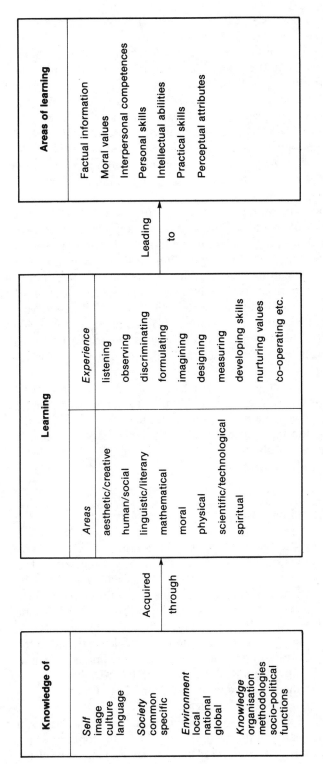

Figure 5.4 Content and learning experiences for a prejudice reduction curriculum

these cast their net of definitions as widely as does this book in fixing the meaning of prejudice as encompassing racism, sexism, credism and classism.

Yet it hardly needs repeating that the materials used by teachers are thereby given an authority in the eyes of pupils, and their parents, which means that the material must be free of all these prejudices outlined here. Because the material is so 'powerful' this process cannot be left to chance and must be organised at a number of different levels. Firstly, guidelines for deciding about texts and materials, expressed both as criteria and procedure, need to be set down at institutional and, if appropriate, department or class levels. Both criteria and procedures need to be negotiated with the community and it may be that, in some cases, for example, in the selection of minority languages material for the library, the community may be involved directly.

But there are also other aspects of resources which are often overlooked: such as space, time, environments, timetabling and staff deployment and use of the resources of pupils and of the community. For example, does the timetable allocate less time, or unpopular times, or less able teachers, or poorer workshop facilities to groups on a cultural basis, or to subjects which express minority cultures? Is the school sending a subliminal message about the strength of its commitment to prejudice reduction by the time and space available for issues of prejudice reduction? Do syllabuses have a sufficient common framework to express that commitment forcefully and coherently across time, subject and space? Is the grouping policy compounding poorer resources for pupils who already have enough problems and who may come disproportionately from minority backgrounds?

To summarise this section concerning the logistics of the prejudice reduction curriculum, it is necessary to consider critically, not only the more obvious resources and to prune them to take 'defensive' action, as appropriate, but also to consider the 'hidden curriculum' of logistics, the time, space, environment, timetabling and staff deployment dimensions equally vigorously, testing them against the school's policy for multicultural education and prejudice reduction.

MODES OF TRANSACTION (Including ways of teaching and learning)

Under the heading of modes of transaction we are considering an area closely interlinked with all five components of the curriculum previously discussed in this chapter. It will be clear, for example, that the methods of teaching planned by teachers imply a social and learning rationale, as well as views about the content which has been selected, the learning experiences envisaged and the resources which will be necessary to implement them. Here, such factors as those referred to in the previous components are important: varied learning and motivational strategies matched to the children's cultures; manifestly culture-fair approaches to monitoring and assessment; a variety of materials and stimuli of oral, aural, visual and tactile kinds, explanations available to pupils and parents on their performance and the modes of feedback and accountability of teachers for their actions and judgements.

But, by 'modes of transaction' is meant, also, something broader than classroom teaching methods, namely, all planned interaction and informal contact which happens 'in the name of the school'. It is important that the style of such contact is exemplified by the school and its staff, so that respect for persons is writ large in the actions and behaviours of all staff and pupils at all times — in the playground, on the sports field, in the staffrooms, in the corridors, during lunchtime, at staff meetings and pupil assemblies, on the occasion of parents' evenings, school festivals and drama productions. In other words, each action of every group and individual must express the ethos of the school at all times, and, in particular, its commitment to prejudice reduction.

In the classroom the ethos of the school must imbue each and every mode and objective. This is true whether the approach is information-oriented, experimental, creative, inquiry-based, awareness-raising, collaborative, skill-training, gaming or simulation; whether addressing the growth of forms of expression, the nurturing of values and attitudes, the development of thinking and learning techniques, interpersonal relationship or social actioning, that school ethos, as argued, in chapter 4, will have both intellectual and social components: let me summarise them as a 'learning community' and a 'caring community' focus, combined into a design for living and learning in a school community, which is well disciplined and ordered and conducive to both intellectual and social growth. As I emphasised in chapter 4, high expectations, both intellectual and moral, as well as an emphasis on teamwork and collaboration in all aspects of the school's life, are indispensible to the development of healthy modes of transaction which reflect the school ethos and aims. Needless to say, a willingness, and ability to explain, to give feedback and to accept the need for accountability and for democratic decisions are also important ways in which the school inducts pupils into moral maturity, and this extends to the relationship nurtured with parents and the wider community. It is important, for example, that pupils, parents and teachers know where they stand with regard to involvement in decision-making and what the parameters for participating are before the negotiations begin.

An important element in the modes of transaction is the generation of a tradition of appeal to the rational judgement of pupils within a democratic classroom and school ambience. Coercive methods are pedagogically unsound and inimical to the aims and ethos of a school committed to prejudice reduction. Factual indoctrination is likewise inappropriate, dysfunctional and likely to be ineffective except in the presence of the authority. Here, the insights apply from the material on the learning rationale presented in an earlier section of this chapter, namely that the prejudice reduction curriculum must aim for higher levels of intellectual functioning. It must also aim, through the presentation and rational discussion of moral dilemmas, problems and issues, to motivate pupils to derive their values reflectively in order to achieve autonomous moral development. Clearly, that will be dependent on the age and cultural background of pupils, which will have deep implications for the modes of instruction and teaching methods of educators. Instructional processes do make a difference.

I have tried to portray in figure 5.5. the complex factors referred to in this chapter that should underlie the modes of transaction, bearing in mind that the more detailed approaches to teaching are dealt with in greater depth in chapter 6. The figure emphasises the unity of the school's ethos, including both the intellectual and social components, working interactively. Within the overall focus provided by that ethos, the figure proposes ten priority areas of variables, which are drawn in part from the

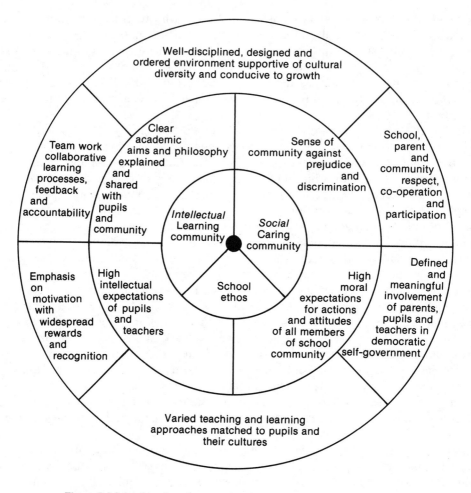

Figure 5.5 School modes of transaction for prejudice reduction: a rationale
© 1987 James Lynch

school effectiveness research which I have quoted more extensively in chapter 4. These ten variables may be considered to promote prejudice reduction and at the same time to facilitate and improve pupil achievement. Thus, once again, we find that a well-disciplined and ordered environment that is supportive of cultural diversity and committed to the reduction of prejudice, is also one that is conducive to both intellectual and social growth. Within that context, the attitudes and behaviour of teachers and their teaching/learning approaches are a crucial variable. As Brophy and Good trenchantly point out, basing their judgement on an extensive review of the literature: 'The myth that teachers do not make a difference in student learning has been refuted' (Brophy and Good, 1986, p. 370). And that also applies to prejudice reduction.

EVALUATION STRATEGIES

The final component of the prejudice reduction curriculum, evaluation, addresses all the six previous components, critically and reflectively and then feeds back into them. It does not just imply critical monitoring of pupils' academic performance, nor even of their social and academic performance, although it includes both of them. The evaluation strategy has to be focussed on all the policies, practices and behaviours of the whole school community and reflexive onto itself, i.e., also focussed on the effectiveness of the evaluation strategy itself. Having said that, we are concerned particularly in this chapter with the curriculum, seen as the planned learning of information and activities and the component parts of that curriculum proposed in this chapter. In other words, the evaluation strategy is an integral part of the school curriculum strategy, which in turn is part of the overall school strategy.

There are many approaches to evaluation and a number of different perceptions of areas of scanning which need to be included. For example, it hardly needs repeating that effective evaluation should include the perceptions of pupils, teachers and parents with regard to how well the school is functioning both socially and intellectually. It has to be recalled also that, ultimately, the purpose of evaluation is to lead to renewed and effective action, so that any strategy for evaluation must include procedures for feedback to staff, parents and pupils as appropriate. The instruments for evaluation may also be varied, ranging from tape or video-tape recordings, through to observational techniques, protocols of discussions, anecdotal records, logbooks, objective tests, teacher-prepared assessments to test memory, judgement, skill in usage of material, artefacts produced by teachers or children, collections of student work, minutes or accounts of meetings, interview schedules, questionnaires, diaries, checklists, attitudinal tests, examinations, assessment inventories and formal or informal reports.

Whilst each school will make its own selection of approaches, techniques, instruments and components and objectives, it is possible to identify some basic principles and a number of exemplars for possible models. In general, for example, the prejudice reduction evaluation strategy will need to be a process model of evaluation rather than a 'product efficiency' one. That is to say, it must go beyond data, however obtained, to an examination of the values and assumptions that underly that data and must focus on the teaching and learning as a whole, set within a particular dynamic, cultural and institutional context, accountable to certain supra-institutional, cultural ethics and in accord with the school's policies and ethos. Criteria for the evaluation of teaching and learning will be addressed to the aims outlined in this chapter, which in turn are responsive to the underlying social and learning imperatives in accord with explicit principles of procedure. None of this precludes change in any of the elements, and the criteria for judgement of teaching and learning presuppose institutional and wider community and systemic policies and criteria sustaining the commitment to prejudice reduction.

The vast literature generated by projects in the School Effectiveness Movement in the United States provides a number of very useful practical examples of evaluation approaches. There is neither time nor space to detail every one here, let alone all 39 associated projects, but one good example is the School Effectiveness Programme of the Santa Clara County Office of Education in San Jose, California, This is an interesting approach because of the way in which schools have anonymous data from comparable schools against which to judge themselves. There, based on a conceptual framework of school effectiveness built up from the literature and research, 14 effectiveness variables have been identified and broken down into their component parts. For example, the school environment/climate variable is further broken down into such items as the norms which guide behaviour, e.g., high expectations, organisational processes, e.g., shared decision making and open communication, and structures, e.g., discipline procedures. From performance on these variables a basic school profile is built up, based on data from parents, pupils and teachers. Using these data and the anonymous data on similar variables from other schools, schools have standards against which to judge their performance, after which assistance is given to the school in analysing its data and interpreting it, prioritising its needs, formulating a plan and obtaining support and further feedback (Santa Clara County Office of Education, 1983, 1984).

Another example is the manual developed by the California State Department of Education for both primary and secondary schools, which is intended to enable schools to study themselves and to review their effectiveness. The two manuals are very detailed and include guidance to schools on a seven-part programme review process, including the school's self study against the quality criteria set down by the state; preparatory work for the review; the review itself and how to conduct it; the comparison with the 'quality criteria', the preparation of the report; the proposals and suggestions for change and the reporting-back phase to the school community (California State Department of Education, 1985, 1986). These activities are organised under four active headings; preparing, including training; reviewing; reporting and revising. The review includes observations in classrooms, interviews, both formal and informal; scrutiny of documentation; meetings; and appraisal of pupil learning; determination of additional data needed to complete the review.

The importance of basing such evaluation strategies on valid and vigorous research and sound practice is emphasised in another state programme, that developed by Connecticut. In a description and appraisal of the programme, three officials from the State Department of Education emphasise both the modifiability of factors involved in effective schools and the need for vigorous and precise, qualitative and quantitative methods for gathering and analysing information (Gauthier, et al., 1983 p. 404). They also comment on the contiguous nature of school effectiveness and programmes dealing with race, sex, equality and national origins. In other words, more effective schools are more effective in those areas as well.

In the field of developed instruments, which would be suitable for the purpose of overall evaluation, we are probably fairly reliant on American material at the moment. For instance, the National Study of School Evaluation in the United States produced a set of evaluation guidelines for multicultural education as long ago as 1973. It includes statements of philosophy, objectives, principles and criteria to evaluate them. The guidelines offer detailed criteria for appraising the school structure — including the racial balance, attitudes and commitment of staff; the school organisation and grouping; the formal curriculum; learning materials; special education and provision; extra-curricular activities; pupil services, including pastoral and counselling provision; decision-making; and pupil-community involvement. The material includes provision for an overall evaluation of the school's involvement in multicultural education, a mechanism to encourage change and a student opinionaire.

A different, but similarly detailed evaluation checklist was published in 1976 by the National Council for the Social Studies. This comprises a series of 23 basic criteria. They range across areas such as the school ethos, its policies and procedures, the school staff, in-service provision, reflection of different cognitive styles in learning strategies and materials, student self-image, knowledge of the multicultural nature of society, the promotion of values, attitudes and behaviours conducive to multicultural education, education for effective and potent citizenship, interpersonal and interethnic relations, ethnic representativeness of the curriculum coverage, interdisciplinarity and open-mindedness of the curriculum, aesthetic dimension, minority language, use of local community resources and commitment to continual evaluation. Each of these areas is further subdivided into a number of sub-categorisations.

A further example, developed in the United States by the teacher's organisation, the National Education Association (1980), is the 'Profile of Excellence' addressed to the establishment of racial equality in schools, and produced in 1980. It addressed six components with a number of criteria which, if fulfilled, would secure equality of education for all pupils. The six components are called governance and administration, personnel and staffing, curriculum and instruction, school facilities, student services and school community relations. The third component, curriculum and instruction, includes a definition of curriculum and instruction and the underlying assumptions concerning racial equality. There is then a checklist of criteria for adequacy, where the teacher is asked to respond as to whether performance on that variable is adequate, excellent or deficient. Specific evidence is asked for as justification for the response given and an explanation requested for deficiencies cited. Finally, a request for recommendations for improvement is included. The curriculum and instructional areas covered include the availability of a school policy statement, the involvement of persons of different racial backgrounds, provision of in-service education, attentiveness to the racial and cultural identities of pupils, racism, and its effects. This latter is by no means as detailed as the others cited but its techniques have greater appeal for teachers. It is more open-ended and invites participation in reflecting on answers, identifying strengths and weaknesses and proposing deliberate strategies for change.

These examples represent just one model, there are others however. The guidelines developed by the Multiethnic Inspectorate of the Inner London Education Authority (1981) furnish a useful, if limited and somewhat dated, exemplar for teachers who would like to see a model of how they can begin to evaluate their school's response to the demands of multicultural education. A checklist is provided for such areas as school policy, equality of opportunity, racism, curriculum, classroom strategies, resources, language, ethos and atmosphere, support and care of pupils, staff development, parents and their communities and school to work. As a pathfinder towards a more sophisticated approach the document has the advantage of an attractive and simple layout.

The former Schools Council Programme One, which was dedicated to 'Purpose and Planning in Schools', resulted in a very useful publication which could assist schools to generate their own criteria and to evaluate their provision according to them (Nuttall, 1981). It gives a classification of strategies for introducing self-evaluation, based on initiatives taken by LEAs but emphasises the need for a school to pick up the idea of evaluation, to internalise it and to make the process its own, reflective of its own unique features, and that seems to me the essence of the approach which I have tried to adopt in this chapter. Just as it is necessary for pupils to internalise moral values and to make them their own, so also is it only if teachers internalise their own evaluation strategy for prejudice reduction that it will have their necessary commitment and understanding.

I would not wish to suggest that developing a prejudice reduction evaluation strategy is easy. It is a complex and controversial process, which may have to grow from very modest beginnings. At first it may be only partial. This section has sought to offer indications of possibilities rather then programmatic guidance on approaches to this question. Ideally such evaluation will address all seven components of the curriculum discussed in this chapter and include different techniques and approaches based on the perceptions of parents, pupils and teachers. To begin with it may be more modest. In any case, however, it will be important to have a well-thought-out policy and procedure to ensure effective feedback and, as appropriate, action.

Looking back across the seven components of the curricular strategy for prejudice reduction presented in the chapter, there is much evidence that is inconclusive and tentative and areas where any evidence is sparse. But, a number of provisional guiding principles for the work of educators seem to emerge from the considerations in this chapter. Clearly, any list will be incomplete, and yet there seems to be convincing evidence or argument that a prejudice reduction curricular strategy should:

1. Derive from the overall intellectual and social ethos of the school;
2. Include a societal and learning rationale that comprehends cultural diversity and the automatic need in that kind of society for prejudice reduction;
3. Take account of the cognitive biography of pupils;
4. Express a commitment to democratic values;
5. Include cognitive, affective and behavioural objectives, including planned teaching approaches to correct for misinformation, inappropriate attitudes and unsuitable behaviour;
6. Span the full range of learning experiences and areas of knowledge;
7. Appraise the logistics of teaching and the full range of resources for their congruence with the prejudice reduction policy;
8. Employ methods of teaching which appeal to the reflective judgement of pupils to derive their own values;
9. Eschew indoctrination approaches;
10. Aim for the higher levels of intellectual functioning and moral reasoning;
11. Include a built-in evaluation strategy, including provision for feedback and action.

SUMMARY

To summarise, I have proposed, in this chapter, a model of a curriculum rationale for prejudice reduction deriving from seven components: a societal rationale; a learning rationale; aims; content and experiences; modes of transaction; resources; and evaluation. I have emphasised that there are other variables involved in the overall institutional commitment such as those identified in chapter 4 on whole school policies and that I have been concerned in this chapter particularly with a curriculum strategy for prejudice reduction. I have concluded the chapter with a list of provisional guiding principles which emerge from the chapter. I have also underlined that I am not proposing a causal model of prejudice reduction, nor am I suggesting that the seven components are discrete. Quite the reverse, although the model draws on the literature, more work and refinement are necessary, as is also empirical support. Moreover, the components are overlapping, interdependent and interactive. If

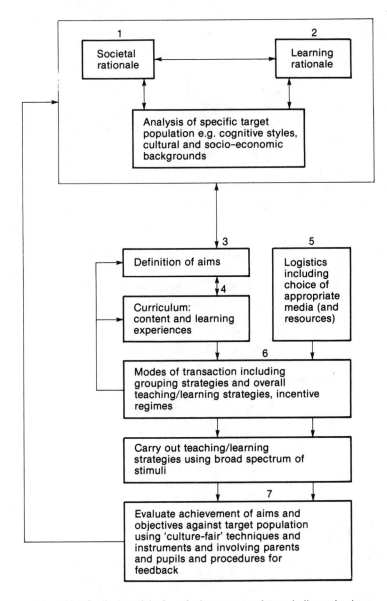

Figure 5.6 Cyclical model of curriculum strategy for prejudice reduction

alternative and better models of the rationale for a curriculum strategy for prejudice reduction are proposed, this chapter will have served its purpose, namely to stimulate thought and discussion of a coherent, ordered and democratic basis for such a curriculum, which rests on sound pedagogical principles. Figure 5.6 seeks to portray the relationship between the seven components diagrammatically and should be seen as an integral part of the overall rationale of the institution and its ethos. In the next chapter, I want to look more closely at teaching approaches to the prejudice reduction curriculum. In particular, I want to offer a categorisation and some detail of teaching/learning approaches which have been found to be, or are argued to be, effective, before moving in chapter 7 to discuss the very important prerequisite to successful teaching — adequacy of resources and other materials.

ACTIVITIES

1. How plausible do you consider to be the model of curriculum presented in this chapter? Assess critically both its logic and its usefulness, and seek to improve both the overall model and the interrelationship of the parts. Draw out the implications for prejudice reduction and set down the major 'guiding principles' which they imply for your teaching.
2. Look again at the section labelled modes of transaction. How close are the principles identified to those in the effective school's literature? How would you bring the two closer together and focus them more sharply on prejudice reduction?
3. Draw up a model using the components of a whole-school policy, as presented in chapter 4, as a setting for the curriculum rationales presented in this chapter. Formulate the model as a 'philosophy of teaching and learning' and prepare an action list for discussion at a staff meeting with your colleagues.
4. Consider the 'learner and learning rationale' proposed in this chapter and reflect on your own teaching. What additional information do you need to be able to take greater account of the 'cultural styles' of your pupils? Make a plan of how you could set about obtaining that information.
5. Using the aims for a prejudice reduction curriculum, as proposed in this chapter, formulate an appropriate curriculum evaluation strategy.

REFERENCES

Banks, J.A. (1981) *Multiethnic Education: Theory and Practice*. Boston: Allyn & Bacon.
Banks, J.A. (1985) *Teaching Strategies for the Social Studies*. New York: Longman.
Banks, J.A. (1986) 'Multicultural education: development, paradigms and goals', in Banks, J.A. and Lynch, J. (eds) *Multicultural Education in Western Societies*. London: Holt, Rinehart & Winston.
Bloom, B.S. (1956) *Taxonomy of Educational Objectives: Handbook I: Cognitive Domain*. New York: David McKay.
Brophy, J. and Good, T.L. (1986) 'Teacher behaviour and student achievement', in Wittrock, M.C. (ed.) *Handbook of Research on Teaching*. New York: Macmillan, 328–75.
California State Department of Education (1985) *Elementary Program Review Training Manual 1985–6*. Sacramento, CA: Superintendent of Public Instruction.

California State Department of Education (1986) *Secondary Program Review Training Manual* Sacramento, CA: Superintendent of Public Instruction.

Clark, R.M. (1983) *Family Life and School Achievement: Why Black Children Succeed or Fail.* Chicago: University of Chicago Press.

Goodlad, J.J. (1979) *Curriculum Inquiry: The Study of Curriculum Practice.* New York: McGraw Hill.

Graham, P.A. (1980) Whither equality of educational opportunity? *Daedalus.* **109**, 115–32.

Grant, C.A. and Sleeter, C.E. (1986) *After the School Bell Rings.* Philadelphia: Falmer

Gauthier, W.J., Pecheone, R.L. and Shoemaker, J. (1985) Schools can become more effective, *Journal of Negro Education.* **54** (3), 388–408.

Her Majesty's Inspectorate (1985) *The School Curriculum from 5 to 16.* London: HMSO.

Inner London Education Authority, Multiethnic Inspectorate (1981) *Education in a Multiethnic Society: An Aide-memoire for the Inspectorate.* London: ILEA.

Klein, G. (1986) *Reading into Racism.* London: Routledge and Kegan Paul.

Kleinfeld, J. (1975) Effective teachers of Eskimo and Indian students, *School Review.* February, 301–44.

Kohlberg, L. (1969) Stage and sequence: the cognitive-developmental approach to socialization', in Goslin, D.A. (ed.) *Handbook of Socialization Theory and Research.* Chicago: Rand McNally.

Kohlberg, L. (1973) The claim to moral adequacy of a highest stage of moral judgement, *The Journal of Philosophy.* **70** (18), 631–32.

Kohlberg, L. (1979) 'Justice as reversibility', in Laslett, P. and Fishkin, J. (eds) *Philosophy, Politics and Society.* New Haven: Yale University Press, 257–72.

Lynch, J. (1983) *The Multicultural Curriculum.* London: Batsford.

Lynch, J. (1986) *Multicultural Education: Principles and Practice.* London: Routledge and Kegan Paul.

Musgrave, P. (1979) *The Sociology of Education* 3rd edn. London: Methuen.

National Council for the Social Studies (1976) *Curriculum Guidelines for Multiethnic Education.* Arlington VA: NCSS 42–48.

National Education Association (1980) *Profiles of Excellence: How to Establish Racial Equality in Schools.* Washington DC: NEA.

National Study of School Evaluation (1973) *Evaluation Guidelines for Multicultural/Multiracial Education.* Arlington VA: National Study of School Evaluation.

Nisan, M. and Kohlberg, L. (1978) *University and Cross-Cultural Variance in Moral Development: A Longitudinal and Cross-Cultural Study in Turkey.* Cambridge MA: Centre for Moral Education, Harvard University.

Nuttall, D.L. (1981) *School Self-Evaluation: Accountability with a Human Face?* London: Schools Council.

Ogbu, J. (1978) *Minority Education and Caste.* New York: Academic Press.

Peters, R.S. (1981) *Ethics and Education.* London: Allen & Unwin.

Philips, S.U. (1983) *The Invisible Culture.* London: Longman.

Ramirez, M. and Castaneda, A. (1974) *Cultural Democracy, Biocognitive Development and Education.* New York: Academic Press.

Rosenthal, R. and Jacobson, L.F. (1968) *Pygmalion in the Classroom: Self-Fulfilling Prophecies and Teacher Expectations.* New York: Holt.

Santa Clara County Office of Education (1983) 'School effectiveness: a conceptual framework', San Jose, CA: Board of Education.

Santa Clara County Office of Education (1984) 'School factors which promote student achievement', San Jose, CA: Board of Education.

Stodolsky, S.S. and Lesser, G. (1975) 'Learning patterns in the disadvantaged, in *Challenging the Myths: The Schools, the Blacks and the Poor.* Cambridge MA: Harvard Education Review (Reprint Series, No. 5).

Tyler, R.W. (1949) Basic Principles of Curriculum and Instruction. Chicago: University of Chicago Press.

United States Commission on Human Rights (1973) *Differences in Teacher Interaction with Mexican American and Anglo Students.* Washington DC.

Vasquez, J. (1979) *Locus of Control, Social Class and Learning*. Los Angeles, CA: National Dissemination and Assessment Centre, California State University.

Weinstein, C.E. and Mayer, R.E. (1986) 'The teaching of learning strategies', in Wittrock, M.C. (ed.) *Handbook of Research on Teaching*. New York: Macmillan, 315–27.

White, J.H. (1984) *The Psychology of Blacks*. Englewood Cliffs NJ: Prentice-Hall.

Wilson, J., Williams, N. and Sugerman, B. (1967) *Introduction to Moral Education*. Harmondsworth: Penguin.

Chapter 6

Teaching Approaches

INTRODUCTION

In chapter 5, I have sought to construct a curricular rationale for prejudice reduction comprising seven major components: societal rationale; learning rationale; aims; content and experiences; logistics; modes of transaction; and evaluation. Further I have emphasised the way in which such an exercise has to be seen in the context of the whole-school policies, proposed in chapter 4. I have discussed each of the components in turn and have illustrated them separately, while constantly drawing attention to the symbiotic — or even synergetic — nature of the curricular components, and their contribution to a school ethos which is conducive to and supportive of both social and intellectual growth. I concluded the chapter by suggesting a few guiding principles for educators, who wish to draw together a curriculum rationale appropriate to a school's commitment to prejudice reduction, and consistent with its broader policy for cultural pluralism.

Chapter 5 has been preparatory for this chapter in the sense that it has identified principles, propositions and concepts which must underpin the classroom action of teachers. Drawing on those principles and the literature concerning prejudice acquisition and reduction scanned in earlier chapters, I would like, in this chapter, to identify more closely some of the teaching/learning strategies for prejudice reduction which that literature and research may support. I want to propose a categorisation of these approaches, referring to the prerequisites for success, the advantages and the disadvantages of each category of approach, formulated in such a way as to encourage teachers to review their own teaching and to include a varied range of different approaches to prejudice reduction, appropriate to the age, cultural background and intellectual level of the children. It is hoped that a variety of overlapping and interactive approaches to teaching for prejudice reduction will be adopted rather than one method being seized on by teachers as being 'right'. In any case, teachers usually do translate curriculum into instruction by blending together many elements, styles and approaches. I have, therefore, grouped together 12 major curricular approaches which teachers may adopt with relative ease in their classrooms. For ease of labelling,

I have called these: direct teaching; coalition formation; moral education; case histories; interethnic contact; principle-testing; drama and simulation; materials approaches; discourse; collaborative/co-operative learning; coaching and expectation training; and awareness training. I would like to emphasise, once again, the interrelationship between these approaches and the whole-curricular and whole-school context and initiatives introduced and described in chapters 4 and 5. The 12 approaches should not be considered as either complete in themselves or as separate one from another. There is overlap between and among them, hybrid versions are possible, even desirable, and each is interdependent with the ethos and other components of the school system and the curriculum as a whole. Additional approaches and alternative categorisations are certainly possible. What I have done is to select 12 generic approaches from the literature surveyed earlier in this book, for which there is evidence of success, although admittedly incomplete and circumstantial, even thin in some cases.

Before I discuss each of the generic approaches in greater detail, I should like to say a word about the classroom climate and peer relationships. While there is a large and growing literature on school climate and its relationship to pupil's academic achievement (Brookover et al., 1979; Crain, Mahard and Narot, 1982), there is very little work on the way in which alternative classroom social structures affect interethnic and other peer relations and prejudice, although there is some data indicating that pupil's perceptions of the social climate of the classroom are related to academic outcomes (Walberg, 1969; Walberg and Anderson, 1968). Co-operative learning methods have also been shown to produce positive effects on pupil's perceptions of social relations in the classroom (Sharan, 1980; Slavin, 1980), and a democratic classroom climate has been argued to be conducive to gains in both academic and social domains. This latter accentuates in particular the development of positive civic attitudes (Ehman, 1980; Torney, Oppenheim and Farnen, 1975).

Each of the approaches I propose in this chapter is interdependent with the classroom ethos that a teacher is able to generate and sustain, and the values, attitudes and behaviour of that teacher both in and outside the classroom. While differing approaches to classroom instruction, including different patterns of communication and interaction, may be expected to yield different social and academic outcomes, only some of these approaches may be expected to result in improved interethnic relations and prejudice reduction. The function of this chapter is briefly to describe those approaches from which, the evidence suggests, prejudice reduction may result. That result will, however, be dependent, among other things, on the climate the teacher succeeds in constructing as the foundation for building his pedagogy. One aspect of that ethos about which we know a great deal, is the way in which teachers who set and communicate high expectations for all pupils stimulate high academic performance (Good, 1982; Good and Brophy, 1984). Another is that 'business-like' teachers who are effective classroom managers may more easily attract pupils' attention and more successfully encourage their academic achievement (Brophy, 1979; Walberg, 1984).

I do not wish to imply a simple, directional causality from teachers to pupils. Hamilton (1983) warns against this, and I accept that both teaching and learning are complex and continuously interactive processes in the construction and daily reconstruction of classroom reality. For the subliminal and unobserved in the

classroom, such as the thoughts, feelings, attitudes and perceptions of the participants, are often as important in determining ethos and the effectiveness of teaching as
the planned inputs of the teacher. In other words, the effectiveness of the approaches
that I suggest will be 'framed' by the prior knowledge, experience and attitudes of
pupils and teachers, as well as by the broader curricular and institutional social
contexts referred to above. Moreover, notwithstanding my earlier comment about the
paucity of work on the effects of classroom climate on pupil's attitudes, I am conscious
of how vast is the literature on the study of teaching (Shulman, 1986). With all the
preceding caveats, let us now take a closer look at the 12 approaches.

DIRECT TEACHING

There can be no doubt that good, direct teaching can be efficacious in contributing to
prejudice reduction. It can, for example, fulfil the important fundamental function of
correcting for misinformation, as well as challenging the historical and cultural
material about ethnic groups that is often at the base of stereotyping. It can facilitate
more positive identification with the folk culture and life histories of great personages
from ethnic minorities as well as nurturing a recognition of the creative and positive
contributions of all cultural groups to a culturally diverse society. It may enable pupils
to begin to come to terms with that diversity and to feel comfortable in interacting
with peers from other groups, and thus provide the initial criteria for distinguishing
fact from opinion. Underpinned by appropriate learning theory, the approach may
thus hold promise.

While direct teaching has been shown to be less powerful a pedagogy than some
others in facilitating the development of interethnic friendships and healthier
attitudes, it also has the advantage of representing a continuity with the teacher's
existing teaching and frame of reference. It can thus be the first 'dipping of the toe', by
the teacher into the field of prejudice reduction and a 'trailer' to more potent but also
more complex methods of teaching. For example, most teachers may begin by
relaying the facts of prejudice and its injurious effects, but gradually move to involve
the pupils in social inquiry which will yield concepts, generalisations and theories as
well. From there, hypothesis development and testing may lead on to higher levels of
questioning and valuing. From these follow the acquisition of important decision-
making skills for non-prejudiced and reflective decision-making, weighing and
evaluating the accuracy of generalisations, judiciously identifying alternative courses
of action and responses to the generalisations of others and defending rationally
particular values or courses of action. Thus, while knowledge is a necessary
component, as emphasised in chapter 5, higher levels of knowledge and opportunities
for personal values identification and clarification are indispensable to sound
decision-making and the ability to make reflective, morally autonomous and socially
responsible judgements.

The important thing to bear in mind is that a heavily didactic or indoctrinating
approach to the development of a reflective commitment to the values of a democratic
cultural diversity is a contradiction in terms. It is pedagogically unsound and it denies
the pupils the freedom that is their democratic right — to choose between what are
often equally healthy values. In any case, it is unlikely that pupils will espouse,

internalise and use to guide their action, values which have been forced onto them, nor will they have acquired a method or process for identifying, clarifying and explicating their own values, when the 'enforcer' is no longer present. Direct teaching is not the same as directive teaching (Torney-Purta and Schwille, 1983).

A number of important models have been developed in the social studies areas in the United States, including those by Hunt and Metcalf (1968), Oliver and Shaver (1966) and Newman (1970), to enable pupils to analyse value problems. Superka et al., (1976) have summarised the major approaches, many of which include moral dilemma episodes and structured rational discussion (demanding the application of reason) in addition to evidence, testing principles, analysing analogous cases and guided research. Banks (1985) has developed a value inquiry model, which encompasses nine stages: observation–discrimination; description–discrimination; identification–description; identification–analysis; hypothesising; recalling, e.g., naming alternative values; predicting, comparing and contrasting; choosing; and justifying, which includes stating reasons, sources and possible consequences of value choice. (Banks, 1985, pp. 413–21). Simple question and answer strategies, combined with normal direct teaching techniques and reinforcement and motivation strategies on a whole-class basis may be used in order to commence this process, taking into account the age and background of the children.

Some of the essential and basic information and knowledge for prejudice reduction is, however, very difficult to bring to life in the classroom. Knowledge, for example, of national and local legislation, of institutional regulations and more broadly of human rights at the international level can be unexciting, and this applies even where an attempt is made to expose the underlying rationale and values. Pupils can be very quickly 'turned off' with detriment to the more complex and desirable developments referred to above, even where a human interest is injected into the discussion of rights. For that reason, a number of authors have proposed the identification of particular issue areas associated with a high pupil activity pedagogy (e.g., Pettman, 1983). Others have provided episodes each of which focusses on a particular component of moral reasoning with activities in which moral problems are presented and each of which requires a value judgement and justification for that judgement (Main, 1978).

Without inferring that teachers may impose a ready-made value system on children, neither should they underestimate the power which they have to change attitudes merely by dint of being an authority figure. Clearly a message from a source of high credibility will be more likely to produce attitude change than one from a source of less credibility. Addressing the five known determinants of attitude change, for example, Flay (1978) lists them as:

1. The power of the message;
2. The existing attitude (to be changed);
3. The level of commitment to the existing attitude;
4. The credibility, expertise or trustworthiness of the changer;
5. The level of salience and ego-involvement of the person addressed.

So, the very fact that teachers commit their teaching to prejudice reduction means that it is likely to communicate a powerful message to pupils, quite apart from the particular message which they are conveying on that occasion.

While it is beyond the scope of this book to describe it in detail, the work of the Institute for Research on Teaching at the College of Education of Michigan State University, which was created in 1976 to conduct research on teacher thinking and decision making, has relevance for those teachers who wish to improve the effectiveness of their teaching and to expand their criteria for professional judgement to include prejudice reduction. The research programme addresses the following two basic questions. How do the ways teachers think about themselves and their pupils, their subject matter and the settings for their work affect the nature and quality of teaching and learning? How can the nature and quality of these cognitive processes be improved? (Institute for Research on Teaching, 1986.) Moreover, some authors in the United States have begun to produce catalogues of different models of teaching, operating at different emotional and intellectual levels. In order to meet the increasingly heterogeneous needs of their pupils, educators need to expand their repertoire of teaching methods. This is particularly so, where, as in prejudice reduction teaching, the teacher has to aim for cognitive, affective and conative gains.

One such catalogue is produced by Joyce and Weil (1986). This categorises approaches as informational processing (including inductive thinking), inquiry training, use of advance organisers, memorisation, stage-appropriate teaching, problem analysis and research approaches. A second group or family is concerned with learner-centred strategies including non-directive teaching, the enhancement of creative thought, personal awareness enhancement and shared responsibility. The third family encompasses social approaches, such as group investigation, role playing, policy discussion, interpersonal skill development and social science inquiry, while a fourth group concentrates on the behavioural approach, which may include mastery learning, feedback usage to modify behaviour and assertive training. This latter may be particularly useful in enabling pupils to cope with potentially stressful situations while improving both self-concept and academic achievement. Direct teaching approaches as much as other pedagogies will, of course, need to use rational democratic means. But the evidence is good that where there is appeal to the rational judgement of participants within the context of a democratic curriculum, improvements in attitudes can be achieved (Trager and Yarrow, 1952; Johnson, 1966; Litchner and Johnson, 1969; Stenhouse, Verma and Wild, 1982).

Are there any principles which emerge from the research and writing in the field of combating prejudice by means of direct teaching and the presentation of information? I believe that, based on existing good practice, a number of tentative principles may be identified which teachers may easily adopt into their existing teaching style such as that:

- the more democratic the classroom regime, the greater the feeling of trust between teacher and taught, the more positive the teacher attitude on the issue, the more likelihood of positive outcomes;
- collaborative methods of content presentation are more efficacious;
- high activity pedagogical approaches are more potent than passive ones;
- the teaching/learning strategies must adopt rational methods and appeal to the judgement of pupils;

- 'expert' resources should be invoked to support the appropriate value positions;
- methods must aim to help pupils clarify their own value positions;
- the material presented should aim to 'stretch' pupils conceptually and cognitively;
- material should evoke identification and empathy with victimised individuals and groups adopting an 'us' rather than 'them' approach;
- the content should not be too far outside the existing cognitive and affective frame of reference of the pupil;
- the material should include demonstrated social support for the issue;
- the material should include evidence of active counter measures by the victim against the persecution or discrimination in question;
- the presentation should include situations involving value dilemmas;
- there should be an emphasis on similarity rather than difference;
- everyday material and content on family life should be included;
- to be helpful there should, if possible, be an age similarity between the pupils and the 'victim(s)';
- the material should emphasise positive rather than negative aspects;
- the content should clearly demonstrate inconsistences and incompatability of 'value application.'

The commencement of teaching for prejudice reduction affords a good opportunity to teachers to reappraise the range and orientation of their current teaching approaches against a list of principles, such as that provided above, and to expand and extend it according to their own perception of their distinctive professional context and needs, their considered view of their pupil's needs and with reference to more recent research. It is, in other words, a good opportunity to 'retread' their teaching styles as a whole and to incorporate new criteria addressing prejudice reduction. For, just as the process of prejudice reduction has to be built into the day-to-day life of the school, so it has to be built into the continuous process of professional development of teachers' competence by the teacher. We shall return to this topic in chapter 8.

COALITIONS

There is no *subject* in the school curriculum called prejudice reduction. Nor is there likely to be. As I have emphasised throughout this book, prejudice reduction is a curriculum commitment which is the responsibility of all staff and pupils and of all subjects taught in the school curriculum. The school curriculum changes only slowly, and it is often difficult to find appropriate points of insertion for new areas and new criteria. All the more important, then, is the forging of creative coalitions with those areas of innovation which may be evolving. There are, for example, a number of projects that are introducing such areas as international education, human rights education, peace education, world studies, global and development education, environmental education and citizenship education. All of these have considerable bodies of knowledge, concepts and philosophy in common with education for prejudice reduction. Moreover, existing subject areas such as geography, humanities, history and religious education may already be striving in a similar direction and towards similar objectives.

An early paper by Hicks attempts to explore precisely that area of commonality and overlap which already exists between development education and multicultural education (Hicks, 1979). Moreover, Banks has always maintained that the commitment of multiethnic education has to be to educate pupils into a personal identity which arises from and transcends ethnic, national and global identifications (Banks, 1981, 1986), and Lynch has argued for a more international context, including teaching for human rights (Lynch, 1986a). Several international organisations have also been involved in developing curriculum territory which is fertile ground for prejudice reduction. The UNESCO ASPRO Project, the Council of Europe, Teaching for Human Rights Programme and the World Bank materials are examples here.

In a three-year project carried out on behalf of the Scottish Consultative Committee on the Curriculum and based at Jordanhill College of Education in Glasgow, for example, a conceptual framework was adopted which linked environmental education, development education, peace education, international education and multicultural education in a composite curriculum initiative for secondary schools in several Scottish districts. The project was very successful, not least because of the unity of conceptual and political strength provided by such areas working in co-ordinated and co-operative manner rather than competing with each other for scarce curriculum time (Dunlop, 1985). The Schools Council/Rowntree project on World Studies based at St Martin's College, Lancaster and the World Studies Teacher Training Centre at York University are slightly better known. They have produced some excellent material (Hicks and Townley 1982), including the reproduction of such seminal documents as the UNESCO Recommendations on Education for International Understanding and Peace. A teachers handbook for World Studies is now available (Fisher and Hicks, 1985).

In the United States, some of the anti-prejudice curriculum materials broaden towards their conclusion to include a worldwide perspective for the application of the principles learned. A new educational programme from the Anti-Defamation League of B'nai B'rith, entitled *Being Fair and Being Free* does precisely that, causing pupils to look, towards the end of the course, at problems abroad evoked by prejudice and the rejection of pluralism (Anti-Defamation League, 1986), while King (1980) has embraced a long-standing commitment to developing 'worldmindedness' as a major part of her approach to multicultural education. Several school boards have developed guides for teaching about human rights (e.g., Detroit Public Schools, 1981), featuring instructional materials and activities, representing a variety of perspectives, and addressing issues such as prejudice, racial and ethnic stereotyping, sex roles and ethnocentrism and social skills and responsibility. Authorities in the United Kingdom, Canada and Australia have also produced similar material.

MORAL EDUCATION

On several occasions in this book I have referred in some detail to the usefulness of the approaches pioneered in the field of moral education by Kohlberg (Kohlberg and Hersch, 1977). I have described in detail the stage typology of the structure of moral development and the principle that pupils must be taught with material that is aimed at a level of moral development one stage in advance of their existing level for advancement to take place (Arbuthnot and Faust, 1981). I must emphasise what I said in the Introduction of this book, namely that all educators are involved in an essentially moral task that encompasses the initiation of children into rational modes of thought and healthy moral values. Thus, regardless of the subject or level, the work of Kohlberg speaks to teachers and has implications for their teaching approaches. The major prerequisites are a knowledge of the stage developments and their invariant sequence and the capability to reason at least one stage in advance of their pupils — what Arbuthnot and Faust (1981) call the '+1 reasoning requirement'. Clearly this is not likely to be a problem when working with young children, but with older children, and particularly young adolescents aged 12 to 14, who are reasoning at stages 3 and 4, it can become a real inhibition to effective moral education, although not rendering it totally ineffective.

Since moral development is achieved by the introduction of moral dilemmas or questions which can be solved by reasoning one stage above the pupil's current stage of moral development, a first step — as in all good teaching — has to be an assessment of the pupil's current level of reasoning. This can be achieved with certain rudimentary skills and techniques that will enable the teacher to make a professional guesstimate, on the basis of which reversible judgements may be made. For example, within the context of other indicators, such as the child's intelligence and general level of maturity, children between the ages of five and eight will be within stages 0–2 with the majority at stage 1. In the age range 9 to 11, the spread will be stages 1–3 with the majority in stage 2; in early adolescence, ages 12 to 14, the range will be stages 1–4 with a likely majority at stage 3. Within the final years of compulsory schooling, 15 to 16, any of the stages 1–5 may be found but a reasonable expectation is that a majority are at stages 3 and 4. In post compulsory education any of the six stages may be found with a minority of below five per cent still at stage 1 and a minority of less than one per cent at stage 6. Clearly, with advancing age, the process of estimating the stage of moral development becomes more difficult and the need is therefore greater for the teacher to pick up the right cues, for example, the use of social perspectives in pupil reasoning, in the way they respond to moral questions and dilemmas. Arbuthnot and Faust offer a series of 'clues' to this process by advising teachers to:

- develop good listening habits;
- carefully collect relevant information;
- be sparing with questions rather than overburdening pupils;
- ask open rather than closed questions;
- avoid direct 'why' questions;
- evoke 'revealing' information, i.e., revealing in terms of the stage typology such as evidence of social awareness;
- use rephrasing techniques to test pupils;
- refer to the major characteristics of the typology.
  (Arbuthnot and Faust, 1981, pp. 111–27).

In a sense, even at a fairly superficial level of acquaintance, Kohlberg's work reminds educators that pupils cannot simply be told how to think about moral issues, or given a structure of moral values which they then use. Moral development results from a process of accommodation and construction whereby pupils will seek to solve problems by assimilating them into their current mode of moral thinking, and only when that is not possible will a new strategy be developed which represents the next higher stage of moral development. It is the function of the educator to facilitate this process of challenge and consequent accommodative response. But then, that is not an unfamiliar technique to good teachers. Of course, teachers will use different techniques to achieve this advancement, dependent on the age and stage of the pupil. On the other hand, whatever the technique, it will probably involve a strategy including five phases: setting the scene, forming the groups, choosing the dilemma, initiating discussion, projecting into the future life and action of the pupil.

Kohlberg's work has certainly not been uncontroversial and the case for the existence of stage 6 has been 'softened' over more recent years, dependent to some extent on the scoring manual used (Kohlberg, Levine and Hewer, 1984). Then, too, Kohlberg is aligned with a philosophical view of morality that argues that there is an objective moral good which human beings 'know', and which is formal, universal and without exception, and which, in its true form, is simply a theory of perfect reciprocal justice (Flanagan, 1984). Nor is his argument watertight *vis-à-vis* criticisms of the sex bias of his sample, the closed nature of the moral dilemmas posed, the entirely verbal nature of the evidence or the alleged failure to meet Piaget's stage criteria and thus its entitlement to be classified as a developmental stage theory. True, talk is cheap and action comes more expensive. But with all these limitations and caveats, Kohlberg's work remains a rich potential informant of teaching strategies for prejudice reduction. Teachers do not have to accept his theory as the whole story on morality. They may, however, develop pedagogical strategies which draw on it to serve their pursuit of prejudice reduction, by means which appeal to the rational moral judgement of their pupils. For this, of course, teachers also need to be aware of their own moral values and value-related decisions (Shaver and Strong, 1982; Strike and Soltis, 1985).

CASE HISTORIES

There are a number of different ways in which case histories may be used in the development of varied and stimulating approaches to prejudice reduction. They may be used as illustrations of the lifestyles of members of minority communities to correct for misinformation and stereotyping or to provide for positive identifications and an understanding of the contributions of all ethnic and cultural groups to the totality of human culture and the national culture in particular. They are a useful way of introducing the 'great names' of human endeavour regardless of sex, race, class or creed, and can be utilized as a non-threatening way of enabling pupils to explore their own feelings of prejudice and to understand the insidious existence and working of institutional prejudice. Used in this way, they provide a indirect and democratic means to achieve more long-term gains in healthy attitudes than short-term, single-shot racism awareness training.

I have already referred to the use of life histories of famous blacks by Singh and Yancy (1974) that led to significant reductions in racial prejudice and the way in which tendencies to evaluate black more positively than white and to overcategorise these to cultural groups, can be similarly modified (Best et al., 1975). An interesting application of the use of case histories is that used by Katz in presenting case histories involving a person or persons suffering from prejudice to those holding the same prejudice, with good results reported. Clearly, while great care is needed in such a process, and while it may be difficult to identify precisely the prejudices of individuals, such a technique can facilitate the development of qualities of humanity and empathy at the same time as placing prejudiced pupils in a position of logical dissonnance. Enhanced by dramatic representation, simulation and role reversal such techniques may prove to be very effective.

Case histories may include more recent material referenced to human rights and their violations: the reports of Amnesty International provide eloquent sources for such work. The cases of Martin Luther King, Steve Biko, Andrei Sakharov, Nelson and Winnie Mandela, or cases referred to the European Court of Human Rights involving racial or sexual discrimination or harassment, are fruitful sources of case study material which can be used for dramatisation or as evidence. More broadly, issues of international commerce and intercourse may illuminate a North–South perspective which takes issue with exploitation and greed in the use of resources based on the neglect of democratic principles of justice espoused by the exploiting countries. They may, of course, be used to show the 'good versus good' dilemmas which are the stock-in-trade of a pluralist society, and to enable pupils to identify and clarify their own attitudes and perceptions of other groups: an essential first step in progressing up the ladder of prejudice reduction.

Case histories may also be used on a comparative basis to contrast and compare differing views of the same event. Taxel (1982), for example, illustrates this from discussions with his students of two versions of the history of the Revolutionary War, one of which totally ignores the contemporary institutionalisation of slavery and the other of which discusses the same phenomenon from the point of view of a nine-year-old slave. The incident of the *Komagata Maru*, a Japanese ship which unsuccessfully attempted to land its Sikh passengers in Canada in 1914, is reported as having been used with good effect to assist Canadian youth to understand racism and similar dilemmas in immigration policies in Western democratic societies (Hubbard 1982). Another Canadian writer, however, argues that while employing films, drama and fiction involving a realistic enactment of a social situation that invites young people to identify with the minority group can be effective, the 'victims' presented should be of approximately the same age as the subject (Kehoe, 1984). He also draws attention to the need for the victim to be seen fighting back, so as to avoid providing vicarious gratification to those with repressed prejudice towards minority groups in general or the specific group involved in the case study. Evocations of empathy are also dependent on the victim being presented in an attractive light and the level of trust between teacher and learner.

A number of principles emerge from Kehoe's work which may be helpful to teachers in selecting and using case studies as well as in direct teaching. I have amended and amplified them slightly, but the following list incorporates the main ones.

- A positive teacher attitude on the issue, not a neutral one;

- the existence of positive relationships of trust between teacher and taught;
- a good match between new material and the existing frame of reference of the pupil;
- the provision of recognised 'expert' sources;
- an 'us' rather than 'them' presentation;
- a demonstration of public agreement with the value position to provide for 'social pressure';
- a goal of positive achievement rather than negative emphasis;
- the inclusion of everyday materials and details of family life where possible to emphasise the normality of the victim;
- an emphasis on similarity rather than difference;
- an age similarity between victim and learner;
- a demonstration of 'fight back' on the part of the victim;
- the illustration of inconsistency of treatment or value application.
  (Kehoe, 1984, pp. 64–5 amended.)

INTERETHNIC CONTACT

We have already seen in chapters 3 and 5 the important role which interethnic contact may play in reducing and overcoming prejudiced attitudes. There is now convincing research, stretching back well over a quarter of a century, testifying to the efficacy of this technique, subject to certain conditions. Broadly stated the requirements are that:

- the contact must be equal status;
- it must be manifestly supported by the authority of the institution;
- the contact within the group should be on a collaborative basis;
- there should be a similarity of competence level among the group members;
- the contacts should be continuous rather than transitory;
- there should be opportunities to interact with outgroup members as individuals;
- the composition and work of the group must be manifestly important, typical, real and voluntary.
- there should be explicit superordinate goals for the group as a whole;
- the work of the group must stand a good chance of success;

I have emphasised that individuals may collectively influence group norms and it is certainly important to take into account both individual and social dimensions in tackling prejudice. But, it should not be assumed that *any* planned contact will improve norms and values; it may, in fact, have the opposite effect. Moreover, the teacher needs to take into account that contact itself may raise or exacerbate anxieties (Stephan and Stephan, 1985). In planning such interethnic contact, teachers will, therefore, need to take into account the prior intergroup experience of pupils and the conditions under which it took place; the level of knowledge and information of the individuals concerning each other's outgroups, including the existence of stereotypes and exaggerated perceptions of similarity or dissimilarity; the type of structural group situation that they are planning, including the aims and composition of the group, pre-existing relationships and the type of collaboration which they have in mind.

So teachers may well find that preparatory work is necessary for successful intergroup contact to achieve prejudice reduction. Direct teaching to provide accurate information and erase false stereotypes may be a helpful facilitator of later success. Historical and cultural material, case histories to evoke empathy and opportunities for identification may be important precursors to group contact, if the contact is to have the desired effect and not a contrary dysfunctional one. In a sense, the point illustrates once again the need for teachers to adopt a spectrum of interrelated, different, but compatible elements and approaches into their teaching strategies (Brophy, 1982).

Pre-preparation may also take the form of priming and expectation training with regard to cognitive and affective dimensions, both to increase knowledge and to encourage the development of competences and skills, informational as well as social. One way to ease pupils into group work is the use of dyadic working methods, which tend to be less threatening and a good way of introducing pupils to the skills of peer-tutoring. Teachers may also, through more carefully deliberating on and planning their own dyadic relationships with individuals from different ethnic groups, facilitate the process by their actions rather than their words (Gay, 1974). Games and competitions may also be useful techniques in preparing pupils for group work and, as in the work of Slavin (1983), may be used as part of co-operative work to improve interethnic relationships as well as to accelerate attainment. Thus, given the kinds of caveats aired above and the fulfilment of the conditions previously listed there, the evidence seems to indicate that interethnic contact through co-operative learning methods is a superior way of teaching to whole-class instruction in fostering co-operative behaviour between and within groups, in improving relationships and ethnic attitudes, as well as nurturing better learning programmes (Sharan et. al., 1985).

In sum, interethnic contact is an efficacious and promising means of achieving prejudice reduction. Teachers will, however, need to exercise care in the way they prepare for and frame such contact, making sure that the conditions referred to in the earlier part of this section are met. Given that these conditions are fulfilled there are, additionally, various subroutines of interethnic contact which can be used to further enhance pupil gains in both cognitive and affective domains, ranging from games and tournaments to the reinforcement of co-operative group work by the provision of information which meets the conditions already itemised in the section on direct teaching, to the inclusion of coalitions with other subject and thematic areas, use of case studies and simulation and role-playing exercises.

PRINCIPLE-TESTING

Earlier in this chapter I reiterated the point that it is by identifying, discussing and resolving moral dilemmas according to explicit rational criteria, that individual pupils can clarify their own values and increase their moral maturity. In this section I want to look at one particular technique whereby that can be achieved, principle-testing: part of a discussion technique for values education, developed by Metcalf, which challenges pupils to achieve consistency in the application of moral principles or, if they cannot, to provide rational justification for any inconsistency (Metcalf, 1971).

This approach has been shown to be successful in altering and amending pupils' attitudes to minority group members (Kehoe and Todd, 1978).

There are a number of 'guidelines' for principle testing which may enable teachers to improve their techniques and thus heighten the effects of their teaching and Kehoe (1984) has given examples of sample lessons and subject matter. These guidelines address respect for persons, democratic process, rationality, mutuality/reversability, parallel case, universalisation, denial of relativism, subsumption, prejudgement, consistency, provisionality and avoidance of pre-emptive solutions. It is important, however, to emphasise once again that, as in the case of all the other approaches described in this chapter, I am presupposing the existence of a democratic classroom ethos, that is, one where there is an open opportunity for pupils to discuss moral issues and to resolve them in a rational and honest way. That does not imply that one opinion is as good as another, but it does embrace a commitment to tolerance. This means that pupils can work out their own new and hopefully healthier values as part of an educational process which appeals to their judgement rather than as part of an imposed submersion in indoctrination.

Turning, now, to the techniques of principle-testing, it is important to point out that pupils may need to acquire certain basic understandings of the rules and techniques of the 'game'. Some of these may be introduced by direct teaching techniques as a priming operation for principle-testing proper. Pupils must, for example, understand that the existence of an 'open discussion forum' does not give them the right to express views which are hateful or offensive to their fellow pupils or staff. *Respect for persons* is a prime basis for principle-testing and implies the acceptance of the worth and value of all individuals, even if they sometimes express irrelevant, inconsistent or just plain incorrect views. It implies that pupils show courtesy, even in disagreement, to each other's life-views, cultures, customs and languages, but it does not imply that these will remain unscrutinised or undiscussed. Indeed, they may be generative of principle dilemmas which are grist to the mill of a principle-testing approach: ritually slaughtered meat, religious observances, special clothing all provide a rich source of 'conflicting goods' in a pluralist society.

Closely clustered with the prime ethic of respect for persons is a knowledge and acceptance of *democratic process* and *rationality*. These imply a commitment to such courtesies as taking turns to speak, giving the other person a chance, accepting the principles inherent within a democratic society, such as the rule of law, private property, active citizenship and a commitment to rational discourse, in the balanced and honest marshalling of evidence and presentation of arguments.

Mutuality and reversibility are both principles and techniques. They involve the pupils' ability to actively or imaginatively take the part of the victimised person, or the judge who has to resolve the dilemma. As a technique it is useful for the teacher to be able to invite a pupil to put themselves in his or her place i.e., the person around whom the dilemma centres. Closely associated with this technique is quoting a *parallel case*, not as a pre-emptive resolution of the problem, but as an illustration and yardstick against which the rationality of a particular principle may be tested. Pupils can be invited to say whether the same principle should apply and, if not, why not.

Universalisation is a broadening of the parallel case to the question of what would happen if we all acted in a particular manner. In a sense, it is an invitation to *reductio ad absurdum* as a technique of highlighting the irrationality or inconsistency of a particular principle. The reverse is an invitation to pupils to consider what it would be like if no one undertook a particular task or accepted a particular responsibility. The principle of *denial of relativism* is in a sense a subcategory of rationality insofar as it is intended to challenge the often heard and more frequently implied view that one opinion is as good as another, and that everyone is entitled to their own opinion. The rational challenge to this is that some views are better grounded in reason than others and are therefore more supportable, more rational and better, than views which represent unreflective and inconsistent grounding.

A subtest of this is the technique called *subsumption*, which represents the test of whether a new idea, concept or proposed principle may be subsumed under an already existing one, previously accepted by the group. The technique may be used to challenge pupils to show that the view they hold or the principle they are advocating may be consistent with some more general value principle. This enables the social pressure of a previous endorsement by the group of a given principle to be legitimately used. This is also a useful approach to the avoidance of *prejudgement*, by which a principle is applied to a person or situation in advance of the facts being known: an infringement of the principle in a democratic society that someone is innocent until proven guilty. Of course, prejudgement also affords other guidelines already enunciated, such as that the fact attributed to the case must be ascertained as true and accurate, the principle should be rationally grounded, the information and arguments used must be relevant, there should be mutuality of application, in other words the judgement should be acceptable to the 'judge' for application to her or himself.

Consistency is, naturally, the test of the application of relevant arguments to support a principle, or the application of a principle to a case in the same way on every occasion. *Provisionality* assumes the imperfection of human knowledge and a willingness to revise judgement and principle application, if they can be shown to no longer apply rationally or be inconsistent with new knowledge or principle. A number of researchers have used consistency as the main cutting edge of their work to change attitudes by showing inconsistency between values and attitudes (Rokeach, 1968, Kehoe, 1975). The work suggests that, because values are a more 'potent' component of a pupil's cognitive structure, in a case of demonstrable inconsistency between a value and attitude the attitude is likely to yield because, supported by logical argument, both psychological tension and a desire for cognitive consistency may be evoked, thus moving the attitude to become consistent with the value. A curriculum unit developed at the Ontario Institute for Studies in Education (OISE) may prove a useful model for values education and moral reasoning. It comprises various pupil readings and activities on prejudice, relating to different ethnic groups in North America, to anti-Semitism and to immigration policy. Each of the six episodes contained in the unit focuses on a particular component of moral reasoning, requiring a value judgement about a moral problem and a justification of that judgement (Main, 1978).

Finally, it is important to avoid providing pupils with a *deus ex machina* to solve dilemmas for them. As repeated on several occasions already, it is important for them to work out their own 'principle' position and to identify and clarify their own values. Thus, even where there is a legal resolution to a problem being discussed, it is a good idea not to share it with pupils on each occasion, or if it is shared for the judgement itself to be the subject of principle-testing. In other words, teachers will wish to avoid pre-emptive closure on discussions which may be productive of moral growth. After all, it is the process, not the product, which produces such growth. Given the above guidelines, principle-testing, well prepared for and taught within a democratic classroom environment, can be a powerful method of prejudice reduction which is well within the reach of most teachers to implement successfully.

DRAMA

Drama has been most often used in conjunction with other approaches to prejudice reduction (eg., Ijaz and Ijaz, 1981), but it is such a flexible teaching method that it may usefully be applied in both singular and hybrid forms (Nixon, 1980). On the other hand, it is not always successful and it needs to be carefully planned and interpreted into the longitudinal approach to prejudice reduction throughout the child's school life and into the repertoire of teaching methods of the teacher. In the form of role-playing and simulation, it may be evocative of reasoning and empathy such as are essential to any systematic and logical approach to prejudice reduction (Gray and Ashmore, 1975). Role-playing and simulation are similar to drama insofar as each person is asked to play a part which is different from his or herself. A word-for-word script is not provided, however, only a role description in general terms. The person playing the role has to imagine what the character they have 'adopted' might say or do. To become proficient takes practice and patience and it should not be assumed to be immediately within the capacity of all pupils, but, given perseverance and appropriate guidelines for pupils and staff, it can represent a very rich, developmental, diverse and satisfying group of approaches (Shaftel and Shaftel, 1967, 1982; Belch, 1974).

Flexibly defined and utilised drama may include both drama in education and theatre in education, and, under drama in education, it may include both formal productions of pre-existing plays or ones 'made up' by the pupils. It can be one of the most divergent, multiform and creative means for achieving prejudice reduction, and it may be utilised in all subject areas, with all levels and backgrounds of children. It represents an extension of the existing worlds of both pupils and teachers and may be used to incorporate a variety of cultural conventions and approaches. It may be pre-packaged in the form of tape clips or films for discussion or totally improvised and made-up by pupils.

In the form of dressing-up, drama already comprises an essential component of work in many kindergarten, reception or infant classes. In the form of dioramas, puppets, masks and shadow plays it may be used to link aesthetic and communication skills and manual dexterity preparation for pupils with technological dimensions relating to the articulation of the members of the human body — all contributing to creative role-playing for prejudice reduction. Masks may also be used to effect, where, because of developmental stage or cultural background, pupils are diffident about role-playing and acting. Equally, combined with mime, music or dance or profile performances against a screen, role-playing may be broadened to achieve greater effect or to incorporate traditions from diverse cultural groups. The use of a single or two-way telephone may also be usefully incorporated into role-playing on a dyadic or group basis, with, for example, senior pupils adopting the role of counsellors or advisors in conflict resolution and management.

An audio or video record of such activities as well as an opportunity for pupils to demonstrate and 'play out' their prepared material may afford scope to broaden and deepen the experience and to reinforce newly acquired values. Such records may be useful for subsequent analysis by teachers of their own practice or for analysis and discussion by pupils. Shared with parents and the community, appropriate records may also deepen the experience and achieve much needed parental and community involvement and support.

Kehoe argues that role-play of a previously unacceptable position may increase its acceptability. He reports two approaches, one where the subject's task in the role-play was to write an essay in favour of strenuous efforts to create better opportunities for minorities, and another in which subjects acted out cases of discrimination and ways to promote better race relations. Voluntarily undertaking action opposed to the person's beliefs may result in even greater positive attitude change (Kehoe, 1984, p. 93). Chapman describes an experiment linking together the use of the simulation game 'Starpower' with a discussion phase aimed at the development of more positive attitudes in college students towards blacks and women. The experiment sought to evaluate the effectiveness of the combined strategies in terms of attitude and behaviour change. The author found that experimental subjects in both cases indicated significantly more positive attitudes to blacks, more willingness to support black student activities and, in the case of males, significantly more positive attitudes towards women and men in what are described as non-traditional sex roles (Chapman, 1974).

As in the above descriptions, drama may be used in conjunction with other approaches, such as case studies, to encourage moral 'reversibility', that is feeling what it is like to be 'inside the skin or clothes' of the other, victimised, person. It does, however, need substantial preparation and can usefully be preceded by both direct instruction and co-operative group work. Often too, the problems faced by adolescents between two cultures may be usefully role-played in dramatic representation and value confrontation. Pupils may also be invited to prepare their own dramatisation of a given dilemma and later with greater sophistication to make up their own dilemma and dramatise that. In this way pupils may be asked to volunteer to role-play the defence of a particular ethnic group or someone suffering racial or sexual discrimination, in cases where they may or may not find the case to fit their values.

Sometimes drama is a separate subject on the school's curriculum, but there is no reason why that should rule out the use of drama, simulation and role-playing in other subject areas, provided that the work is preplanned as an integral part of the whole, continuous prejudice reduction strategy in that area and talked out after the dramatic representation. It can be an effective vehicle for prejudice reduction with younger children (Grimmestad and De Chiara, 1982), and it can also play a part in extra-curricular activities in order to focus interest and attention on the plight of victimised groups and individuals as an alternative to talk or discussions. Moreover, it is evident that the same conditions apply as with other approaches introduced earlier: attention to the age and conceptual and moral stage development of the pupils; sensitivity to a diversity of cultural mores which may restrict 'dressing up' activities; maximum involvement of parents and the community; appeal to the judgement of the pupils and a concern with the process as much as any product, realising that pupils must be free to identify and clarify their own values through dilemma discussions and resolution, or they are unlikely to make progress up the 'ladder of prejudice eradication'. Above all it is important to avoid reinforcing stereotypical representations of minority groups as having a monolithic culture and to encourage pupils to see beyond the dramatic incident, used as generalisation, to the real individuality of all people from all groups.

Conversely, to the pupils themselves making dramatic presentations or role playing, as a recent School Curriculum Development Committee points out, the visit of a group of artists or craftspersons to demonstrate the dance, music or visual arts of their culture can deeply enrich the lives of all in the school. Many theatre in education groups in major multiracial cities actually have specific multicultural aims (Craft and Klein, 1986). Teachers, too, may benefit from 'dramatic' involvement as part of their professional development. A pack developed at the University of Nottingham, for example, and entitled 'Lifestyles' is intended to enable teachers to develop a greater sensitivity to cultural differences and to alert them to the dangers of stereotyping. It is intended for use in workshop-type activities and takes the form of a kit based on the lifestyle of several British families of different national and religious origins (Nottingham University, 1984).

Some authors have sought to collect resources and to provide guiding principles to support teachers' efforts in using drama in multicultural education and prejudice reduction approaches in schools. Nixon, for example, sets down a useful set of guidelines for what he terms 'anti-racist teaching' which are worthy of scrutiny for their applicability to prejudice reduction in particular school situations and are susceptible to further refinement and development (Nixon, 1985). Moray House College of Education in Scotland has undertaken a survey outlining the uses of drama in multicultural education and it includes documentation of classroom plays and resources for theatre in education in the United Kingdom (Moray House College of Education, 1985).

One of the disadvantages of some of the above initiatives and material is their one-off, or solo, nature. They need to be integrated into other curricular approaches and to be further developed for longitudinal progress. Project 'Reach' developed by the Arlington School District in the United States seeks to do just that. It is aimed particularly at all-white schools, or schools with few ethnic minority pupils, and, using a spiral curriculum which includes dramatic opportunities, it seeks to educate pupils through four phases. These centre on human relations skills, cultural self awareness, multicultural awareness and cross cultural awareness. Each phase is seen as a necessary prerequisite to its successor, for example, the human relations phase engages pupils in activities related to group dynamics and interpersonal relations. These are seen as a necessary preparation for them to be able to deal with issues of cultural difference and cross cultural communication later in the programme. The overall pack of materials includes helpful 'role cards' and directions and guidance to teachers on how to prepare for and guide role-playing activities.

The handbook includes a group of positive and negative group roles, such as task gatekeeper, problem solver, facilitator, spark plug, encourager and feelings gatekeeper on the one hand, and dominator, verbal distracter, withdrawer and group lemon on the other (Arlington School District, 16, 1982). The pack is in developmental order, and is systematic and progressive in its approach to gradually building up skills and information by an integrated pedagogical approach, which includes drama, excursions to such places as Black Arts Groups, role-playing, simulation exercises and guidelines on preparing and talking out the experiences. Probably the most detailed treatment of role-playing and games, including both the theory and the practice as well as the material and lists of sources and resources, are those provided by Belch (1974) and Shaftel and Shaftel (1967, 1982), all of which were produced in the United States, but are readily available in other countries.

Thus, scripted or unscripted drama, theatre visits and visits to the school by drama-in-education personnel, role-playing and simulation all form a very important component in an integrated approach to prejudice reduction. They do, however, need care in preparation and follow-up and the selection of appropriate materials and themes. Used in an *ad hoc* fashion they may do more harm than good, and teachers need to plan very carefully both the graduation of learning and their expectations of pupils. Teachers will also need to lay down guidelines for such activities. Role playing, for example, is play and not reality and pupils revert to their normal personality when the work is completed, although hopefully with increased awareness of issues of prejudice and discrimination. Nor must such 'games' ever be used to settle grudges or to 'get back' at another pupil. If there are deep-rooted antagonisms between pupils, particular care must be taken in deciding whether this is not a technique which might be postponed until other strategies have been used to begin the process and soften the values conflict. Only professional teachers will know their pupils well enough to decide this. Given the above preconditions, all the evidence points to drama as an effective means to prejudice reduction.

MATERIALS APPROACHES

As the whole of chapter 7 is devoted to resources for prejudice reduction, it is not the aim to duplicate in this section what appears there. On the contrary, the aim is, in line with the other sections in this chapter, to indicate pedagogical approaches rather than draw attention to specific resources. There is a long history of the use of materials as a basis for prejudice reduction strategies from text books, fiction, case studies and other written material to the utilisation of puppets, dioramas, dressing-up, masks, shadow plays and profiling and telephones, and from the early use of film to the later utilisation of audiovisual aids, videotapes and television (Peterson and Thurstone, 1933; Middleton, 1960). Nor is there any reason why, with the widespread introduction of microcomputers into the classroom, approaches to prejudice reduction should not be combined with, and supported by, the most recent advances in information technology, either in the form of provision of accurate information, or computer-adaptive learning and testing.

The need to avoid bias in the materials used hardly needs mentioning. And yet it is the first step in tackling the issue of prejudice reduction. An overall and thoroughgoing scrutiny of existing materials is an essential prerequisite to starting, but it is also a learning exercise in itself. Ideally it should involve consultation with parents, pupils and the community and it certainly involves collegial discourse about the criteria and their application. A rational policy with explicit, negotiated guidelines is, once again, the safest way of avoiding a 'crank', bookburning approach that may do no one any good and may indeed do direct harm. It is to be expected that, in the process, there will be a great divergence of view that will need to achieve some working resolution. This process can, though, actually be used to facilitate greater awareness and maturity as well as involving pupils in appraising the material which they encounter at school. In turn, this may be one of the best preparations for enabling them to develop a sense of critical appraisal of the material they will experience in their wider world, on television, on radio, in the cinema and in the Press. They may thus learn the difference between factual statements, claims and value judgements, and may begin to devise strategies and criteria for evaluating the credibility of previously accepted sources of information in the media. Naturally, teaching children to question and to take issue has to be related to their age and stage of development, but there is no reason why it should not commence as soon as they enter school and continue until they leave — and hopefully, of course, into adult life too.

Materials should not be regarded as a mere adjunct to teaching for they fulfil an important function in providing, through vicarious means, experience that the teacher cannot provide and that the child cannot usually experience at first hand. Developing a global dimension to the work of combating prejudiced and stereotypical views of developing countries may, for example, demand insights. Possibly these are best presented through the use of such kits as the World Bank's 'Towards a Better World Series', much more skilfully and effectively than by the teacher seeking to produce all his or her own material (World Bank, 1986).

Nor should teachers underestimate the extent to which the multicultural classroom provides them with opportunities for materials otherwise unavailable. Holiday snaps and films, cultural artefacts and clothing, pictures of family, friends and places may all provide helpful assistance in overcoming stereotypes and helping children to feel comfortable with difference. But beware! Caution also needs to be exercised, not only to look after materials borrowed, but to monitor their suitability. For example, proselytising material that is prolific and very readily available may not be the most appropriate material for dampening prejudice. Material from the community should thus be welcomed, but must, of course, be subject to normal safeguards of safety and political acceptability levied against all materials used in schools, and should also be appraised against the guidelines for assessing material, referred to above. This is one central value of such guidelines, that they make such a process more objective and depersonalised.

In the United Kingdom the Humanities Curriculum Project has often been considered to be a model of the kind of large-scale material production approach to curriculum development so popular in the 1960s and 1970s. The project was, in fact, more than a materials approach. It encompassed a whole pedagogical philosophy and has deeply influenced approaches to, and thinking about, teaching. This is so even though the central concept of 'the neutral chairman' as the archetypical role for the teacher became rather controversial — probably as much through being misunder- stood as though being understood and disagreed with. The project produced units on the family, war, education, poverty, relations between the sexes, work and race. The teacher is expected to take responsibility for discussion groups of pupils. She or he feeds in documentary evidence and acts as a feelings gatekeeper to protect individual pupils against group pressure, and is expected to develop a climate of open and vigorous enquiry, but not to endorse a particular point of view (Stenhouse, 1980; Schools Council, 1970; Rudduck, 1979). The breakthrough was thus not just in the preparation of a multimedia pack, including relevant training, but also in the development and delivery of an appropriate philosophy of teaching including the usage of material.

A similar recognition of the need for built-in training was at the heart of the MACOS Project developed by Bruner in the United States, and other more recent materials such as the REACH project, quoted earlier in this section, have attempted to deliver a full package, including training. The point here is that well-intentioned but misguided use of 'powerful' material may be worse than useless, it may be actually harmful. The more powerful the material, the more need therefore for careful preparation including appropriate training, a theme to which the whole of chapter 8 is devoted.

One aspect of the careful preparation which is necessary in the use of materials approaches to prejudice reduction is a knowledge of the material saturation point. In certain cases, it is sometimes considered that the more material of different kinds that can be used the better the chances of the student learning and the more effective the teaching. The contrary may be the case and too much material through too many media may blur the issues, obscure the concept and encourage 'material deafness', a casual approach to evidence and a neglect of more important stimuli on the part of pupils.

DISCOURSE

Discourse as a method of prejudice reduction is both essential to the pupil's future as a citizen in a democratic society, committed to change by persuasion rather than coercion, and difficult to achieve in a school context. It necessitates great skill on the part of the teacher and presupposes a certain level of maturity and debating competence on the part of the pupils. It is, of course, derived from and overlapping with many of the other teaching approaches adumbrated in this chapter, and includes phases of values identification and clarification, and thus many of the teaching strategies aimed at achieving these goals. By discourse is meant the achievement of conflict resolution by means of rational discussion and democratic decision. The approach involves an ability to argue coherently and logically and to present a case, using rational evidence and reasoned means of presentation. It presupposes a certain level of communicative equality on the part of the adversaries in discourse, which, in turn, necessitates coaching of pupils to realise that only by rational discourse on a basis of equality can the truth content of information, assertions, statements and advocated positions be effectively tested. It will be evident that discourse within a democratic ethos in classrooms and society is an important means of advocacy of a case.

A number of educators in the United Kingdom have sought to develop strategies to initiate children into discourse. Jeffcoate (1979), for example, gives a number of graphic insights into classroom practice, initiatives and strategies for discourse development, and Rudduck (1979) has provided a detailed and extensive series of publications arising from the Schools Council Humanities Curriculum Project on the problems and techniques of discussion teaching. She considers important issues such as why both pupils and teachers find discussion difficult and what alternative roles are available to the teacher in discussion lessons, for example, as instructor, consultant, devil's advocate, participant and neutral chairperson. She proposes criteria for the analysis of discussion and ground rules for assessing progress and provides initial and provisional means of identifying and diagnosing problems encountered. Clearly each of these different discussion roles for the teacher implies a different approach to authority and different instructional strategies that will effect the 'construction' of valid academic knowledge in the classroom. In reality, of course, many of the roles overlap and blend together as the teacher uses his or her judgement in responding to the dynamic momentum of relationships in the classroom — combining improvisation and spontaneity in pursuit of the 'art of effective teaching' for prejudice reduction (Gage, 1984).

One constant is, however, the need for the availability of good 'value dilemma' material as a basis for the discourse. In the United States, the literature is replete with handy and attractive activities for classroom use (Simon, Howe and Kirchenbaum, 1978), particularly with regard to the values clarification aspect of discourse. There are a variety of interpretations of the exact practical meaning of value analysis, but it is a 'greedy' method of teaching insofar as it does require an extensive range of different materials to develop in individual pupils the ability to make rationally and morally defensible judgements by means of the acquisition of a set of skills essential to that task. Pupils are encouraged to carefully identify the value questions, to collect and marshall relevant facts, to arrive at a value decision and to examine the implicit principle by four tests: role exchange, universal consequences, new cases and subsumption (Metcalf, 1971). Coombs and Meux (1971) have developed a series of approaches to values education and the Association for Values Education and Research (AVER) at the University of British Columbia has also produced a range of value exercises, including distinguishing between factual and value claims, use of syllogism to ensure that conclusions follow from premises, reason-assembly charts and moral principle testing activities, although the results on the effectiveness of the use of the materials in prejudice reduction are mixed (AVER, 1975, 1979).

The discourse approach, though, which itself is a hybrid, also includes the increasingly important area of moral education, where there is an increasing amount of material available. By now, the reader will be familiar with the dilemma discussion approach whereby, through the creation of cognitive disequilibrium brought about by engaging pupils in discussions about moral dilemmas and exposing them to the next highest stage of moral reasoning, development through the stages of moral reasoning can be stimulated. Suffice to say that the research about that aspect of the discourse methodology is more supportive of effectiveness than is the case with values clarification (Enright, et al., 1983, Leming, 1985). But there is an interesting footnote by Higgins, quoted by Lemming, which seems to suggest that enhancement of moral judgement development may be more difficult when the teacher has curricular priorities and when the moral dilemmas are defined by a particular academic content (Leming, 1985, p. 137; Higgins, 1980, p. 100). The idea of 'right answers' and firm social historical facts may naturally inhibit the 'free flight' involvement of pupils in discourse and restrict their 'realistic' engagement with moral dilemma resolution, and thus their progress in moral reasoning.

In addition to the discussion, value analysis and moral reasoning components of the discourse method, co-operative learning, inquiry (discussed in the next section of this chapter) and social and community action and involvement are dimensions which may be included, these latter as behavioural 'proving grounds' for newly won discourse skills. Obviously, careful planning and subsequent reflection, as well as consideration of the age and background of the pupils are necessary and the conditions for intergroup contact need to be weighed in depth, before embarking on such an activity. The major objective of this dimension is to assist in the process of issue definition, social negotiation, moral reasoning, responsible judgement and action by exposing the pupil to the reality of life in the wider community for active and responsible citizenship. The research on this active aspect of discourse is, however, very limited and the findings tentative though encouraging (Newmann and Rutter, 1983).

One or two general principles of the discourse method emerge from our fleeting glance at some of the major components of this hybrid approach. These are: the overwhelming need for a democratic classroom climate; the availability of a large amount of suitable material which is progressive and developmental; the adoption of flexible and changing but appropriate roles by the teacher, acting not as arbiter but as logistics person and facilitator as well as person- and outcome-gatekeeper; the need for careful planning and maturation on the part of all concerned; finally, the provision of realistic proving grounds for the practising of newly acquired skills in different cultural and social realities. It would be dishonest to assert that the approach, as a whole, is a proven facilitator of prejudice reduction, although some component parts have a convincing record, but it is a promising approach which is fully consistent with democratic values and includes components which are well tested and proven.

CO-OPERATIVE LEARNING APPROACHES

Co-operative and collaborative approaches to learning have been the subject of considerable attention over the last decade. We have already considered, in chapter 5, the research evidence concerning their value and it is unnecessary to repeat that material here. In a sense, the approach is well established as a means to redress the previous, competitive emphasis on individual achievement in schools, but, more recently, it has also be come one of the major dimensions of the effective schools movement. Many of the techniques used and researched have had value issues at their centre and the research evidence is very promising in both cognitive and affective domains (Slavin, 1982, 1983). As chapter 5 explained, there are a number of different variations, some eliminating competition entirely, others using a combination of competition and co-operation. The first example includes the use of student teams, comprising pupils of different backgrounds and abilities, who may themselves decide how to study material presented to them by the teacher for learning. Individual quizzes are administered and a team score computed, with students receiving a bonus for being above the previous score. The tournament variation uses the same teams, worksheets and format and the students play academic games competing to give the right answer or challenge the responses of members from other teams.

A third variety is the Jigsaw method (Aronson, 1978) where pupils are assigned to six-member teams and are presented with material divided into five parts (to cover absences). Pupils from different teams covering the same material meet in expert groups to discuss their material and then return to their teams. Team reports are prepared and students 'quizzed' about the material, on which they receive individual scores. This approach has been modified slightly to allow all students to cover the whole, but for each to become an 'expert' in a topic. Under this variation individual scores are then combined into team scores, and there is a system of public recognition and a co-operative reward structure for the academic performance of the group. One model attempts to eliminate competition completely by co-operative group inquiry emphasising data gathering by pupils, interpretation through group discussion and the synthesis of individual contributions into a group product (Johnson and Johnson, 1975).

The results of the field experimental research on co-operative techniques in the classroom, when compared with non co-operative methods, and covering a very large number of studies, are clear:

- superior academic learning, achievement and productivity;
- improved self-esteem;
- better relationships between pupils of different racial and ethnic backgrounds and between handicapped and non-handicapped pupils;
- greater mutual concern and trust (Johnson et al., 1981).

Quite unequivocally, teachers may seek to adopt co-operative methods in the knowledge that they are possibly among the most potent approaches for the improvement of race relations. There are, of course, conditions but, given prudent planning and normal monitoring procedures, including attention to the task orientation of the group, co-operative methods must feature in each teacher's prejudice reduction teaching 'arsenal'.

PRE-PREPARATION AND EXPECTATION TRAINING

I have already referred in chapter 3 to the work of such educators as Cohen (1980), who, as part of a co-operative group approach to teaching for prejudice reduction, have attempted to develop deliberate strategies of pre-preparation and expectation training to prime group members who were dominated by others. While there may be moral reflection on the fairness of such an approach on the part of some teachers, there can be little doubt that it is a legitimate part of a teacher's repertoire of motivation and teaching techniques for all pupils, and especially those with special difficulties, either social or academic, to provide for supplementary teaching.

It will be apparent that social confidence is an essential characteristic for full participation in group methods. A positive self image may influence the processing of social information, by causing selective attention, affecting the inferences which are made in social situations and the retention of information (Stephan, 1985). Further, social confidence may be enhanced by the expectation of the achievement of success in the academic sphere. Moreover, when stereotyped expectations of the behaviour and ability of some pupils by others are transmitted and cause loss of confidence in those pupils their consequent performance confirms the expectations. It is a vicious circle that it is important to break. Priming, coaching and expectation training are possible strategies of pre-preparation which may aid a teacher to break the circle, and on whose effectiveness we have evidence.

Such pre-preparation may, however, also need to include the majority in a group, because of the way in which in-group members of a group tend to 'average out' any negative impression, behaviour or performance on the part of one of their own, but do not have the necessary complexity of cognitive structure to do so for outgroup members. Such a necessity may be 'absorbed' into the teacher's preparatory work for groups in the form of whole-class discussions of the rules of the game including fairness and evenhandedness. The important point is, as Stephan (1985) argues, cognitions other than just prejudice have to be taken into account. Furthermore, it is important that enhanced self image and participation in the group is confirmed, for in the very process of explicit confirmation of the social and academic behaviour of one individual may be the seeds of the disconfirmation of a falsely low expectation on the part of others within the group. Thus, the effects of expectancy training may result in not only individual growth, but also greater social co-operation in the group, with the promise of both social and economic gains for all (Humphreys and Burger, 1981).

In a sense, the approach has much in common with the need to teach children how to learn from teaching, which was referred to in chapter 5. But Cohen's approach goes further. His approach has been to aim to counteract expectations created by diffuse characteristics such as race, sex, and ethnicity by challenging them with conflicting characteristics related to a specific task or competence, as a potential basis for preventing 'weakly assertive' pupils being submerged in group work. In an earlier study by Cohen, Lockheed and Lohman (1976) such initiatives led eventually to prolonged equal-status behaviour on the part of members of two different ethnic groups who had previously seen each other as being of different status. While the research linking expectation training to prejudice reduction is modest, the results may promise greater equality of participation and more accurate mutual evaluation and benefit. This is not least the case with co-operative group work, as part of other broader strategies of prejudice reduction, such as co-operative groups. Thus, the approach has a significant role to play in breaking the role cycle which influences the way in which in-group behaviour, based on particular expectations, leads out-group members to behave in ways which confirm those expectations. Its disadvantage may be that in some cases, enhanced self confidence may lead to a lowering of the 'liking' threshold by other members of the group. In other words, they may like the newly self confident individual less. Teachers will need to be aware of this potential negative reaction and to counter it with increased social support and confirmation for all members of the group.

AWARENESS TRAINING

One approach to prejudice reduction that has become very popular in recent years, but which remains almost totally unevaluated, is that which has arisen from the work of Katz in the United States (Katz, 1978). While it does not treat prejudice generically, but focuses on only one form, racism, it has led to a mushrooming of programmes in countries as diverse as Canada and the United Kingdom under the title of Racism Awareness Training (RAT) (Twitchen and Demuth, 1985). There is a fairly rich literature on attempts to reduce prejudice in group interaction settings, with some adopting techniques taken from group therapy while others involve discussions and other structured interaction situations, including sensitivity training. In some cases, parties to intensive political conflicts have been brought together and human relations workshop approaches have been developed in the United States, although Stephan (1985, p. 644) reports that no empirical data are available on their success.

The problems with the approach as interpreted in the United Kingdom are manifold. Firstly, most of the studies carried out using this kind of technique have been done with adults. Secondly, the philosophy surrounding the use of these techniques in England states *ex cathedra* that racism is a white person's problem, when it is apparent that, pervasive and pernicious though institutional racism is, it is not the prerequisite of all individuals in any one group. Thirdly, the approach fails to take adequately into account the regenerative nature of racism and other forms of prejudice in a culturally diverse society, and therefore the way in which prejudices are continually produced and reproduced with each new generation. In some cases, too, the approach has led to attempts to short-circuit democratic procedures and measures and to adopt a coercive and confrontational approach which may in fact only serve to exacerbate deep-rooted anxieties and make real attitudes and behaviour change less likely (Jeffcoate, 1984, pp. 150–51). Moreover, it seeks by a short-term, one-off process to tackle prejudice, and neglects the need for continued reinforcement of prejudice reduction measures and indeed the other hard-won research gains in what we know about prejudice reduction. It plays cavalier with the evidence we have about the nature of prejudice and how to attenuate it.

Notwithstanding the above criticisms, as part of an overall integrated teaching strategy it could have a promising, if modest, part to play in the composite democratic educational challenge to prejudice in a pluralist society. It derives from a credible social learning theory, which seeks to use group support and norms to enhance the learning of new values and could be an effective, if as yet unevaluated, introductory means of making pupils aware of the facts of prejudice and discrimination. Judiciously organised according to normal educational principles of procedure, it can be a means of pupils' sharing their experience and becoming more aware of the vicissitudes of the society in which they live. Awareness is, however, only the first step in changing attitudes and behaviour, so it can only be seen as an interim 'first-step' approach. Pretensions to therapeutic objectives on the part of teachers should, however, be avoided, and pupils with major personality problems in respect of prejudice should be referred for specialist assistance. If such group techniques are adopted as part of an overall, integrated approach to prejudice reduction it is important that certain guidelines are adhered to. The discussions should not, for example, focus on the relatively high level of prejudice of members of the groups; a focus which may support and enhance those prejudices. The group leaders should make clear their disapproval or prejudice, and the content of the groups' work should provide positive information about other groups. Participation should of course be voluntary.

Teachers are neither skilled therapeutic experts nor final undisputed arbiters of morality, and the approach therefore needs to be embedded in a democratic classroom ethos, where there is an opportunity for open discussion of value dilemmas and conflicts. Teachers should be wary of buying the 'big bang' brand of prejudice reduction which could, in unskilled hands, do real damage, would be unlikely to gain democratic support and may actually accentuate and increase prejudice (Myers and Bishop, 1970). For teachers are placed in a position of trust, *vis-à-vis* their pupils, and while that trust can form a very useful basis for 'holding the hands of pupils' until they learn to look after themselves in the rigours of discourse, it must never be used to adopt dubious and potentially injurious methods and approaches (whose efficacy remains, in any case, to be demonstrated) and in pursuit of implicit political objectives which are beyond the remit of schools in any society.

SUMMARY

Building on the seven-part curriculum strategy for prejudice reduction, presented in chapter 5, and basing my proposals on the need for an appropriately democratic school and classroom climate, I have sought, in this chapter, to identify, describe and evaluate 12 approaches to teaching for prejudice reduction. I have emphasised the incomplete nature of the list and the way in which the approaches described blend into each other, arguing that effective teaching as an art form demands spontaneity and improvisation to use an integrated style of teaching appropriate to the skills and personality of the teacher and pupils, their needs and backgrounds. Notwithstanding that personal element in teaching, there are certain guidelines that can be sifted from the 12 approaches that may enable teachers to improve their teaching effectiveness and to aim more centrally and successfully for prejudice reduction. Figure 6.1 seeks to illustrate the dynamic process of blending elements from the 12 approaches described into the personal pedagogical style of the teacher. Naturally, it must be seen in the context of the curriculum strategy for prejudice reduction proposed in chapter 5, and particularly the learning rationale, taking into account the varying styles and cultural biographies of pupils in a multicultural classroom.

As in previous chapters, my argument here is that an integrated personal teaching style, such as that available from the components in this chapter, may be expected to lead to cognitive, affective and behavioural gains reflective of a lower degree of prejudice. This in turn should be linked wtih higher self-esteem for all pupils, a greater sense of personal efficacy, lower learning anxiety and also, therefore, higher academic performance, provided that serious account is taken of the points in the learning rationale in chapter 5 about a variation of culturally sensitive cues and rewards and the need for culture-fair modes of assessment and evaluation.

In chapter 7, I want to consider the kinds of resources which are necessary for implementing the curricular and teaching strategies described in chapters 5 and 6. I shall range wide to exemplify rather than provide a comprehensive catalogue of all resources within each category, which, in any case, would demand a book in its own right. In chapter 8 I shall be considering that most important of all resources for prejudice reduction: the teachers. I shall be suggesting how, through appropriate forms of professional development, they may reappraise their own professional horizons and effectiveness and, as part of that process of critical professional reflexivity, bring prejudice reduction more centrally into their pedagogical sights.

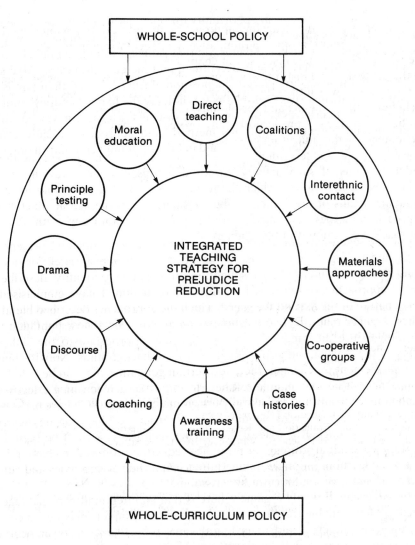

Figure 6.1 Components of an integrated teaching strategy for prejudice reduction

ACTIVITIES

1. Consider the 12 approaches to prejudice reduction introduced in this chapter and list their advantages and disadvantages. Which of them are included in your current repertoire and, if not all, which would you like to include, why and how?
2. Are there additional approaches that you would wish to include in the categorisation introduced in this chapter? How far do you think that insufficient emphasis has been placed on inquiry approaches? Try to draw up an alternative classification that better suits your own style and place the approaches into some kind of sequential hierarchy.
3. Describe the relationship, as you see it, between the curricular strategy outlined

in chapter 5 and the teaching approaches introduced in chapter 6. Try to formulate the relationship diagrammatically in such a way as to take account of the whole-school issues discussed in chapter 4.

4. In the context of the institution within which you work, try to draw up a series of criteria against which the effectiveness of the various approaches may be gauged, including both academic and social outcomes. Cross-reference your list with one of the lists of factors proposed by any project involved in the effective schools movement, or the indicators proposed by the 'Rutter Report'.

5. Consider the available evidence on racism awareness training, the conditions for and limitations of such activity proposed in this chapter. Draw up a list of guidelines for the ways in which the techniques may be used in your institution, including details of the content to be considered, and the age at which such an approach may best be introduced. Specify its relationship with the other approaches considered in this chapter.

REFERENCES

Anti-Defamation League of B'nai B'rith (1986) *Being Fair and Being Free*. New York: ADL.

Arbuthnot, J.B. and Faust, D. (1981) *Teaching Moral Reasoning: Theory and Practice*. New York: Harper and Row.

Arlington School District (1982) *Project REACH* (Teacher Guide and Training Manual) Washington: Arlington School District 16.

Aronson, E. (1978) *The Jigsaw Classroom*. Beverley Hills: Sage.

Association for Values Education and Research (1975) 'Final report of a study in moral education in Surrey, British Columbia', Vancouver, BC: University of British Columbia, AVER, Faculty of Education (Report No. 6).

Association for Values Education and Research (1979) 'Evaluation of the AVER "Prejudice" unit in a senior secondary school', Vancouver BC: University of British Columbia, AVER, Faculty of Education (Report No. 7).

Banks, J.A. (1981) *Multiethnic Education: Theory and Practice*. Boston: Allyn & Bacon.

Banks, J.A. (1985) *Teaching Strategies for the Social Studies* 3rd edn. New York: Longman.

Banks, J.A. (1986) 'Multicultural education: development, paradigms and goals', in Banks J.A. and Lynch, J. (eds) *Multicultural Education in Western Societies*. London: Holt, Rinehart and Winston.

Belch, J. (1974) *Contemporary Games*. Detroit MI: Gale Research Co. Vol I: Directory, vol II: Bibliography.

Best, D.L., Smith, S.C., Graves, D.J. and Williams, J.E. (1978) The modification of racial bias in pre-school children, *Journal of Experimental Psychology*. 20 193–205.

Brookover, W. Beady, C., Flood. P., Schweitzer, J. and Wisenbaker, J. (1979) *School Social Systems and Student Achievement*. New York: Praeger.

Brophy, J.E. (1979) Teacher behaviour and its effects, *Journal of Educational Psychology*, 71 (6) 733–50.

Brophy, J.E. (1982) *Classroom Organisation and Management*. East Lansing MI: Michigan State University, The Institute for Research on Teaching (Occasional Paper No. 54).

Chapman, T.H. (1974) 'Simulation game effects on attitudes regarding racism and sexism', Maryland University, Cultural Study Centre, Research Report.

Cohen, E.G. (1980) 'A multi-ability approach to the integrated classroom', paper presented at the American Psychological Association, Montreal, Canada.

Coombs, J.R. and Meux, M. (1971) 'Teaching strategies for value analysis', in L.E. Metalf (ed.) *Values Education*. Washington, DC: National Council for the Social Studies.

Craft, A. and Klein, G. (1986) *Agenda for Multicultural Teaching*. London: School Curriculum Development Committee.

Cohen, E.G., Lockheed, M.E. and Lohman, M.R. (1976) The centre for interracial co-operation: a field experiment, *Sociology of Education*. **49**, 47–58.

Crain, R., Mahard, R. and Narot, R. (1982) *Making Desegregation Work*. Cambridge, MA: Ballinger.

Detroit Public Schools (1981) *Elementary, Middle and High School Guides for Teaching about Human Rights*. Detroit MI: Michigan Department of Curriculum Development Services.

Dunlop, J. (1985) *IMEP Working Papers* 1–3. Glasgow: Jordanhill College of Education.

Ehman, L.H. (1980) Change in high school students' political attitudes as a function of social studies in classroom climate, *American Educational Research Journal*, **17**, 253–65.

Enright, R.D., Kapsley, D.F., Harris, D.J. and Shaver, D.J. (1983) Moral interactions in early adolescence, *Theory into Practice*, **22**, 134–44.

Fisher, S. and Hicks, D. (1985) *World Studies 8–12: A Teachers Handbook*. London: Oliver & Boyd.

Flanagan, O.J. (1984) *The Science of Mind*. Cambridge MA: The MIT Press.

Flay, B.K. (1978) 'Catastrophe theory model of attitude change', paper presented at the Annual Convention of the American Psychological Association, Toronto, Ontario: ERIC Document ED 170 541.

Gage, N.L. (1984) What do we know about teaching effectiveness, *Phi Delta Kappan*. **66**, 87–93.

Gay, G. (1974) 'Differential dyadic interactions of black and white teachers with black and white pupils in recently desegregated social studies classrooms: a function of pupil ethnicity'. Washington, DC: National Institute of Education.

Grimmestad, B.J. and De Chiara, E. (1982) 'Dramatic Plays: A Vehicle for Prejudice Reduction in Elementary School', *Journal of Educational Research*. **76** (1) 45–9.

Good, T.L. (1982) How teachers' expectations affect results, *American Education*. **18** (10), 25–32.

Good, T.L. and Brophy, J.E. (1984) *Looking in Classrooms* 3rd edn. New York: Harper.

Gray, D.B. and Ashmore, R.D. (1975) Comparing the effects of information, role-playing and value discrepancy treatments on racial attitudes, *Journal of Applied Social Psychology*. **5** (3), 262–81.

Hamilton, S.F. (1983) The social side of schooling, ecological studies of classroom and schools, *Elementary School Journal*. **83** (4), 313–34.

Hicks, D.W. (1979) Two sides of the same coin, an explanation of links between multicultural education and development education, *New Approaches to Multicultural Education*. **7** (2), 1–5.

Hicks, D.W., and Townley, C. (1982) *Teaching World Studies*. London: Longman.

Higgins, A. (1980) 'Research and measurement issues in moral education intervention', in Mosher, R.L. (ed.) *Moral Education: A First Generation of Research and Development*. New York: Praeger.

Hubbard, K. (1982) The Kamagatu Maru incident: a moral dilemma, *History and Social Science Teacher*. **17** (4), 227–30.

Humphreys, P. and Berger, J. (1981) Theoretical consequences of the status characteristics formulation, *American Journal of Sociology*. **86**, 953–83.

Hunt, M.P. and Metcalf, L.W. (1968) *Teaching High School Social Studies* 2nd edn. New York: Harper and Row.

Ijaz, M.A. and Ijaz, I.H. (1981) A cultural programme for changing racial attitudes, *History and Social Science Teacher*. **17** (1) 17–20.

Institute for Research on Teaching (1986) *Communication Quarterly*. **7** (4) East Lancing MI: College of Education, Michigan State University.

Jeffcoate, R. (1979) *Positive Image: Towards a Multicultural Curriculum*. London: Writers and Readers Co-operative.

Jeffcoate, R. (1984) *Ethnic Minorities and Education*. London: Harper and Row.

Johnson, D.W. (1966) Freedom school effectiveness: changes in attitudes of Negro children, *The Journal of Applied Behavioural Science*. **2**, 325–330.

Johnson, D. and Johnson, R. (1975) *Learning Together and Alone*. Englewood Cliffs NJ: Prentice Hall.

Johnson, D.W., Mariyama, G., Johnson, D., Nelson, D., and Skon, L. (1981) The effects of co-operative, competitive and individual goal structures on achievement: A meta-analysis, *Psychological Bulletin.* **89**, 47–62.

Joyce, B.R. and Weil, M. (1986) *Models of Teaching* 3rd edn. Englewood Cliffs, NJ: Prentice Hall.

Katz, J.H. (1978) *White Awareness: A Handbook for Anti-Racism Training.* Norman: University of Oklahoma Press.

Kehoe, J.W. (1975) Demonstrating the relationship betwen values and attitudes as a means of changing attitudes, *Alberta Journal of Educational Research.* **21** (3), 207–212 (September).

Kehoe, J. (1984) *Achieving Cultural Diversity in Canadian Schools.* Cornwall, Ontario: Vesta Publications.

Kehoe, J.W. and Todd, R.W. (1978) The effects of principle-testing discussions on student attitudes towards selected groups subjected to discrimination, *Canadian Journal of Education.* **3** (4), 73–80.

King, E.W. (1980) *Teaching Ethnic Awareness.* Santa Monica, CA: Goodyear.

Kohlberg, L. and Hersch. R.H. (1977) Moral development: a review of the theory, *Theory into Practice.* **XVI** (2), 53–59.

Kohlberg, L., Levine, C., and Hewer, A. (1984) 'The current formulation of the theory, in L. Kohlberg *Essays on Moral Development. Vol II: The Psychology of Moral Development: The Nature and Validity of Moral Stages.* San Francisco: Harper and Row pp. 212–319.

Leming, J.S. (1985) 'Research on social studies curriculum and instruction: interventions and outcomes in the socio-moral domain', in Stanley, W.B., *Review of Research in Social Studies Education: 1976–1983.* Boulder, CO: ERIC Clearinghouse for Social Studies/Social Science Education and Washington, DC: National Council for the Social Studies.

Litchner, J.H. and Johnson, D.W. (1969) Changes in attitudes towards Negroes of white elementary school students after use of multiethnic readers, *Journal of Educational Psychology.* **60** 148–52.

Lynch, J. (1986a) *Multicultural Education: Principles and Practice.* London: Routledge and Kegan Paul.

Lynch, J. (1986b) 'International dimensions on multicultural education', paper presented at a Conference on Multiculturalism in Canada: Exploring Ethno-Cultural Issues, Harrison, British Columbia, April 25.

Main, J. (ed.) (1978) *Prejudice (Student Handbook)* (Value Reasoning Series) Toronto, Ontario: Ontario Institute for Studies in Education.

Metcalf, L. (1971) *Values Education.* Washington DC: National Council for the Social Studies.

Middleton, R. (1960) Ethnic prejudice and susceptibility to persuasion, *ASR.* October, 679–686.

Moray House College of Education (1985) *Drama in Multicultural Education: A Survey.* Edinburgh: Moray House

Myers, D.G. and Bishop, G.D. (1970) Discussion effects on racial attitudes, *Science* **169**, 778–89.

Newmann, F.M. (1970) *Clarifying Public Controversy: An Approach to Teaching Social Studies* Boston MA: Little Brown.

Newmann, F.M. and Rutter, R.A. (1983) 'Effects of high school community service programmes on students' social development', Washington, DC: National Institute of Education, (Research Report).

Nixon, J. (1980) Teaching about race relations, *Secondary School Theatre Journal.* **19** (3) 16–18.

Nixon, J. (1985) Drama and anti-racist teaching: guidelines for action, *Curriculum* **6** (3) 5–12.

Nottingham University School of Education (1984) *Lifestyles Pack.* Nottingham: University Park.

Oliver, D.W. and Shaver, J.P. (1966) *Teaching Public Issues in the High School.* Boston MA: Houghton Miflin.

Peterson, R.C. and Thurstone, L.L. (1933) *Motion Pictures and The Social Attitudes of Children.* New York: Macmillan.

Pettman, R. (1983) *Teaching for Human Rights.* Richmond, Victoria: Hodja Educational Resources Co-operative Limited for the Australian Commission on Human Rights.

Rokeach, M. (1968) *Beliefs, Attitudes and Values*. San Francisco CA: Jossey-Bass.

Rudduck, J. (1979) *Learning to Teach Through Group Discussion*. Norwich: Centre for Applied Research in Education.

Schools Council (1970) *The Humanities Curriculum Project: An Introduction*. London: Heineman Educational Books.

Shulman, L.S. (1986) 'Paradigms and research programmes in the study of teaching: a contemporary perspective, in Wittrock, M.C. (ed.) *Handbook of Research on Teaching* 3rd edn. New York: Collier Macmillan.

Shaftel, F.R. and Shaftel, G. (1967) *Role Playing for Social Values*. Englewood Cliffs NJ: Prentice Hall.

Shaftel, F.R. and Shaftel, G. (1982) *Role Playing in the Curriculum* 2nd edn. Englewood Cliffs NJ: Prentice Hall.

Sharan, S. (1980) Co-operative learning in small groups — recent methods and effects on achievement, attitudes and ethnic relations, *Review of Educational Research*. **50**, 241–71.

Sharan, S. et al., (1985) 'Co-operative Learning Effects on Ethnic Relations and Achievement in Israeli Junior High School Classrooms', in Slavin, R.E. et al., *Learning to Co-operate: Co-operating to Learn*. New York: Plenum Press.

Shaver, P. and Strong, W. (1982) *Facing Value Decisions: Rationale Building for Teachers*. New York: Teachers College Press, Teachers College, Columbia University.

Simon, S.B., Howe, L. and Kirchenbaum, H. (1978) *Values Clarification: A Handbook of Practical Strategies for Teachers and Students* 2nd edn. New York: Hart Publishing.

Singh, J.M. and Yancy, A.V. (1974) Racial attitudes in white first grade chldren, *The Journal of Educational Research*. **67**, 370-2.

Slavin, R.E. (1980) Co-operative learning, *Review of Educational Research*. **50**, 315-42.

Slavin, R.E. (1982) A 'policy choice: co-operative or competitive learning', in Wayne, E.A. (ed.) *Character Policy*. Washington, DC: University Press of America.

Slavin, R.E. (1983) *Co-operative Learning*. New York: Longman.

Stenhouse, L. (1980) *Curriculum Research and Development in Action*. London: Heinemann Educational Books.

Stenhouse, L. Verma, G. and Wild, R. (1982) (eds) *Teaching about Race Relations: Problems and Effects*. London: Routledge and Kegan Paul.

Stephan, W.G. (1985) 'Intergroup relations', in Lindzey, G. and Aronson, E. (eds) *The Handbook of Social Psychology*. New York: Random House.

Stephan, W.G. and Stephan, C.W. (1985) Intergroup anxiety, *Journal of Social Issues*. **41** (3), 157–75.

Strike, K.A. and Soltis, J.F. (1985) *The Ethics of Teaching*. New York: Teachers College Press, Teachers College, Columbia University.

Superka, D.P., Ahrens, C., Hedstrom, J.E. with Ford, L.J. and Johnson, P.L. (1976) *Values Education Sourcebook: Conceptual Approaches, Materials Analyses, and an Annotated Bibliography*. Boulder CO: ERIC Clearinghouse for Social Studies/Social Science Education.

Taxel, J. (1982) *Sensitizing Students to the Selective Tradition in Children's Literature*, Paper presented at the Annual Meeting of the American Educational Research Association, New York: March 1982. ERIC Document: ED 213647 S0013929.

Torney, J. Oppenheim, A. and Farnen, R. (1975) *Civic Education in Ten Countries*. New York: John Wiley and Sons.

Torney-Purta, J. and Schwille, J. (1983) The trend toward more directive moral education in the United States, *International Journal of Political Education*. **6**, 101–11.

Trager, H.G. and Yarrow, M.R. (1952) *They Learn What They Live*. New York: Harper.

Twitchen, J. and Demuth, S. (1985) *Multicultural Education* 2nd edn. London: BBC.

Walberg, H. and Anderson, C. (1968) Classroom climate and individual learning, *Journal of Education Psychology*. **59**, 414–9.

Walberg, H. (1984) What makes schooling effective? A synthesis and a critique of three national studies, *Contemporary Education: A Journal of Reviews*. **1** (1), 22–34.

Walberg, E. (1969) Social environment as a mediator of classroom learning, *Journal of Educational Psychology*. **60**, 443–8.

World Bank (1986) *Catalogue of Educational Materials*. Washington DC: World Bank.

Chapter 7

Resources for Teaching to Reduce Prejudice

INTRODUCTION

In the preceding chapter I have tried to lay the groundwork for the introduction of prejudice reduction as one of the central priorities of schools — indicating the reasons why it is necessary and how its introduction, development and evaluation may be accomplished. In chapters 5 and 6. I have concentrated more centrally on issues of teaching, considering, in turn, a seven-part rationale for the curriculum and a series of approaches to teaching, from which an integrated teaching strategy for prejudice reduction may be compiled. In succeeding chapters, I want to review the resource implications of that priority, those strategies and approaches. In this chapter, I shall be discussing the physical resource considerations, indicating the availability of exemplary material rather than seeking to cover the field comprehensively. I shall be drawing on resources from a number of different countries, including the United States, the United Kingdom, Canada and Australia, because each nation has typically emphasised different aspects of the challenge and only in a few major respects do those coincide. Then, in chapter 8, I want to consider the human resource dimension, reflecting on the challenge to staff development which the adoption of prejudice reduction implies for systems, institutions and individuals.

A total overview of all materials within the field of prejudice reduction would be an unreasonable task within the confines of one chapter, and particularly if all the materials concerned with cultural diversity and multicultural education were to be considered for inclusion. I have, therefore, sharpened my focus in this chapter to material more specifically addressing prejudice reduction, which itself may be generative of further 'leads' with regard to resources, for example, in the form of a substantial bibliography, glossary, list of materials or addresses. In categorising the components of prejudice reduction, I have had reference to the difficult logistics problem with which it presents teachers and to the media through which prejudice reduction may be accessible. For convenience' sake, I have labelled the categories of resource under the following titles: reference resources, teaching material (including value dilemma and clarification resources) moral education writings and community assets not covered under the above headings. It will be apparent that the list is to some extent arbitrary and that no theoretical or empirical validity is implied, but rather a rule-of-thumb attempt to organise 'support services' from a very complex and diverse field in such a way to make them comprehensible and more accessible to a lay educator audience.

REFERENCE RESOURCES

Because the field of prejudice is so vast and yet fragmented, and because so many disciplines and areas of interest impinge or play on the field, it is sometimes a daunting task to begin and it is easy to become discouraged. One fairly immediate way of breaking the ice is to go to the *Thesaurus of ERIC Descriptors*, which should be available in most major libraries (Houston, 1984). Under the term 'prejudice' (p. 199), the reader is directed to use the term 'bias', which appears on page 26 where the scope note (SN), or definition, is given, as are terms for which it is used (UF), narrower terms (NT), related terms (RT) and broader terms (BT). Under 'bias' the number of references contained in ERIC is given by direct reference to the *Current Index to Journals in Education*, which is a serial publication appearing monthly, where, through the subject index, entries in the category of the descriptor chosen may be seen. Through the accession number cited at the conclusion of the entry, the reference may be sought under the main entry section where a brief abstract is given together with the ERIC Clearing House number. The article may be ordered in full according to the procedures outlined at the beginning of each issue of the *Index*. Similar is *Resources in Education*, which covers resources such as books, unpublished conference papers etc., material, that is, other than journal articles. This also appears monthly and, additionally, there are *Annual, Semiannual* and *Cumulative Indexes*; these latter are on microfiche and cover authors and titles but not subjects.

A reader may, of course, request an on-line or off-line bibliographic search of the ERIC database. A listing, with abstract, of an off-line print-out of approximately 300 items would cost in the region of £30 (or US$45) including on-line negotiation time. The disadvantage to such a search is that it would encompass a predominance of United States' sources and would need to be complemented by a manual or computerised search of other appropriate indexes such as those quoted below.

There are also other indexes, such as the *Education Index*. This does cite prejudice as a major term, and is published monthly, except for July and August, with a bound cumulation each year. There is a British equivalent of this, the *British Education Index* (1961–), which appears annually and again references bias rather than prejudice. There are also Canadian and Australian equivalents of this publication, the *Australian Education Index* (1957–) which appears bimonthly and references bias and not prejudice, and the *Canadian Education Index* (1965–), which appears five times a year. This latter references prejudice in the English language descriptors, and the word is cross-referenced from the French as well. The French equivalent *Sciences de l'education, Bulletin signalétique* (1947–), which appears quarterly with an annual accumulation, does reference prejudice in both English and French descriptor indexes. There is also a trilingual *International Index of Bibliography on Education* (1981–), published quarterly, but this does not reference either prejudice or bias as key descriptors. The 'German speaking' equivalent is the *International Bibliographie der Zeitschriftenliteratur* (1965–), published biannually. It covers all disciplines and aims to be international in its coverage; it indexes prejudice among its major descriptors. There is also an extensive citation index, the *Social Science Citation Index* (SSCI) (1966–) which lists prejudice and gives several subterms as well.

The *Public Affairs Information Service* (PAIS)(1916–) has a wealth of references under such terms as prejudice, intercultural education, minorities, blacks, race relations, including discrimination, and sex discrimination. The *Social Sciences Index* (1974–) includes extensive references under such terms as prejudice, race discrimination and prejudice, sexism and ethnocentrism. The *British Humanities Index* (1962–) has the terms sex and sexism as well as extensive entries under subcategories and under race.

There are also two major indexes of dissertations, which are accessible either manually or online, and cover, respectively, the United Kingdom and North America, with selected European dissertations from 1976. The *Comprehensive Dissertation Index* (1973), which covers the period 1961–1972 in 37 volumes, and the *Ten Year Cumulation* (1973–82) in 38 volumes, cover all dissertations in North America in the periods indicated. There are annual supplements, a subject index, grouped by disciplines into four volumes and a keyword index. There are also regular up-dates, and free special subject bibliographies, and catalogues are published grouping together dissertations in given areas such as *Women's Studies* (1985). There are on line search services through Lockheed's Dialog or Bibliographic Retrieval Service Inc (BRS), which give access to titles from 1981 as well as an abstract of dissertations from July 1980. An associated publication *Dissertation Abstracts International* (1969–) is published quarterly by University Microfilms International and section A covers the humanities and social sciences, while, since Autumn 1976, a section C has been published quarterly that provides abstracts of a portion of European dissertations.

Abstracts are, in fact, a second major source of information and reference material on an up-to-date basis. The various abstracting journals give indispensable and accumulated references in a different form from those provided by an index but including similar bibliographical and key word facilities. An abstract is really a bibliography in which mainly contributions to periodicals, but also some books and conference papers are summarised, whereas an index is a systematically arranged list that gives enough information for each item to be traced by such terms as author, title, subject, content, but does not usually include an abstract as such (Prytherch, 1984).

General abstracting services are available from a number of sources such as *Sociological Abstracts* (1953–). This publication appears five times a year and includes a numerical subject categorisation comprising terms such as sociology of sexual behaviour, feminist studies and a detailed index which includes references under such terms as prejudice and racism. *Abstracts in Anthropology* (1970–), of which four issues are published each year, covers terms such as minorities, ethnicity, class differentials and sex roles, and indexes terms such as racial inequality and sexism. The *Exceptional Child Education Resources* (1969–), a quarterly journal of abstracts, stored in the Exceptional Child Education Resources (ECER) database of the Council for Exceptional Children, includes terms such as sex discrimination and blacks. The *Child Development Abstracts and Bibliography* (1927–), published three times a year, includes prejudice and sex differences as some of the terms relevant to the concerns of this book. *Psychological Abstracts* (1927–) provides a monthly compilation of summaries under 16 major classificatory categories, and it indexes terms such as bias, feminism, prejudice and social discrimination. There is an associated *Thesaurus of Psychological Index Terms* (1985), now in its fourth edition, which is a compilation of vocabulary used in the field generated from the files of *Psychological Abstracts*. *Sociology of Education Abstracts* (1965–) published quarterly indexes such terms as blacks, cross ethnic relationships, culture, race and sexism.

More specifically, on the issue of sexism, the two abstracts, *Women Studies Abstracts* (1972–), published quarterly in the United States and the newer *Studies on Women Abstracts* (1983–), published bimonthly from the United Kingdom, are indispensable sources. On the race dimension, the *Sage Race Relations Abstracts* (1975–), the newer *Multicultural Education Abstracts* (1982–) and the *Social Work Research and Abstracts* (1965–), published four times a year and containing entries under both race and sex issues, all afford an important and ready access to relevant contemporary information and sources, including some concerned with prejudice.

A further source of information is to be found in the various handbooks, such as the *Handbook of Research on Teaching*, the third edition of which (Wittrock, 1986) has several articles which have been used in the preparation of this book and which provide seminal contributions to such areas as teaching strategies (Schulman, 1986) and moral and values education (Oser, 1986). The *Handbook of Social Psychology* (Lindzey and Aronson, 1985) also has excellent summative articles on fields directly or indirectly concerned with prejudice and its reduction, which cover the most recent research and publications. An example in the 1985 edition is the detailed and seminal article by Stephan on intergroup relations (Stephan, 1985). In similar vein, although not actually named a handbook, is the *Review of Research in Social Studies Education* (1966–1983) (Stanley, 1985), which forms Bulletin 75 of the National Council for the Social Studies. The 1985 edition contains a very useful chapter by Leming (1985) which deals with research in the socio-moral domain, the first section of which covers moral or values education and is thus of direct relevance to the theme of this book.

The various yearbooks are also a possible source of immediate information, useful definitions and further 'leads'. The *Review of Educational Research* (1931–) and the *Review of Research in Education* (1973–) are also of assistance, both being publications of the American Educational Research Association, (AERA). The latter is a Yearbook and while neither prejudice nor bias were indexed in recent years, it has up-to-date surveys of the *état présent des choses* in areas germane to teaching strategies. The former is a quarterly journal of the AERA.

There is, too, a range of encyclopedias and dictionaries covering the field of education generally such as the now somewhat dated *Encyclopedia of Education* (1971), the more recent *Encyclopedia of Educational Research* and the *International Encyclopedia of Education* (1985). In a very detailed index this latter cross-refers the reader from prejudice to bias. There are, however, very detailed entries for race and racial, including discrimination, and, under sex, bias and sexism. The *Harvard Encyclopedia of American Ethnic Groups* (1980) lists race, ethnicity and prejudice as well as including details of all ethnic groups in the United States with definitions. It is an indispensable resource to anyone working in this and related fields. The newer *Dictionary of Race and Ethnic Relations* (Cashmore, 1984) includes both shorter, concise definitions and more substantial entries and is cross referenced. The index includes entries under such topics as prejudice and racism, but not sexism. Finally *The Bibliographic Guide to Educational Research* (Berry, 1980) is an invaluable resource and concise guide, and (Woodbury, 1982) has compiled a guide to sources of educational information, which can be a useful starter, and contains an index which includes entries under bias, racism and sexism.

Looked at internationally, there is a plethora of journals and periodicals that deal with issues of cultural pluralism, which are listed under key words such as race, sex, discrimination, social work, ethnic relations, sociology, anthropology, psychology and social psychology. Many of these are concerned with ethnic studies, with race relations or with multicultural education more broadly and they aim at different audiences and at different levels. Some are oriented to and written by academics, while others address narrower community concerns. Some are manifestly political, while others seek to be more detached. Some are published by organisations of educators, some by national ethnic communities, some by professional associations and some by particular local ethnic communities. There are, of course, many overlaps in their foci and coverage. In sum, there is a pluralism of periodicals, magazines and journals whose interests impinge on the area of this book, and probably the best way for the neophyte to begin a more systematic scan is to address one of the indexes or abstracting services given above and work through the key words as indicated, noting those journals which seem to be appearing frequently. A fairly complete list of journals may be found in *Ulrich's* two volume *International Periodical Directory* (1985) which has a title index and entries which indicate the major topics covered by a journal.

With that proviso, the major race relations periodicals such as *Ethnic and Racial Studies* (1978–), the Institute of Race Relations quarterly *Ethnicity* (1976–), *Race and Class* (1959–), the publications of the Commission for Racial Equality, London, *Education* (1978–) and *New Community* (1971–), and such journals as *Race Today* (1968–) and *Research in Race and Ethnic Relations* (1979–), represent the 'academic' end of the market, while *Dragons Teeth* (1979–) and the *Bulletin: Interracial Books for Children* (1969–) represent the more practical part of the market. This latter additionally includes issues concerning sexism, as does the journal *Sex Roles* (1975–). There is in fact an increasing number of journals focussing on feminist issues, such as *Women's Studies* (1974–), which appears three times a year, the *Women's Studies Quarterly* (1972–), *The Psychology of Women Quarterly* (1976–) and the journal of the Women's International Democratic Federation, *Women of the Whole World* (1951–), which is published in the German Democratic Republic.

Of course, there are the heavier academic journals arising from a disciplinary interest, many of which are longstanding, such as the quarterlies, *Psychology* (1964–), *The Psychological Record* (1937–) and the *Psychological Review* (1894–), as well as the more school-and-curriculum-oriented *Psychology in Schools* (1964–). There are analogue journals with a sociological orientation, such as the quarterlies *The Sociological Review* (1908–), *Sociology of Education* (1927–), *Social Psychology Quarterly* (1937–), *Sociological Inquiry* (1930–) and the *Social Science Quarterly* (1920–). *Human Relations* (1947–), published by the Tavistock Institute in London, seeks to contribute to the integration of social science studies, and there are a number of journals in the field of human and civil rights such as the *Human Rights Quarterly* (1981–). The mass circulation *Social Studies* (1909–) attracts many articles on teaching the social studies and issues concerned with values and moral education, as does its Canadian counterpart, *The History and Social Science Teacher* (1965–). Concerned with the teaching of all subjects is the journal *Multicultural Teaching* (1982–), which appears three times a year and contains brief contributions with a more practical orientation and book reviews. The range of journals is thus vast and daunting, but it is not insurmountable and the assiduous worker has many aids to assist the quest.

While they are not, strictly speaking, reference sources, there are a number of definitive studies, which are indispensable supports to the study of prejudice reduction. The early work of Adorno et al (1950), the classic study of the roots of prejudice by Allport (1954), the book by Clark (1955), in which he explains how prejudice affects all children, and the excellent, detailed and still reliable work of Simpson and Yinger (1965) are essential first bases in getting to grips with prejudice. This latter work, and in particular in chapters 22 and 23, summarises, organises and critically appraises most of the previous work and gives an essential map and overview of the field up to the mid 1960s. A similarly impressive summary of research and theory developed over several decades is offered by Williams and Morland (1976). The book edited by Katz (1976) updates the field to the mid 1970s with well-researched chapters and extensive bibliographical references covering the elimination and reduction of prejudice.

With the continued diversification and specialisation of the field from the early 1970s and a certain quiescence of interest in prejudice reduction in the late 1970s, it has become more difficult to include a single source which gives a good overview of the field. The article by Stephan (1985) in the *Handbook of Social Psychology* is, however, a reliable and detailed starting point, while the brief summary by Banks is an extremely readable starter for those totally new to the field (Banks, 1985) and the books by Milner (1975; 1983) offer readable contributions on topics such as children's racial attitudes, the socialisation of attitudes, identity and education. Both authors' contributions are certainly suitable as introductory texts for students. The extract from the *Harvard Encyclopedia of American Ethnic Groups* by Pettigrew et al. (1982) is also a concise, readable and authoritative theoretical and historical survey of prejudice, while the contributions by Gilligan (1982) and Tetreault (1985) are important 'starters' for sexism. More specifically on sex-role stereotyping, the collection edited by Weiner (1980) and the authoritative but now out-of-print study, with an extensive annotated bibliography, by Maccoby and Jacklin (1974) are good for basics, while Gilligan's writings have attempted to correct the way in which the psychology of man has left out women in the many developmental theories which have been produced by psychologists (Gilligan, 1982).

TEACHING MATERIALS

With regard to teaching resources, there is rather a dearth of good materials and it is often a matter of adapting material intended for other but related purposes, such as teaching the broader aspects of cultural diversity. Having said that, a number of organisations contribute to the field, including the ERIC Clearinghouses, and in particular the one on Bilingual Educational in the United States, and the Local Authorities Race Relations Information Exchange (LARRIE) in the United

Kingdom. These are national organisations, which aim to provide material, information, contacts and a data bank. At an international level, the Commonwealth Institute, with offices in London and Glasgow, has library and other services and produces excellent teaching materials and aids, which are very appropriate for discussion approaches to prejudice reduction. The Centre for Peace Studies at St Martin's College, Lancaster, and the Centre for World Development Education have a similarly international focus. Other centres tend to limit their horizons to a more predominantly national audience, such as the Policy Studies Institute, which publishes material on racial discrimination, The Runnymede Trust, which publishes a monthly bulletin, *Race and Immigration* (1969–), the Institute of Race Relations, which has published several books on racism, and the Council for Education in World Citizenship (CEWC).

Some sectional organisations such as the Afro-Caribbean Resource Centre (ACER), which has developed both packs for pupils and materials for teachers, including videos, the All Faiths for One Race (AFFOR) and the All London Teachers Against Racism and Fascism (ALTARF) the Minority Arts Advisory Service (MAAS) produce material that, with judicious scrutiny, can be used for teaching for prejudice reduction. International organisations such as UNESCO, the Council of Europe, Oxfam and the World Bank, also produce material and guidelines often useful for teaching. Local authorities such as the ILEA in the United Kingdom and School Boards such as Arlington in the United States do likewise. Also in the United States, the Council on Interracial Books for Children, through its Racism/Sexism Resource Centre for Educators, and the Anti-Defamation League of B'nai B'rith promote and develop materials and initiatives which support prejudice reduction.

Turning more specifically now to teaching materials including those addressing moral and values education, the Western Education Development Group at the Faculty of Education, University of British Columbia (WEDGE) has produced a range of multicultural material, but of particular note is the excellent book by Kehoe (1984a) on enhancing the multicultural climate of the school, which includes a successful mix of academic research, activities, ideas and 'tools' for teaching and evaluation, interview schedules and other instruments. In similar authoritative, practical and helpful vein are Kehoe's other books *Multicultural Canada: Considerations for Schools, Teachers and Curriculum* (1984b) and *Achieving Cultural Diversity in Canadian Schools* (1984c), which, in spite of their titles, should be useful to all teachers. This latter, in particular, contains principle-testing discussion lessons, various measures and instruments, lesson plans and role-plays, as well as examples of how to 'lead off' and continue teaching involving prejudice reduction. Coincidentally, the University of British Columbia is the site of the Association for Values Education and Research, which produces a manual for teachers on prejudice (AVER, 1978). A fundamental source in that field is also the book on values education by Metcalf (1971), which is now considered a classic in the field.

The Council on Interracial Books for Children, Inc., (1986) produces an annual catalogue of resources to combat racism, sexism and other forms of bias, including filmstrips, lesson plans, curricula, books, pamphlets and a bulletin, including resources for anti-sexist and anti-racist teaching strategies and the, by now, well-known and used guidelines for selecting bias-free textbooks and storybooks. Less directly relevant but with potential in the areas of learning and teaching styles, co-operative group work in the classroom and teaching thinking skills, is some of the material marketed by the Association for Supervision and Curriculum Development (1986).

A more substantial catalogue of material is available from the Anti-Defamation League (ADL) in New York (1986a). This catalogue contains details of curriculum books which comprise activities and modules, such as those by Shiman et al. (1979) and the ADL and University of Nebraska (1980), as well as the National Council for the Social Studies compendium on racism and sexism (NCSS, 1980), in addition to details of other handbooks, readings, activities and audio-visual material directly concerned with prejudice. Two sets of materials are particularly worthy of mention, one for primary and middle school children and the other for secondary school pupils. *The Wonderful World of Difference* (ADL, 1986b) is a coherent interdisciplinary package of 20 activities, addressing detailed objectives concerned with respect for persons, cultural diversity, difference and similarity and the nature of prejudice and the threat this latter comprises for society. It includes a selection of duplicable worksheets and is intended for pupils aged 6 to 14 years.

The analogue secondary package is called *Being Fair and Being Free* (ADL, 1986c). It is a joint project between the ADL, the United States Channel Five Television Company, WCVB and the Greater Boston Civil Rights Coalition, which includes teacher training and curriculum materials for educators, prime-time television transmissions and adjunct projects to heighten public awareness and consciousness — including a state-wide poster contest which led to the production of an important study guide (ADL, 1986d). This document includes an extensive and detailed range of teaching suggestions and resources, including readings, sample lessons, curricula, a bibliography and a filmography.

In the United Kingdom, the National Union of Students has reissued its anti-racism pack (National Union of Students, 1985), but it is little more than a collection of papers and pamphlets and would need 'weeding' before being of use in teaching. A similar stricture applies to the *Profile on Prejudice* offered by the Minority Rights Group (MRG, 1985) which again would need careful sifting and screening, but contains some material which may be supportive to teachers in their preparation. Much more useful for teaching is *Report No 59* of the Minority Rights Group (1983) which contains a number of excellent articles, including both anti-racist and anti-sexist contributions, a model school policy statement and a good resource section, comprising theoretical, literary and autobiographical books, which can be used effectively in prejudice reduction.

AFFOR (All Faiths for One Race) is one of the very few United Kingdom organisations which has produced a teaching pack (Phillips-Bell and Ruddell, 1982). The pack includes 12 structured lessons and teaching materials. AFFOR has also produced a study of race reporting in the newspapers which should be very useful for lesson preparation (Baker et al., 1980). Much more modest, but none the less worthy of note, is the anti-racialism pack produced jointly by the British Youth Council and the Joint Committee against Racialism (British Youth Council, 1983). There is also much helpful material in a reader for the social studies produced by New Society (1983). The Catholic Commission for Racial Justice (1983) has also produced some selected background information and the Commission for Racial Equality has a bibliography on racism and prejudice in Britain containing almost 50 items

(Commission for Racial Equality, 1984).

A number of authors have attempted to put together texts specifically addressing teachers and teaching, of which the ones by Katz (1978), Colangelo (1979), Stenhouse et al. (1983) and the book produced for the Australian Human Rights Commission (Chambers and Pettman, 1986), are probably the best known. The publication by the School Curriculum Development Committee (Craft and Klein, 1986), although not specifically aimed at prejudice reduction, is a handy, readable and well-organised 'handbook' for teachers, which includes bibliographies and names and addresses of organisations, bookshops and media suppliers. The second edition of the Twitchin and Demuth (1985) book also has a wealth of material and sources including, in its second edition, a chapter devoted to anti-racist strategies, while the handbook on sex equality for schools by Sadker and Sadker (1982) is an indispensable tool for teachers, including sample lessons, models for gender equality in the curriculum and a resource directory.

As argued in chapter 6, coalitions with such areas as human rights and World Studies can yield important material and other essential resources useful in value discussions and principle-testing. *The World Studies Journal* (1979–), the results of the Schools Council/Rowntree *World Studies Project 8–13* (Fischer and Hicks, 1985) and the earlier *Teaching World Studies* by Hicks (1982) are invaluable resources in this respect. Of equal worth are the Human Rights instruments available from such organisations as the United Nations (1978), UNESCO (1978) and the Council of Europe (1978; 1986), which in some cases also produce teaching materials, e.g. Starkey (1986), and from those countries with an explicit Charter of Rights and Freedoms and Human Rights Commissions (Canada, 1984a; 1984b). Aid organisations such as Oxfam (1986) and profit-making international agencies, such as the World Bank (1986) also produce catalogues of their materials for schools. Even those nations which do not have such an explicit document have sometimes produced useful listings of sources (Department of Education and Science, 1979), and a number of academics in countries such as Canada and Australia have begun to draw up textbooks for teaching about human rights (e.g. Ray and D'Oyley, 1983; Pettman, 1983), in some cases assisted by their respective Human Rights Commissions. Sometimes, provincial councils, national commissions and voluntary bodies have also put together packs of materials that are important aids to teaching about human rights anywhere (e.g. British Columbia, Council of Human Rights, 1986; Lee, 1985). Others are available from the Civil Rights Commissions, such as the United States, or Human Relations and Rights Departments, at the state or city level (e.g. Pennsylvania Department of Education, 1975).

A small but increasing number of State Departments of Education and School Boards are assembling packages of material, sometimes quite extensive, that aim to respond to cultural diversity and to teach human relations skills and cross-cultural competences. Examples include the Brookline School Department's *Multicultural Resource Handbook* (1977) and Arlington School District's Project *REACH* (Respecting our Ethnic and Cultural Heritage) (1982). Others with slightly different orientation have been produced by Detroit Public Schools (1981), Columbia University, New York (1982), and, with a particular emphasis on value reasoning (including readings and activities on prejudice) the Ontario Institute for Studies in Education (Main, 1978a; 1978b). Somewhat dated in a rapidly moving field but still worthwhile for preparation is the informational guide on sex stereotyping, sex bias and sex discrimination by Etheridge and Rice (1976). Of future relevance are the recent projects at school board level such as the one called 'Crossroads', supported by the Rockefeller Foundation in Seattle, from which teaching material is expected to emerge.

Several sources have attempted to produce overall guidelines for developing a school policy or for reviewing its current functioning, many of which may be adapted for prejudice reduction purposes. The School Curriculum Development Committee GRIDS Project (Guidelines for Review and Internal Development in Schools) has produced both a primary and secondary handbook (McMahon et al., 1986) and ALTARF has collected a number of accounts of schools preparing and putting their own policies into action (All London Teachers Against Racism and Fascism, 1984). In the United States, some of the evaluation instruments produced by State Education Departments and School Boards involved in the 'Effective Schools Movement' are also susceptible to adaptation to include prejudice reduction objectives.

A very important aspect of any policy for book and materials is their selection according to explicitly agreed criteria, reflective of a major concern with prejudice reduction across the board. While there is no single instrument which covers racism, sexism, credism and classism, attempts have been made to provide checklists for class bias (National Association of Teachers of English, 1982), on racism (National Union of Teachers, 1980; Klein, 1986), and by the Council on Interracial Books for Children, in the form of filmstrip, audio-tapes and booklets concerned with identifying sexism and racism in children's books and literature (Council on Interacial Books for Children, 1980, 1986). Helpful indicators are also included in the work of the National Committee on Racism in Children's Books and, more obliquely, in the books written by Cohen and Manion (1983) and Saunders (1982), both of which have strong positive, supportive and practical orientation, such as is likely to appeal to teachers, although neither is focussed directly on prejudice reduction.

As I have pointed out in an earlier publication (Lynch, 1983) the library is also an indispensable resource which needs to be brought into line with the overall policy on materials for multicultural education, and of course that applies to prejudice reduction too and to the whole gamut of educational materials such as records, cassettes and all other kinds of cultural artifacts which may be provided or brought into school. One now more broadly accepted and utilised technique of teaching which, as argued in chapter 6, may be of significant support to teachers in their efforts to introduce prejudice reduction strategies into their schools, is role-playing. While only a small proportion of all 'games' focus on the use of role-playing in developing values, citizenship, intergroup education and similar areas contiguous to prejudice reduction, a number of authors have focussed especially on their use in the classroom. The book by Hawley (1975) focusses on values exploration by means of practical classroom strategies of role-playing, while an early, readable and succinct introduction is the Phi Delta Kappan 'Fastback' by Thompson (1978). The book by Demmery (1981) deals with rather more formal dramatic play in the junior school and has a similar modest format.

A much more extensive contribution by Belch (1973; 1974), though now dated and out of print, offers a two volume directory and bibliography, although unfortunately neither prejudice nor racism merit main subject entries. A more recent publication is the fourth edition of the *Guide* by Horn and Cleaves (1980) which covers only those simulations and games which have specific educational purposes, omitting those used for research and experimentation by a limited specialised audience. The classic book by Shaftel and Shaftel (1982) is a rich assemblage of sources for prejudice reduction work, including resources for preparing teachers to lead role-playing as well as material for implementation by pupils. It also contains a good bibliography.

I have emphasised in chapter 6 the important potential contribution of moral education to prejudice reduction. The giant, so to speak, in that field is Kohlberg and probably the most up-to-date summary statement — although quite extensive — of the state of play in the field is contained in the second volume of his *Essays on Moral Development* (Kohlberg, 1984). A number of his students have refined, criticised and evaluated his work and their contributions are also worth looking at (Davidson, 1977; Gilligan, 1982), this latter, in particular, for its gender critique of Kohlberg's work. Probably the most extensive attempt to implement his theoretical work in an actual course is the two-volume social studies text written by Lockwood and Harris (1985), which seeks to use dilemmas in American history as a means to stimulate value-reasoning and moral progression.

COMMUNITY RESOURCES

In addition to the above academic and semi-academic assets, it is important to realise that major resources are available to the teacher trying to implement a prejudice reduction curriculum from the teaching staff, parents, pupils and the surrounding community. In any case, as part of its policy in response to cultural diversity, the school will be engaged in a continual scrutiny of that community in order to monitor the changing dynamic of its cultural pluralism. The catchment area of a school is rarely static. One dimension of that dynamism is in the churches and other religious organisations, another is the Community Relations Councils, Citizens Advice Bureaux and other voluntary organisations. Equally fundamental, although little documented, is the supplementary provision of schooling often made by ethnic minority communities. While the whole issue of supplementary schooling is very sensitive and there is little documentation of such provision and its varied and diverse aims, we are fortunate in possessing an exemplary study from Australia (Kringas and Lewins, 1979). A recent study by Tomlinson (1984) also gives a unique insight into the complexity of family school relations and is an important resource for schools considering a closer appraisal of the situation in their catchment area. Individual case studies and descriptions do appear from time to time (e.g. Chevannes, 1979; Nagra, 1981). A good source of material is also such journals as the *Journal of Social Issues* and *History and Social Science Teacher*. The all too few Parliamentary Select Committee Reports emerging from the House of Commons also provide a wealth of up-to-date important materials about individual communities, their values, distribution, mores and aspirations (See, for example, House of Commons, Home Affairs Committee 1985).

More broadly, it is possible to pick up terms in the ERIC Thesaurus quoted above such as school community relations (p.227) or supplementary education (p.159) and trace them into the *Current Index to Journals in Education* or the *Resources in*

Education through the annual or cumulative indexes, and thence into the kind of on-line or off-line search described earlier in this chapter.

SUMMARY

In this chapter I have tried to indicate some of the background resources which are available for those wishing to commence teaching for prejudice reduction. Naturally, the other chapters in this book are also resource chapters and their extensive chapter bibliographies have dealt with and indicated the range of materials available. While the selection in this chapter is, therefore, personal and restricted it has sought to identify nodal points in the three areas of reference materials, teaching materials and community resources. In the next chapter, I want to trace through the material resource consideration of this chapter into the human resource dimension and to suggest in what ways, by deliberate strategies of professional development, it may be enhanced and made more appropriate to teaching for prejudice reduction.

ACTIVITIES

1. Set yourself a realistic time span (say the last five years) and construct a search of the journal material in the ERIC Thesaurus and Current Index to Journals in Education, under terms such as prejudice, bias, racism, sexism, ethnicity, etc. Check the overlaps and look at the major references which these sources are citing. Draw up a brief bibliography of those materials.
2. Starting with the Shaftel and Shaftel (1982) book quoted in this chapter list those educational 'games' and role-playing exercises that you think may be of use to you in your teaching. Specify the author, full title, date of publication and the name and address of the publisher. Indicate with which age group and for what activities in which subject areas, each item may be most useful.
3. Try to draw up a catalogue of community resources available to your school, indicating clearly the criteria for inclusion, and the way in which they may be accessed.
4. Collect a list of national and international organisations and the materials they make available aimed at prejudice reduction, including contiguous areas such as racism, sexism and ethnocentrism, and international agreements, declarations, covenants and other instruments.
5. Making reference to the checklists and guidelines for the selection of books and materials indicated in this chapter, such as those by NATE, Klein, NUT and the Council on Interracial Books for Children, which together cover racism, sexism and classism, draw up a composite instrument suitable for use in your school.

REFERENCES

Adorno, T.W. et al., (1950) *The Authoritarian Personality*. New York: Harper & Row.
All London Teachers Against Racism & Fascism (1984) *Challenging Racism*. London: ALTARF.

Allport, G. (1954) *The Nature of Prejudice*. New York: Addison-Wesley.

Anti-Defamation League of B'nai B'rith/College of Education, University of Nebraska at Omaha (1980) *Prejudice Project*. New York: ADL.

Anti-Defamation League of B'nai B'rth (1986a) *Human Relations Material for the School, Church and Community*. New York: ADL.

Anti-Defamation League of B'nai B'rith (1986b) *The Wonderful World of Difference*. New York: ADL.

Anti-Defamation League of B'nai B'rith (1986c) *Being Fair and Being Free*. New York: ADL.

Anti-Defamation League of B'nai B'rith (1986b) *A World of Difference: Teacher/Student Study Guide*. New York: ADL.

Arlington School District 16 (1982) *Project REACH*. Arlington, Virginia.

Association for Supervision and Curriculum Development (1986) *ASCD Products Catalogue*. Alexandria VA: ASCD.

Association for Values Education and Research (1978) *Prejudice Manual*. Toronto, Ontario: Ontario Institute for Studies in Education Press.

Baker, B. et. al., (eds) (1980) *Read All About It*. Birmingham: AFFOR.

Banks, J.A. (1985) 'Reducing prejudice in students: theory, research, strategies', in Moodley, K. (ed) *Race Relations and Multicultural Education*. Vancouver BC: Centre for the Study of Curriculum and Instruction, University of British Columbia.

Belch, J. (1973; 1974) *Contemporary Games*. Detroit MI: Gale Research Company, vol I, Directory (1973); Vol II, Bibliography (1974).

Berry, D.M. (1980) *A Bibliographic Guide to Educational Research*. Metuchen, NJ: The Scarecrow Press.

British Columbia Council of Human Rights (1986) *Human Rights: A Responsibility We All Share*. Victoria BC: British Columbia Council of Human Rights.

British Youth Council/Joint Committee Against Racism (1985) *Education, not Confrontation: Anti Racialism Pack*. London: BYC.

Brookline School Department (1977) *Multicultural Resource Handbook* vols 1 and 2. Brookline MA: Brookline School Department.

Canada, Public Legal Education Society (1984) *The Canadian Charter of Rights and Freedoms: A Guide for Students*. Vancouver, BC: The People's Law School Society.

Canada, Unity Information Office (1984) *The Charter of Rights and Freedoms(A Guide for Canadians*. Ottowa: The Publications Centre.

Cashmore, E.E. (1984) *Dictionary of Race and Ethnic Relations*. London: Routledge and Kegan Paul.

Catholic Commission for Racial Justice (1983) *Racism in British Society: Notes and Report No 12*. London: CCRJ.

Chambers, B.E. with Pettman, J. (1986) *Anti-Racism Handbook for Adult Educators*. Canberra: The Human Rights Commission.

Chevannes, M. (1979) Supplementary education: the Black Arrow Night School Project, *The Social Science Teacher*. **8**(4) 136–7.

Clark, K.B. (1955) *Prejudice and Your Child*. Boston: Beacon Press.

Cohen, L. and Manion, L. (1983) *Multicultural Classrooms*. London: Croom Helm.

Colangelo, N. (1979) *Multicultural, Non-Sexist Education*. Dubuque, IA: Kendall/Hunt.

Columbia University, New York (1982) *Compact Guides to Information on Urban and Minority Education*. New York: Columbia University, Institute of Urban and Minority Education.

Commission for Racial Equality (1984) *Books on Racialism and Prejudice in Britain*. London: CRE.

Council of Europe (1984) *Human Rights Education in Schools: Concepts, Attitudes and Skills*. Strasbourg: Council of Europe.

Council of Europe (1986) *Recommendation of the Committee of Ministers to Member States on Teaching and learning about Human Rights in Schools*. Strasbourg: Council of Europe.

Council on Interracial Books for Children (1980) *Guidelines for Selecting Bias-Free Textbooks and Story Books*. New York, NY: The Council on Interracial Books for Children.

Council on Interracial Books for Children (1986) *Resources to Counter Racism, Sexism and Other Forms of Bias in School and Society*. New York: The Council on Interracial Books for Children.

Craft, A. and Klein, G. (1986) *Agenda for Multicultural Teaching*. London: School Curriculum Development Committee.

Davidson, F.B.H. (1977) 'Prejudice in childhood: a cognitive-developmental description', in Tumin, M.M. and Plotch, W. (eds) *Pluralism in a Democratic Society*. New York: Praeger.

Demmery, S. (1981) *Drama in a Multicultural Society: The Early Years 4 to 12*. London: Educational Drama Association.

Department of Education and Science (1979) *International Understanding (Sources of Information on Organisations 1979 – A Handbook for Schools and Colleges)*. London: DES.

Detroit Public Schools, Michigan Department of Curriculum Development Series (1981) *Elementary, Middle and High School Guides for Teaching about Human Rights*. Detroit MI Michigan Department of Curriculum Development.

Etheridge, R.M. and Rice, E. (1976) Eliminating Sexism: Rewriting the Scripts. Chapel Hill NC: System Sciences.

Fisher, S. and Hicks, D. (1985) *World Studies 8–13: A Teachers Handbook*. London: Oliver & Boyd.

Gilligan, C. (1982) *In a Different Voice: Psychological Theory and Women's Development*. Cambridge MA: Harvard University Press.

Hawley, R.C. (1985) *Value Exploration Through Role Playing: Practical Strategies for Use in the Classroom*. New York: Hart.

Hicks, D.W. and Townley, C. (1982) *Teaching World Studies*. London: Longman.

Horn, R.E. and Cleaves, A. (eds) (1980) *The Guide to Simulations/Games for Education and Training* 4th edn. Beverley Hills: Sage.

House of Commons Home Affairs Committee (1985) *The Chinese Community in Britain*. London: HMSO.

Houston, J.E. (ed.) (1984) *Thesaurus of ERIC Discriptors* 10th edn. Phoenix, AZ: Oryz Press.

Katz, J.H. (1978) *White Awareness*. Norman: University of Oklohama Press.

Katz, P.A. (ed.) (1976) *Towards the Elimination of Racism*. New York: Pergamon.

Kehoe, J.W. (1984a) *A Handbook for Enhancing the Multicultural Climate of the School*. Vancouver BC: Western Education Development Group, Faculty of Education, University of British Columbia.

Kehoe, J.W. (1984b) *Multicultural Canada: Considerations for Schools, Teachers and Curriculum*. Vancouver BC: Faculty of Education, University of British Columbia.

Kehoe, J.W. (1984c) *Achieving Cultural Diversity in Canadian Schools*. Cornwall, Ontario: Vesta Publications

Klein, G. (1986) *Reading into Racism*. London: Routledge & Kegan Paul.

Kohlberg, L. (1984) *Essays on Moral Development — Vol. II. The Psychology of Moral Development: The Nature and Validity of Moral Stages*. San Francisco: Harper & Row.

Kringas, P. and Lewins, F. (1979) *Why Ethnic Schools? Selected Case Studies*. Canberra: Australian National University Press.

Lee, E. (1985) *Letters to Marcia: A Teacher's Guide to Anti-Racist Education*. Toronto, Ontario: Cross Cultural Communication Centre.

Leming, S. (1985) 'Research in the socio-moral domain', in W.B. Stanley, op. cit.

Lindzey, G. and Aronson, E. (eds) (1985) *The Handbook of Social Psychology*. New York: Random House.

Lockwood, A.L. and Harris, D.E. (1985) *Reasoning with Democratic Values*. vol. I, 1607–1876, vol. II, 1877 to the present; plus Instructors Manual. New York: The Teachers College Press, Columbia University.

Lynch, J. (1983) *The Multicultural Curriculum*. London: Batsford.

Maccoby, E.E. and Jacklin, C.N. (1974) *The Psychology of Sex Differences*. Stanford: Stanford University Press.

Main, J. (ed) (1978a) *Prejudice: Student Book*. Toronto, Ontario: Ontario Institute for Studies in Education.

Main, J. (1986b) (ed.) *Prejudice: Teacher's Manual*. Toronto, Ontario: Ontario Institute for Studies in Education.

McMahon, A., Bolam, R., Abbot, R. and Holly, P. (1986) *Handbooks*. York: Longmans Resource Unit.

Metcalf, L. (ed) (1971) *Values Education*. Washington: National Council for the Social Studies.

Milner, D. (1975) *Children and Race*. Harmondsworth: Penguin.

Milner, D. (1983) *Children and Race: Ten Years On*. London: Ward Lock Educational.

Minority Rights Group (1983) *Teaching about Prejudice*. (Report No 59) London: MRG.

Minority Rights Group (1985) *Profile on Prejudice*. London: MRG.

Nagra, J.S. (1981) Asian supplementary schools: a case study of Coventry, *New Community*. **9**(3) 431–6.

National Association of Teachers of English (1982) Checklist for class bias and source recommended books, *English in Education*. **16**(2) 34–37 (Summer).

National Council for the Social Studies (1980) Racism and Sexism: *Responding to the Challenge*. Washington DC: NCSS.

National Union of Students (1985) *Anti-Racist Pack*. London: NUS.

National Union of Teachers (1980) *In Black and White: Guidelines for Teaching on Racial Stereotyping in Textbooks and Learning Materials*. London: NUT.

New Society (1983) *Race and Immigration*. London: New Science Publications.

Oser, F.K. (1986) 'Moral education and values education: the discourse perspective', in M.C. Wittrock, *op cit.*, 917–41

Oxfam (1986) *Oxfam Schools and Youth Materials*. Oxford: Oxfam

Pennsylvania Department of Education and Pennsylvanians for Women's Rights (1975) *Self Study Guide to Sexism in Schools*.

Pettigrew, T.F., Fredrickson, G.M., Knobel, D.T., Glazer, N., Uedda, R. (1982) *Prejudice*. Cambridge MA: The Bellknap Press of the Harvard University Press.

Pettman, R. (1983) *Teaching for Human Rights*. Richmond, Victoria: Hodja Educational Resources Co-operative Limited, for the Australian Human Rights Commission.

Phillips-Bell, M. and Ruddell, D. (1982) *Race Relations Teaching Pack*. Birmingham: AFFOR

Prytherch, R. (ed) (1984) *Harrods Librarians Glossary*. Aldershot, Hants: Gower

Ray, D. and D'Oyley, V. (ed) (1983) *Human Rights in Canadian Education*. Dubuque, Iowa: Kendall Hunt Publishing Company.

Sadker, M.P. and Sadker, D.M. (1982) *Sex Equality Handbook for Schools*. New York: Longman.

Saunders, M. (1982) *Multicultural Teaching: A Guide for the Classroom*. New York: McGraw-Hill.

Shulman, L.S. (1986) 'Paradigms and research programs in the study of teaching: a contemporary perspective', in M.C. Wittrock, op cit., 3–36.

Shaftel, F.R. and Shaftel, G. (1982) *Role-Playing in the Curriculum*. Englewood Cliffs NJ: Prentice Hall

Shiman D.A. (1979) *The Prejudice Book*. New York: ADL.

Simms, R.L. and Contreras, G. (eds) (1980) *Racism and Sexism: Responding to the Challenge*. Washington DC: National Council for the Social Studies.

Simpson. G.E. and Yinger, J.M. (1965) *Racial and Cultural Minorities* 3rd edn. New York: Harper and Row.

Stanley, W.B. (ed.) (1985) *Review of Research in Social Studies Education; 1976–83*. Boulder CO: ERIC Clearinghouse for Social Studies; Washington DC: National Council for the Social Studies.

Starkey H. (1986) Practical Activities for Teaching and Learning About Human Rights in Schools. Oxford: Westminster College.

Stenhouse, L., Verma, G.K., Wild, R.D. and Nixon, J. (1983) *Teaching About Race Relations*. London: Routledge and Kegan Paul.

Stephan, W.G. (1985) 'Intergroup relations', in Lindzey, G. and Aronson, E. (eds) *The Handbook of Social Psychology*. New York: Random House. 559–658.

Tetreault, M.K.T. (1985) Feminist phase theory: an experience-derived model, *Journal of Higher Education*. **56**(4), 363–384.

Thompson, J.F. (1978) *Using Role-Playing in the Classroom*. Bloomington IN: Phi Delta Kappan Educational Foundation.

Tomlinson, S. (1984) *Home and School in Multicultural Britain*. London: Batsford.

Twitchin, J. and Demuth, C. (1985) *Multicultural Education* 2nd edn. London: British Broadcasting Corporation.

UNESCO (1978) *General Conference on Declaration on Race and Racial Prejudice*. Paris: UNESCO.

United Nations (1978) Human Rights: *A Compilation of International Instruments*. New York: United Nations.

Van der Gaag, N. and Gerlach, L. (1985) *Profile on Prejudice*. London: Minority Rights Group.

Weiner, E.H. (ed.) (1980) *Sex-Role Stereotyping in the Schools*. Washington DC: National Educational Association.

Williams, J.E. and Moreland, J.K. (1976) *Race, Color and the Young Child*. Chapel Hill: The University of North Carolina Press.

Wittrock, M.C. (1986) *Handbook of Research on Teaching* 3rd edn. New York: Macmillan (A project of the American Educational Research Association).

Woodbury, M. (1982) *A Guide to Sources of Educational Information*. Arlington DC: Information Resources Press.

World Bank (1986) Catalogue of Educational Materials. Washington DC: The World Bank.

Chapter 8

Staff Development Strategies

INTRODUCTION

In the previous chapter, I have sought to draw attention to some of the major resources, including sources of information and materials for prejudice reduction. I have indicated how they may be found and efficiently accessed. I have emphasised that the material and sources quoted represent a personal selection, rather than a futile attempt to provide a comprehensive coverage of a diverse, disparate and complex field, with contributions from many disciplines, areas of study and organisation. I have also underlined the fact that, in a sense, all chapters in the book may be considered resource chapters, but that the function of that chapter has been to respond to the need for one of them to be a 'starter' in the search for appropriate resources. For, the field is not well known among teachers and our knowledge is as modest as is the need for action urgent.

In this chapter, I continue the theme of resource considerations, but this time focussed firmly on the human resources. I shall be highlighting the essential role of professional development in 'empowering' teachers with new and extended social and intellectual competences in order to undertake teaching for prejudice reduction, in a way which will lead to cognitive, affective and behavioural change for themselves and their pupils. While the field of staff development for prejudice reduction is far from vast, some projects, having in their number some of the earliest work in the field, included a teacher education component (e.g., Trager and Yarrow, 1952), and I want to refer to some of this. Based on a brief analysis of the literature and my own previous work (Lynch, 1986a, 1986b), I shall then propose an outline model of staff development needs and suggest initiatives and strategies, both individual and collegial, that may help to support teachers in extending their criteria for professional judgement to include the combating of prejudice, such as racism, sexism, credism and classism. I shall conclude by suggesting some guidelines for educators in reflecting on and responding in a professional, autonomous manner, to their own needs as they perceive them, rather than expecting them to respond as automatons to 'prepackaged wisdom'.

It is evident that all proposals for the improvement of the quality of education are dependent on the quality of staff development. This is particularly so where that improvement involves not only the learning of new information and skills, but also the nurturing of new values, attitudes and behaviour. Staff development to teach for prejudice also aims for a knock-on effect, in the form of change in the classroom and school practices of teachers, that will result in a change in the beliefs, attitudes, learning and behaviour of pupils: a very large task indeed. For reasons associated with the size and complexity of the task, the basic requirement is, therefore, for systematic and continuing approaches which can support and extend the professional competence of teachers and continually reinforce their newly acquired values, attitudes and behaviours. For that reason, if for no other, it is necessary for each school to have a staff development policy and procedures that are shared, explicit, systematic. comprehensive and regularly monitored.

TEACHER EDUCATION

My central concern in this chapter is not with the work of the teacher education institutions *per se*, but rather with the process of and strategies for the professional development of teachers, aimed specifically at prejudice reduction. Nevertheless, in view of the underdeveloped state of the field, there are a number of precursor projects and studies, conceptualisations and speculative writings from which we shall have to learn. The early work of Trager and Yarrow (1952), for example, included an accompanying teacher education programme with goals aiming to:

- develop teacher interest in and awareness of human relations;
- develop understanding of children's needs, attitudes and values;
- develop democratic values;
- develop willingness to accept responsibility for intercultural education.

The concern with human relations is noteworthy and tends to be absent from more modern approaches to multicultural and anti-racist education. Yet, similar goals were pursued by the Intergroup Education Movement in the United States in the early post-war period (Taba, Brady and Robinson, 1952), but, as Banks (1987) points out, at that time most mainstream scientists had a conception of blacks as deviant and culturally deprived and, thus, as a 'social problem'. It was not, therefore, until 1976 that standards for multicultural teacher education in the United States were laid down for the accreditation of teacher education programmes. These were then published in revised form in 1982 and stipulated the inclusion of experiences which:

1. Promote analytical and evaluative abilities to confront issues such as participatory democracy, racism and sexism, and the parity of power.
2. Develop skills for values clarification including the manifest and latent transmission of values.
3. Examine the dynamics of diverse cultures and the implications for developing teaching strategies.

4.   Examine linguistic variations and diverse learning styles as a basis for the development of appropriate teaching strategies.
      (National Council for the Accreditation of Teacher Education, 1982, p. 14, 1985)

The standard makes it explicit that the student is expected to develop competences for perceiving, believing, evaluating and behaving in differential cultural settings.

In the United Kingdom proclamations have tended to be more ebullient and less specific until more recently. In 1984, for example, the National Association for Multi-Racial Education, now called the National Anti-Racist Movement in Education, and the main validating body for teacher education courses, the Council for National Academic Awards, both published important statements on multicultural and anti-racist education (NAME, 1984; CNAA, 1984). In March 1984, the second version of a significant discussion document in the field of multicultural teacher education was produced by a working group of the Council for National Academic Awards. Its aim was to 'suggest principles in respect of multicultural and anti-racist education', and it included a checklist of items for possible inclusion in courses of teacher education.

The document embraced commitments to:

* the appreciation and the utilisation of the richness of cultural variety in the United Kingdom and the world, in educational curricula at all levels;
* the development of cultural sensitivity towards the cultural identity and practices of various groups; and,
* the development of a clear understanding of the importance of achieving equality of opportunity in social and economic life.

In addition, the document set out what were seen as five necessary areas of professional education, including equipping teachers to:

* prepare all young people for life in a multicultural and racially harmonious society;
* have awareness and understanding of racism;
* have an awareness of intercultural relations;
* be able to teach, recognising the particular needs of ethnic minority pupils and students; and
* interact effectively with colleagues in relation to these issues.

The overall orientation of the paper was to curriculum rather than to institutional or systemic considerations, although there was a brief reference to necessary institutional initiatives. There was no reference to assessment and its role in knowledge control, although there was one reference to examinations in the context of minority languages. On the other hand, neither prejudice acquisition nor pedagogical strategies for prejudice reduction with regard to students on teacher education courses nor the children they teach, were referred to. The document, and the follow-up checklist of items meriting consideration in the development and validation of teacher education courses derived from the discussion document, were, however, in the explicit acceptance of *anti-racist education*, in advance of previous attempts in Britain to map the practical implications of implementing multicultural teacher education.

Also in 1984, the pressure group NAME published an important and far-reaching statement on teacher education. The statement aimed to:

- achieve an urgent demonstration of NAME's view of the need for essential change in teacher education;
- eliminate racism and promote the development of a just and pluralist society;
- emphasise the need for a reflection in education of the perspectives of all communities including a black perspective; and
- offer a range of practical recommendations for consideration and action.

More exclusively focussed on anti-racism than the CNAA document the statement calls for interventionist education to counter racism and achieve social justice. More broadly than the CNAA document referred to above it calls for explicit policies addressing institutional management, staffing, recruitment and the assessment of students, provision of courses and staff development opportunities, course content, evaluation and resources.

The document calls for the conferment of qualified teacher status to be dependent on the demonstration of 'skills, knowledge and personal qualities appropriate to teaching in a multiracial society' and 'the adoption by students of an anti-racist approach in classroom practice'. All courses should be scrutinised to ensure due emphasis throughout on 'anti-racist perspectives' and should include the development of strategies for anti-racist teaching. The document is neither concrete nor specific with regard to what knowledge, skills, competences and approaches might be necessary, nor how the imperatives might be translated in behavioural consequences.

While both documents were neglectful of the field of prejudice reduction and presumably ignorant of the extensive precursor work in that field, they changed the terms of reference for future discourse in their explicit recognition that racism had to be combated in teacher education and in their advocacy, albeit exclusive in nature in its approach to prejudice, of a teacher education committed to prejudice reduction. Furthermore, that commitment was reinforced by the inclusion in the stated criteria of the newly appointed Council for the Accreditation of Teacher Education, of an explicit requirement that:

> Students should be prepared to teach the full range of pupils, whom they are likely to encounter in an ordinary school, with their diversity of ability, behaviour, social background and ethnic and cultural origins. They will need to learn how to respond flexibly to such diversity and to guard against preconceptions based on the race or sex of pupils.
> (Department of Education and Science, 1984, Annex).

While the criterion does not imply any recognition of the need to train teachers to actively combat prejudice, it does at least recognise the need for teachers to guard against it in their own behaviour.

In May 1985, after some vigorous discussions in its corridors of power, the CNAA offered further elucidation of its earlier notes. In a brief set of guidelines on multicultural education in courses for initial and in-service teacher education, it states: 'The serious study of race-relations (and of ethnicity, religion, class and gender relations) should be seen as a necessary part of education in our society'. (CNAA, 1985, p. 2). Having moved to the verge of a recognition of the need to combat prejudice across the board, the document, somewhat illogically, retrenches and draws the conclusion, that such a commitment involves both multicultural and anti-racist education. It then proceeds to ignore the existence of any other form of prejudice, almost as though sexism, credism and classism did not exist and were unrelated except as subcategories of racism,

But what should teacher education and professional development for prejudice reduction include? A number of organisations and individuals have sought to set down what such a commitment might imply, although usually on a broad multicultural canvas and without specifying other than nodal points for tackling prejudice. An early document, published jointly by the former Community Relations Commission and the former Association of Teachers in Colleges and Departments of Education, for example, envisages three broad dimensions diffused throughout the training of teachers; *informational, technical* and *affective* (CRC/ATCDE, 1974). It also set down the need for *experiential* (e.g., contacts with minority groups) and *philosophical* (e.g., the generation of an appropriate ethos) dimensions, and pointed to the need for the involvement of all staff. This is a significant contribution in its recognition of affective and behavioural dimensions as well as cognitive ones and in its identification of the implications for pedagogies, the ethos of the institution and the provision of experiential means of achieving the goals, echoing in some respects the concern of the Intergroup Education Movement with personal and intercultural relations.

In an address to the American Association of Colleges for Teacher Education, Banks envisaged the implications of a multiethnic ideology for teacher education to lie in the development of *cross-cultural competency, greater self-understanding*, and the *establishment of personal contact situations and dialogue*. In these proposals we can see once again the identification of the need for experiential as well as other means of learning evisaged by the CRC Report, together with a commitment to the discourse of a democratic pluralism (Banks, 1979). The personal contact situations would, of course, need to be subject to the same conditions as those introduced and discussed in chapter 6 of this book.

In a more recent paper addressing the issue of what precisely multicultural teacher education means, Gay (1983) points to the fact that most Americans are ethnically illiterate, living in ethnic enclosures isolated from all but superficial and transitory interactions with ethnic others. She proceeds to identify some essential components for pre-service courses for teachers. These include:

- basic information about ethnic and cultural pluralism;
- knowlege acquisition and values clarification about ethnic groups and their cultures;
- how to combat racism;
- linguistic knowledge of black students in its historical, economic, cultural and political contextuality;
- competences for perceiving, believing, evaluating and behaving in different cultural contexts;

- skill development in translating 'multicultural' knowledge into programmes, practices, habits and behaviours of classroom instruction;
- competences in making educational objectives, curriculum content and learning activities meaningful to the experiential background and frames of reference of all students (their values, perceptions, cognitive processes and language);
- skill in achieving teaching and learning-style congruency;
- psychology and sociology of ethnicity, including issues of human behaviour and learning.

She concludes by stating that many of the above areas represent lacunae in current teacher education, and she draws attention to the great benefit of perspective which multicultural education can bring to conventional teacher education. It is clear that what Gay is suggesting is not merely the provision of fundamental substantive and didactic knowledge, but the translation of that knowledge into individual and group methodologies of intereraction in the classroom. This inevitably involves all levels of Bloom's taxonomy up to the highest levels of mental functioning, and the skills to interpret that functioning into responsive behaviour in the instructional process.

For that level of cognitive, moral and professional sophistication, it is clear that educators need to be involved not solely in informational and awareness-raising activities. As with the pupils , whom they must teach to celebrate diversity and reduce and occlude prejudice, teachers need to be involved in enquiring, experiencing, creating, skill-training, modelling, interelating and social actioning activities, addressing the development of dispositions and values, competences, skills and abilities, learning and thinking techniques, interpersonal relations and practical competences, articulated to the prismatic cultural reality of the ethnic pluralism of society and its currently effective prejudices.

In an earlier contribution on the effects of teacher prejudice on student growth and development, bearing on a large body of research and writing, Gay describes teacher prejudice as valuative screens, through which pupil motivation, interpersonal relations, the processes of instruction and curriculum content are 'filtered, interpreted and assigned meaning relative to the perceived characteristics and capabilities of students (Gay, 1979). At best, as Gay suggests this is done through condescendingly aiming to save ethnic minority students from themselves, at worst by ignoring their alternative cultural realities altogether.

In a paper that reviews some of the conceptualisations of multicultural teacher education and appraises the potential relationship between competency-based teacher education, social studies and multicultural education, Gay (1978) seeks to offer a paradigm to achieve greater specificity, coherence, organisation and sequential development in designing multicultural programmes. This paradigm may provide one way of mapping out, by extrapolation, what new staff development teachers need in responding to the introduction of prejudice reduction. Drawing on the traditions of competency-based teacher education, she specifies five areas of competence:

1. *Knowledge*: addressing cognitive understanding.
2. *Performance*: specifying teaching and instructional behaviour and attitudes.
3. *Consequential/behavioural*: identifying student behaviour resulting from teacher behaviours.

4. *Affective*: indicating attitudes to be demonstrated by teachers.
5. *Expressive*: detailing experience to be undertaken by teachers.

In a contribution to the debate about multicultural teacher education, I have suggested in another place (Lynch, 1986b) that the introduction of genuine programmes of multicultural teacher education, committed to democratic dialogue and involving discourse and appeal to the judgement of participants rather than indoctrination, may find a number of helpful guidelines for prejudice reduction staff development in the contemporary literature on multicultural teacher education:

- *culturally*, for example, concerning the socialisation framework for such activities and its heterogeneous cultural composition;
- *morally*, in the need for an appropriate ethos supportive of an active engagement for policies of prejudice reduction;
- *pedagogically*, in the development of intercultural teaching strategies, which can facilitate personal value clarification;
- *experientially*, in the availability of extended professional opportunities for intercultural contact and dialogue.

Taking up the relay of the implications of the introduction of multicultural and anti-racist education for the staff development of teacher educators, Craft has suggested three areas of need, arising from:

1. the particular needs of ethnic minority children;
2. the needs of all children; and,
3. intercultural relations.
   (Craft, 1986, pp. 6–20.)

Under the first category, he identifies the need to respond to language issues (including both home language and dialect), problems of identity, intergenerational stress and the clash of religious and secular, moral and urban values. These will, in some cases, include more hierarchical, even sexist, modes of relationship and the problem of the sharp underachievement of some children from certain minority groups. He suggests that these factors have implications for classroom teaching skills, part of which will be teacher expectations, values and ethos, pastoral care and counselling for home-relations. When considering the needs of all children and the implications for teacher education, Craft underlines the need for a knowledge of, and a healthier, less ethnocentric attitude to, cultural diversity — including an awareness of regional, religious and social-class variations within the majority culture. He draws attention to both content and process implications for teachers, underlining the role of small group work. With regard to intercultural relations, Craft argues that an awareness of the origins of intercultural prejudice and discrimination, having as a part of it stereotyping on ethnic, racial and regional lines and criteria for the selection of non-racist material, are essential aspects of a teacher's professional repertoire, which should also include the techniques for managing classroom discussion of race and racism. He proposes that both knowlege and attitude dimensions should be included, and achieved through practical as well as intellectual modes.

Craft recognises that where diverse cultures interact within a particular nation state prejudice and discrimination in the form of racism, religious bigotry and other institutionalised forms of hostility and social rejection emerge. Teachers and schools in this area have a major, central and unique role in attenuating and overcoming the inevitable intergroup and interpersonal tensions and conflict that result from a culturally diverse society. He recognises that teachers need to be trained for that role, if the negative images, learned by pupils in the society as part of what Cortes (1981) has called the 'societal curriculum' are not to be passively or actively perpetuated by the school. As Banks (1987a) points out, it is not possible for the school to avoid playing a role in the ethnic education of pupils because children already possess stereotypes of different racial and ethnic groups (and of the two sexes and different religious groups) when they come to school. The choice for the school, therefore, is, as Banks argues, to unwittingly take part in the perpetuation of cultural biases and prejudices or to attempt positively to intervene and influence the development of healthier values, attitudes and behaviour. For this to be achieved through curricular means, not only factual information, but also concept attainment, value analysis, decision-making and social action are necessary.

As early as 1972, the Wisconsin Administrative Code was amended to include a requirement that human relations and intergroup relations be included in all initial teacher education courses (Johnson, 1977). The code stipulated the inclusion of experiences aimed at the development of attitudes, skills and techniques, so that knowledge of human relations, with intergroup relations as a part of them, could be translated into learning experiences for pupils. Such learning experiences as a study of the values, lifestyles and contributions of racial, cultural and economic groups to society; an analysis of the forces of racism, prejudice and discrimination, including their impact on majority and minority communities. Structural experiences, too, in which there are opportunities for participants to examine their own attitudes and feelings about issues of racism, prejudice and discrimination and to evaluate the ways these phenomena may be present in teaching materials. With all the above there should also be direct involvement with cultural groups and organisations committed to the improvement of intergroup relations (Johnson, 1977, pp. 187–8).

Contradicting the assertions of the radical critics of multicultural education, that the schools merely service a society that perpetrates inequality and racism, so socialising students into an existing social order, Banks (1987b) argues that it is possible for pupils to be educated for social change and to close the gap between society's social realities and declared democratic ideals. For this commitment to be effective, however, teachers must also become change agents and cultural mediators, interpreting both macro and micro cultures for all pupils and supporting pupils in their understanding of the need for and possibility of social change. This role requires teachers who have clarified and reflective commitments to democratic values, knowledge and pedagogies and who activate those values, skills and that knowledge in their professional lives. While they cannot be partisan, they cannot remain neutral either. They should support, defend, advocate and demonstrate moral attitudes and behaviour, which are consistent with the overarching ideals of a culturally diverse democracy, such as human rights and dignity, justice and equality. To implement a curriculum that will enable pupils to acquire content, attitudes and skills needed to participate in democratic social action, Banks suggests that teachers, as effective cultural mediators and change agents must acquire:

- social scientific knowledge, involving the processual derivation of the goals, assumptions and values of knowledge;
- clarified cultural identifications;
- positive intergroup and racial attitudes; and
- pedagogical skills.
  (Banks, 1985; 1987b.)

But all schools and all teachers do not have the same staff development needs in terms of content, and different strategies may be more appropriate to one school than another. While there will be some elements common to all, the content, strategy and principles will need to take into account the social, cultural and professional context and the specific institutional and individual needs, for not all staff will start from the same springboard. The importance of the proposed components for staff development, which Craft, Gay, Banks and others have contributed, is to be found in the map which they provide both of *areas of need*, cognitive, attitudinal and behavioral; and the *mode of achievement* of the goals which these represent; intellectual and experiential, individual and collegial. In other words, they address both content and strategies, recognising different starting points and different needs, and taking into account what we know about educational change and professional growth within a culturally diverse society committed to democratic procedures and processes to change attitudes values and skills.

THE CONTENT OF STAFF DEVELOPMENT

Scanning the various proposals for multicultural staff development rehearsed above, it is possible to extract elements which would be fundamental to any staff development policy encompassing the combating of prejudice as envisaged in this book. Noting that throughout the book I have argued that prejudice comprises *behavioural*, as well as *cognitive* and *affective* dimensions, it is possible to allocate the needs to those three categories, while emphasising the overlap which exists. Retrieving Craft's distinction between the particular needs of some pupils and the needs a culturally plural society generates in all children, including intercultural relationships, it is possible to identify a six-part typology as indicated and exemplified in table 8.1.

Of course, the picture is much more complex than suggested by the typology and more extensive too. For example, the area of knowledge will need to include not just facts about society but also tenable and supportable concepts, generalisations and theories that are apace of our knowledge and how to transmit it. Returning to the categorisation of knowledge given in chapter 5 as essential for pupils — knowledge of self; knowlege of society; knowledge of the environment and knowledge of knowledge — teachers will also need to have command of those areas or they cannot empower pupils to acquire them. Moreover, the knowledge cannot remain personal, but has to

Table 8.1 *Typology of content for a staff development policy for prejudice reduction*

	Examples of Particular Needs	*Examples of Needs of all*
Knowledge including: facts concepts generalizations theories	Facts of linguistic and cultural diversity, of the cultural characteristics of pupils and of appropriate learning theories	Facts of cultural pluralism, of prejudice and discrimination
Attitudes	Clarified and reflective positive attitudes towards different racial, credal and social class groups and towards both sexes	Commitment to democratic values such as human dignity, justice and equality
Behaviours	Effective teaching strategies matched to afford equality of learning opportunities of each pupil regardless of race, class, creed, sex and handicap	Effective and satisfying intercultural relations with all children in classroom and school, with parents and the local community

be acquired in a way and form which is communicable to pupils. In other words, the teacher needs to have the knowledge of how to implement the knowledge in a more broadly professional context with colleagues, parents and the community, and also in a more narrowly pedagogical or didactic context in the classroom or workshop. So a fifth 'knowledge' has to be added for teachers, that of *professional and pedagogical knowledge*. Further, each of the aims for pupils expressed in chapter 5 will have implications in themselves and, at one remove pedagogically, so to speak, for teachers. Teachers will need to master the aims and the consequential aims which flow from them for their professional practice. That task will certainly be a big challenge for many teachers, but it will, as I argued in chapter 6, be a good opportunity for them to 'retread' their understanding of teaching, their pedagogical methods and their assessment and evaluation approaches: something in which good teachers are, in any case, continually engaged.

But what goals would underlie such content? It may help what is a complex and interactive network of components, if I give a few further examples and then itemise what seem to me to be major objectives. Teachers need to know about prejudice in a culturally diverse society and to be acquainted with the facts of discrimination in their own society and community. But they also need to be aware of the kinds of curricular and pedagogical strategies outlined in chapters 5 and 6 so that they can incorporate these facts into their teaching in such a way that learning results in the form of new values, attitudes, skills and behaviours in their pupils. They not only need to have clarified their own values in a reflective process, to be aware of their own moral values and value-related decisions (Shaver and Strong, 1982; Strike and Soltis, 1985), but to know how to enable their pupils to do that in a way which will result in positive gains. They not only need to enjoy effective and satisfying intercultural relationships themselves, but to enable their pupils to develop likewise.

Recalling the aims for pupils formulated in chapter 5, and the additional requirement referred to above for teachers to develop the pedagogical competence to achieve those aims, what goals should a staff development policy for prejudice reduction encompass? Intended only as an incomplete starter and as a basis for collegial discussion, it might encompass the aims for pupils from chapter 5 and thus include the following:

1.   Cognitive
- an up-to-date awareness of the cultural composition of society, including both macro and micro cultures, the school and its community;
- knowledge of the ways in which prejudice is acquired, generated and disseminated and with what effects, in a pluralist society, both structurally and personally;
- knowledge of the national legislation and national, local and institutional regulations and policies concerning prejudice and discriminatory behaviour;
- knowledge of the theories, concepts and generalisations concerning prejudice acquisition and reduction;
- knowledge of the pedagogical literature and strategies appropriate to prejudice;
- awareness of flexible response strategies to individual, group and structural discrimination on the grounds of sex, race, creed and class;
- openness to collegial collaboration and co-operation in pursuit of prejudice reduction, including those outlined in chapter 6;
- knowledge of knowledge, its creation, dissemination and function in society;
- knowledge of their pupils and their cultures, including linguistic background.

2.   Affective
- positive self and professional image;
- ability in moral perspective-taking;
- commitment to combating and challenging prejudice and discrimination inside and outside school;
- active support for democratic cultural pluralism including respect for persons, social justice and human educational equality of opportunity;
- acceptance of the unique value of each individual;
- appreciation of the role of rational discourse in prejudice reduction;
- ability to accept mutuality and reversibility in moral decision-making;
- critical self and professional value-awareness;
- commitment to continuing self and professional improvement including enhancement of the criteria for evaluation of practice;
- high academic expectations of self and all pupils.

3.   Behavioural (Conative)
- skills in nurturing and encouraging non-prejudiced attitudes and behaviour in pupils and colleagues;
- competence in teaching for prejudice reduction;
- expertise in intercultural and intergroup relations, including feeling comfortable with diversity;
- manifestation of mutuality in actions in school and community;
- critical, reflective approach to all social situations and the underlying value exchange.

So much for an outline set of goals for professional development. But through what *strategies* might such a staff development be achieved and according to what *principles* might it be devised and implemented? Bearing in mind that the proposals rehearsed at the beginning of this chapter contain much which has not yet been implemented, even though some of them date from the early 1970s, then the issue of how to implement such a programme of staff development becomes doubly important — to achieve the right *strategy* and *principles* as well as the right *content* and *experiences*. The next two sections of this chapter now pick up the relay of questions associated with these two areas: strategies and principles.

STRATEGIES FOR STAFF DEVELOPMENT

A number of authors have been concerned recently with the current inadequacy of the in-service education of teachers. In the United Kingdom, the Eggleston Report (Eggleston, Dunn and Purewal, 1981) castigated providers for the quantitative and qualitative inadequacies of activities offered. As a consequence of the Swann Report and the introduction by the Department of Education and Science of national funding for in-service provision to respond to ethnic diversity, and the introduction by some local authorities and the National Union of Teachers of racism awareness training (RAT) much has improved. There is, though, still little co-ordinated, continuing and focussed provision in the area of prejudice reduction and almost nothing on the staff development strategies that might achieve it. Likewise in Canada, by 1986, several School Boards, including North York, Toronto and Vancouver, and some teachers federations, had introduced activities and programmes addressing anti-racist objectives. But again, there was little specifically focussed on the broader concept of prejudice reduction as formulated in this book. In the United States, apart from the initiatives supported by the Anti-Defamation League, contiguous provision as part of Effective Schools Projects, and more broadly conceived multicultural activities, staff development for prejudice reduction was thin.

In the broader literature, a number of authors have, however, concentrated more closely on the inadequacies of in-service education, from which we may learn in the construction of strategies for staff development for prejudice reduction. In Canada, Small has sought to identify the reasons why continuing professional education (CPE) does not have a glowing record. Pointing to the need for such activities to be carried out through inquiry and experimentation modes, reflective analysis of work-related experiences as well as didactic modes, Small suggests three major reasons for the failure of continuing education for teachers: the wrong focus; the lack of organisational support; provision alien to teacher culture (Small, 1985). He alerts his readers to the need for a social support network or structure to sustain teachers in the difficult implementation phase, particularly after skills workshops, and the importance of collegial support.

In similar vein, and quoting an extensive canvas of American teachers, Neil (1985) also cites lack of follow-up activities as a major cause of the failure of staff development activities, and he refers to Fullan's suggestions that, for real educational change, five elements must be changed including: the organisation of the group; materials; behaviour roles of participants, knowledge and understanding; and the participants' value commitments (Fullan, 1978). These points are particularly important because they draw attention to the process of internalisation of new values and socialisation into new roles that is so crucial to prejudice reduction teaching. Picking up that theme of teacher change as a developmental and experiential process comprising interrelated components, Guskey (1986) proposes a model of the temporal sequence of events which, he hypothesises, typifies the process of staff development to enduring change in teachers' perceptions and attitudes. He sees the three major outcomes of such staff development as change in the classroom practices of teachers, change in their beliefs and attitudes and change in the learning outcomes of pupils. He argues that, contrary to current approaches, changes in teacher classroom practices that demonstrate changed pupil learning outcomes should come before changes in teachers' beliefs and attitudes. This need for the pragmatic verification of teachers' knowledge in the classroom is an essential component of 'attitude-change-demanding' approaches such as prejudice reduction.

Guskey suggests three guiding principles that we can also carry forward into the section of this chapter dealing with principles:

1. Recognise that change is a gradual and difficult process for teachers.
2. Ensure regular feedback to teachers on pupil learning progress.
3. Provide continued support and follow-up.

Based on an extensive international project and focussing more closely on school-based in-service staff development, Hopkins identifies a similar need for continuity and support. Reviewing recent studies and collating the positive and negative finding, he asserts, *inter alia*, that:

- one-shot workshops are ineffective;
- follow-up support for implementation is rare;
- decisions are often taken other than by the teachers involved;
- school-based activities are more suited where complex teacher behaviours are involved;
- the best goal achievement is attained by programmes using demonstrations, trials and feedback;
- teachers appear to learn professional skills and practices best from other teachers;
- collegial and interactive programmes providing individual experiences are more likely to accomplish their objectives;
- the involvement of teachers in planning and decision-making improves the chances of success;
- staff development should be part of an overall plan for improvement.
  (Hopkins, 1986, pp. 266–268, amended).

On the basis of such evidence, it is possible for us to 'map out' an outline model of what staff development for prejudice reduction might look like, in comparison with current provision, insofar as it exists at all. Table 8.2 attempts to summarise the parameters, within which an effective strategy could be organised.

Strategies that have a good fit with the parameters outlined in Table 8.2 are likely to embrace what I have described elsewhere as (Lynch, 1986a): 'working dialogically for

Table 8.2 *Existing and required staff development for prejudice reduction*

Dimension of policy	Existing	Required
Goals	cognitive/awareness	cognitive/affective behavioural
Focus	isolated teachers	institutional
Change	personal	personal/pedagogical/ consequential
Participation	individual	collegial
Integration	aggregative	holistic
Time scale	'one-off'	continuing
Culture	Anglo-dominant	multicultural
Feedback	'perhaps'	from pupils and teachers
Gender	sexist	anti-sexist
Race	racist	anti-racist
Creed	credal hierarchy	multicredal
Values	authoritarian	clarified and reflective
Approach	laissez-faire or coercive	rational–democratic
Treatment of prejudice	implicit or ignored	prejudice reduction commitment

professional growth', which rules out the acceptance of ready-made answers and includes the testing out of the appropriateness of proposed strategies in each setting. Based on the result of a Schools Council supported project in the North of England, which sought to develop just such a dialogical approach with teachers in schools in five different local authority areas, staff development for multicultural education, including prejudice reduction, was seen as:

1. A constant process of professional enquiry and development.
2. The extension by educators of their own reference group and criteria for professional judgement.
3. The development of dialogue between professionals on a basis of equality and between professionals, lay and adminstrative personnel, on the same basis.
4. The existence of overall policy objectives, nationally, in LEAs and in schools, 'worked up' in situ, with the actual implementation fostered, nurtured and monitored at classroom level.
5. Wide discussion of the dilemmas that prejudice reduction evokes for individual schools.
6. Acceptance that accounts of actual enquiry in one setting may provide *one* rich resource for collegial discussion and consideration.
7. Approaches inevitably having a high level of provisionality and subject, therefore, to constant monitoring and dialogue.
8. Acceptance that professional activities most likely to lead to growth are those in which the teachers themselves have defined their own tasks, on a basis of partnership with others.
9. A subtle and organic professional growth which commences where teachers are now rather than grafting on completely new approaches.
10. Activities which appeal to the professional judgement of teachers and incur their support.
(Biott, Lynch and Robertson, 1984).

A less comprehensive and shorter-term project in Canada in the area of racial prejudice was framed by similar parameters, when the City of North York Board of Education arranged a series of seminars on racism awareness for teachers from two families of schools. Part of their learning task was to present similar workshops in their own school and plan the professional development of the staff in that school across an academic year. It was thus an interesting attempt to adopt a 'multiplier' approach, involving staff by:

- providing input from everyday experiences;
- requiring pre-reading of selected texts;
- requesting participants to keep a 'reflection journal';
- encouraging and equipping participants to observe aspects of race relations in their schools;
- requiring syndicate work, including presentation by participants;
- preparing participants for a pilot racism awareness workshop for their own staff;
- expecting participants to plan out the professional development for the staff in their schools for one academic year.

The course stated clearly the expected benefits for participants — a very important consideration at times of tight staffing ratios — and listed the organising principles underlying the work, namely:

- racist behaviour is not natural — it is learned;
- racism is produced both by belief systems and social structures: it is not simply a matter of changing attitudes or changing social structures, but of the recognition of the relationship between both, knowledge about the interests that racism serves, and practices both by institutions and individuals to promote equality;
- racist behaviour has both a cognitive and an affective dimension, so any exploration of racism must allow for the expression of both ideas and feelings about the subject;
- educators respond best to initiatives in race relations when they are directly applied to classroom practice;
- educators find in-service programmes most rewarding when their experience as practitioners is taken into account and not trivialised;
- educators are likely to make changes in their sphere of influence when there is a support system within the school to provide encouragement and feedback.
  (City of North York, 1984).

More comprehensively, Banks et al. (1976) have formulated a series of curriculum guidelines for teacher education that incorporates specific suggestions for supporting teacher education activities, addressing cognitive, affective and pedagogical considerations. Where it is possible for teacher education to be part of an overall reform programme, it is clearly strengthened, and this will particularly be so in attempting to introduce prejudice reduction. But it will not always be the case, and a more modest scale may be necessary to begin the process of reform.

From this brief excursion into the literature of professional development and multicultural education it is possible to perceive both common principles in the literature and common strategies. Perhaps the components of these common strategies might be defined as:

- school-based work but with appropriate support and inputs from 'experts' and/or networks e.g. groups of schools;
- resource support in the school;
- utilisation of the teachers' everyday experience;
- collegiality of planning, implementation and evaluation;
- cognitive, affective and behavioural approaches combined;
- coherent, continuous approaches.

Within these parameters a number of 'tactics' are possible, dependent on the agreement of staff. These may range from diary-keeping, through awareness workshops, discussion groups, simulations, syndicates and curriculum development, to the involvement of teachers in each other's practice by intervisiting. This last can take a number of forms; it may be done on a personal or institutional basis, or through team-teaching approaches and techniques, or by twinning with other institutions and community involvement.

PRINCIPLES FOR STAFF DEVELOPMENT

Given the content and strategies, it is important also to clarify the guiding principles according to which participation is to be agreed. Once again we are faced with a paucity of illustrations but it is, for example, inconceivable that coercion would be contemplated as a means of changing the vast majority of teachers, quite apart from the dysfunctionality of such an approach. Yet, teaching for prejudice reduction cannot be voluntary for reasons given earlier in this book. The individual teacher cannot remain neutral and neither can the school.

An early paper by Grant on how multicultural in-service teacher education may be best achieved uses the well-known conceptualisation of planned organisational change strategies: empirical–rational; power-coercive; and normative–reeducative. Grant emphasises the limited effect of the first two and the importance of the third if the normative culture that guides people in their actions, personal attitudes and cognitive modes is to be changed. Several 'principles' for staff development for prejudice reduction emerge from the insights shown in his writing:

- the need for a framework of empirical–rational and power–coercive measures for normative reeducative change to be effective;
- recognition that the 'problem' may lie in the attitudes, values, norms and external and internal relationships of educators;
- the need for the elimination, or at the very least attenuation, of negative attitudes and pathological norms from the teacher's repertoire of beliefs and values;
- the achievement of fundamental value, habit and meaning reorientation;

- democratic discourse as an indispensable part of the change strategy, involving appeal to the judgement of participants, involvement of the 'clients' in working out the change programme and in its implementation and evaluation;
- mutual and collaborative effort and dialogue to define openly and resolve problems and to bring into consciousness, non-conscious elements, including support and involvement by other dimensions of the pluralist culture;
- three major and overlapping phases: awareness and recognition; acceptance and appreciation; affirmation and full commitment;
- a whole-institution approach.
  (Grant and Mellnick, 1976, amended).

Certainly, some such list of 'rules' would need to be agreed as well as a programme strategy and content if teacher education for prejudice reduction were to be congruent with democratic values, but also to avoid the project being 'hijacked' for whatever purposes by an individual or minority. Given that proviso, however, there is no reason why the principles of procedure should not be agreed collegially as part of the process of values clarification and identification that is at the heart of prejudice reduction and moral ascent by professional educators committed to democratic values.

SUMMARY

In this chapter, I have sought to draw attention to the staff development requirement without which prejudice reduction cannot be implemented by schools. The development activities must be symbiotic with the reform process. I have scanned selected literature from the fields of teacher education and multicultural education, and allocated the ensuing literature to three major headings: content, strategies and principles. Running through each of these three areas are certain underlying commonalities: the commitment to democratic values; the need for partnership, both in the form of collegiality and with the community; the need for organic, systematic and continuing provision and support; the intertwining of staff development with the everyday work of teachers; the requirement to address cognitive, affective and behavioural dimensions as well as the pedagogical implications. In my final chapter I shall pull together the threads of the book, reviewing briefly the overall thrust and content and projecting that into an agenda for urgent action at system, institutional and individual levels.

ACTIVITIES

1. Formulate a set of principles that you think should underlie a school policy for prejudice reduction staff development. Taking the three-part categorisation of planned change, utilised by Grant, detail the extent to which each one might find a place in your overall strategy.
2. Identify the characteristics of a school staff development policy for prejudice reduction and compile them in the form of a document to be tabled at the next

staff meeting. Give careful consideration to the 'political' context and include details of any necessary resource considerations including the participation of 'outsiders'.

3. What do you see as the growth points within your school for the introduction of prejudice reduction strategies. In what ways could these nodal points be 'capitalised' to spread into other areas. Who are the 'gatekeepers' of such a process? How can the bulk of staff best be 'won over' to put staff development for this purpose on their own personal and professional agenda?

REFERENCES

Banks, J.A. (1979) *Multiethnic/Multicultural Teacher Education: Conceptual, Historical and Ideological Issues*. Rosslyn VA: National Clearinghouse for Bilingual Education.

Banks, J.A. (1985) 'Multicultural teacher education: knowledge, skills and process', Paper presented at the Conference on Intercultural Training of Teachers, sponsored by the Swedish Board of Universities and Colleges, Vildmarkshotellet, Kolmarden, Norrkoeping, Sweden (June).

Banks, J.A. (1987a) 'Ethnic diversity, the social responsibility of educators and school reform', in Molnar, A. (ed.) *The Social Reponsibility of Educators*. Alexandria VA: Association for Supervision and Curriculum Development (forthcoming).

Banks, J.A. (1987b) 'The social studies: ethnic diversity and social change, in *The Elementary School Journal* (forthcoming) University of Chicago Press.

Banks, J.A., Cortes, C.E., Gay, G., Garcia, R.L. and Ochoa, A.S. (1976) *Curriculum Guidelines for Multiethnic Education*. Arlington VA: National Council for the Social Studies.

Biott, C., Lynch, J., and Robertson, W. (1984) Supporting teachers' own progress towards multicultural education, *Multicultural Education*, **11** (2), 39–41.

City of North York, Ontario (1984) Racism awareness seminar series. North York, Ontario: Board of Education (Cyclo).

Community Relations Commission/Association of Teachers in Colleges and Departments of Education (1974) *Teacher Education for a Multicultural Society*. London: CRE.

Cortes, C.E., (1981) 'The societal curriculum: implications for multiethnic education' in Banks, J.A. (ed.) *Education in the 80s: Multiethnic Education*. (43rd Yearbook) Washington DC: National Council for the Social Studies.

Council for National Academic Awards (1984) 'Multicultural education: discussion paper', London: CNAA.

Council for National Academic Awards (1985) 'Notes on multicultural education in courses for the initial training and in-service development of teachers', London: CNAA.

Craft, M. (1986) *Teacher Education in a Multicultural Society: An Introduction*. Nottingham: University of Nottingham, School of Education (National Programme for Training the Trainers, Series).

Department of Education and Science (1984) *Initial Teacher Training: Approval of Courses (Circular 3/84)*. London: DES.

Eggleston, S.J., Dunn, D.K. and Purewal, A. (1981) *In-Service Teacher Education in a Multicultural Society*. Keele: The University of Keele.

Fullan, M. (1978) *Implementing Change in Occupational Education*. Ithaca: Cornell Institute of Occupational Education.

Gay, G. (1978) 'Interfacing CBTE and multicultural education in social studies teacher preparation' in Felder, D. (ed.) *Competency-Based Teacher Education: Professionalizing Social Studies Teaching*. Washington, DC: National Council for the Social Studies.

Gay, G. (1979) Teacher prejudice as a mediating factor in student growth and development, *Views in Teaching and Learning*. **55** (2), 94–106.

Gay, G. (1983) Why multicultural education in teacher preparation programmes? *Contemporary Education*. vol. **LIV** (Winter), 79–85.

Grant, C.A. and Mellnick, S.L. (1976) 'Developing and implementing multicultural in-service teacher education', paper presented at the National Council of States on In-Service Education. New Orleans, 17–19 November.

Guskey, T.R. (1986) Staff development and the process of teacher change, *Educational Researcher* **15**,(5) 5–12.

Hopkins, D. (ed.) (1986) *Inservice Training and Educational Development: An International Survey*. London: Croom Helm.

Johnson, J.W. (1977) 'Human relations preparation in teacher education: the Wisconsin experience', in Klassen, F.H. and Gollnick, D.M. (eds) *Pluralism and the American Teacher* (Issues and Case Studies) Washington DC: American Association of Colleges for Teacher Education, Ethnic Heritage Centre for Teacher Education.

Lynch, J. (1986a) *Multicultural Education: Principles and Practice*. London: Routledge and Kegan Paul.

Lynch, J. (1986b) 'An initial typology of perspectives on staff development for multicultural teacher education' in Modgil, S., Verma, G.K., Mallick, K. and Modgil, C. (eds) *Multicultural Education: The Interminable Debate*. Lewes: Falmer Press.

National Association for Multicultural Education (1984) *Statement on Teacher Education*. Birmingham: NAME (July).

National Council for the Accreditation of Teacher Education (1982) *Standards for the Accreditation of Teacher Education* revised edition. Washington DC: NCATE, revised edition (July).

Neil, R. (1985) In-service teacher education: five common causes of failure, *Action in Teacher Education*. **VII** (3), 49–55.

Shaver, P. and Strong, W. (1982) *Facing Value Decisions: Rationale Building for Teachers*. New York: Teachers College Press, Teachers College, Columbia University.

Small, J.M. (1985) Harnessing the wind: continuing professional development for teachers, *Education Canada* (Winter), 10–15.

Strike, K.A. and Soltis, J.F. (1985) *The Ethics of Teaching*. New York: Teachers College Press, Teachers College, Columbia University.

Taba, H., Brady, E.H. and Robinson, J.T. (1952) *Intergroup Education in Public Schools*. Washington DC: American Council on Education.

Trager, H.G. and Yarrow, M.R. (1952) *They Learn What They Live*. New York: Harper and Brothers.

Chapter 9

Postscript

In this book I have argued that, where children are socialised into diverse cultures which interact with each other within a particular nation state, prejudice and discrimination, institutionalised hostility and social rejection emerge. As the major institution of secondary socialisation, the school and the teachers who work there have a unique opportunity and a fundamental responsibility to address the inevitable intergroup conflict and interpersonal tension arising from that diversity of socialisation and enculturation processes. Unless teachers and schools do accept that responsibility, increased social conflict, discrimination, injustice and alienation will result and the gap between the espoused ideals of democratic society and the social reality experienced by minorities will widen: developments which are in the interests of neither minority nor majority communities.

It is particularly important, in a period of extreme conservatism, dominated by a somewhat contradictory, ideological commitment to the pursuit of excellence through a 'return to basics', to emphasise the basic social function of the school in prejudice reduction. For, at such times, it is possible for the commitment of schools to social justice, human dignity and fundamental democratic values and morality to be overlooked, or at least not perceived with the clarity of other preferred objectives. Yet it is the function of a school system in a democratic society to make these ideals attainable for all pupils; if that democratic society is to endure and thrive. Currently, in democratic society, there exists insufficient recognition of the school's role in prejudice reduction and teachers are, thus, ill-prepared to implement it, with consequent legitimation crises in key sectors of society including the schools.

This book has set prejudice reduction at the centre of democratic school responses to cultural diversity. It has been concerned to show how these crises may be attenuated by the introduction of prejudice reduction into schools, not on the basis of any Utopian, revolutionary *tabula rasa* notion, but as a natural evolution from what already exists. It is centrally focussed on how teachers may develop their professional competence by extending their existing skills and the criteria they use for professional judgement, so as to embrace the objective of combating prejudice and discrimination on the grounds of race, sex, creed and class, as part of their ordinary everyday professional lives and teaching activities. At its core is, thus, the fundamental objective of empowering teachers to extend their professional objectives by persuasion, support, encouragement and the provision of appropriate basic information and facts about resources.

There are many ways in which teachers may show their commitment to the reduction and elimination of unhealthy and socially dysfunctional prejudice and discrimination in their work as professional educators, and many of those ways are identified and clarified in this volume. Most of all, however, they may demonstrate their support for democratic values in their everyday teaching, its method as well as its content, the materials which they use and in the relationship which they nurture with colleagues, pupils, parents and the surrounding community. Schools 'show' their commitment to prejudice reduction through their ethos and the way in which they structure, organise and deliver for all pupils an equality of opportunity, deriving from basic democratic values such as human justice, freedom and dignity. In that sense, both teachers and schools can be agents of cultural change and conservation, cherishing and transmitting that which is valuable in society and challenging those values, attitudes and behaviour which are incompatible with democratic values.

Neither schools nor teachers can remain neutral on issues such as prejudice and other morally indefensible attitudes and behaviours such as racism, credism and class stratification. Not to critically address prejudice reduction, is for schools and teachers to support the perpetuation of prejudice and discrimination and, thus to discriminate for some pupils and against others. This course of action would be to pervert and subvert the democratic values that schools exist creatively to sustain, amend and transmit: a morally bankrupt pedagogy that no serious-minded democratic teacher could support, let alone one who is committed to the empowerment of presently victimised and marginalised racial and ethnic groups.

In the introduction to this book I wrote of the need for teachers to empower all pupils to undertake social criticism and action in pursuit of democratic values such as justice, equality and the combating of prejudice. But, to adopt such a role, teachers themselves must be 'empowered' not only with new technical means to achieve well-worn, hand-me-down and often only partially disclosed ends. Teachers must also be enabled to undertake a new critical intellectual relationship with the ends of education in a culturally pluralist democracy. They need to be seen not as the handmaids of dominant groups and their values, but as 'transformative intellectuals' involved in the critical political discourse about new ends as well as new means to create better and more just social relations and a more equitable society, which excludes current injustices, such as racism, sexism, credism and classism (Giroux, 1985a, 1985b; Aronowitz and Giroux, 1985a, 1985b). For as Parker (1986) has argued, the activity of teaching seen as reflective practice has been increasingly squeezed out as dominant groups and governments have sought to relegate teaching to the level of a technical arm of the civil service concerned almost exclusively with means. Such a strategy is, of course, only evocative of a greater crisis in the legitimacy of teaching as a profession causative of an increased legitimation crisis in the wider society, for as long as it is a substitute for the activation of democratic discourse.

For teachers to empower pupils to combat social injustice such as prejudice and discrimination, there has to be a renewed recognition of what the new sociology of education emphasised, namely that the schools are part of a power political structure and that teachers work in the context of ideological and economic conditions. They are thus part of — not neutral from — the overall discourse about legitimate ends for a culturally diverse society and the pursuit of democratic values. They are not, however, mere servants of the status quo, and their role can be as much socially transformative as culturally transmissionist. Their role is both to improve the means by which practice develops through critical self-appraisal and to pursue a more just and humane society through their involvement in the wider discourse about ends. Thus, for teachers and schools to undertake effectively the task of prejudice reduction, there has to be a clear acceptance by dominant groups of the politicisation of teaching and learning in schools. For schools function neither wholly autonomously, as traditionalists would have us believe, nor wholly as the servants of capitalist exploitation, as a Marxian perspective will maintain. Rather they are *par excellence* in a pluralist democracy an arena for discourse among prevailing and countervailing ideologies in competition in the broader society, with the emphasis shifting back and forth in a kind of politico-educational tug-of-war (Carnoy and Levin, 1985).

Yet, time is short for dominant groups in democratic societies to take note of their part in the equation of combating prejudice, if present crises in society are not to deepen. For, currently, they are ambivalent about or connive at the perpetuation of prejudice and discrimination based on birth, sex, race, creed and class, mistaking their own real interests and those of their children. Nowhere, in democratic Western societies, is this discrimination more marked than in nations such as the United Kingdom, where erstwhile privilege of birth trumps the recognition and utilisation of that very ability without which society must decline. Not solely minority groups, but a majority of the nation's most precious resources, its future citizens, is being squandered on unequal competition, the results of which are in any case rigged, so that money and birth weigh heaviest on the scales of human justice and opportunity. Dominant groups must seek, through discourse with victimised groups, a new source of national ideals that all may share, to replace their own crusted, imperial ones. For schools cannot prevail, nor teachers fulfil their allocated task to educate rationally and morally to correct for prejudice and discrimination, while dominant groups continue by their actions to jeopardise those very values they profess to espouse.

A central message of this book is that excellence and justice must not be seen as incompatible objectives for education vying with each other for attention, resources and action. I have tried to show the commonality of purpose between effective schools and schools centrally committed to prejudice reduction, where social and intellectual aims of education coalesce and mutually reinforce each other. In that sense, this book is intended to be both positive and optimistic, pointing the way to democratic evolutionary change, while emphasising the urgency of the necessary educational and broader social measures.

The book commenced by stating the case for deliberate, systematic and continuing approaches to prejudice reduction, based on democratic values and procedures and adopting rational approaches which recognise teaching as a crucially moral task. That process was seen as part of the overall social initiative to harmonise democratic ideals with the social reality of victimised groups. Prejudice reduction was thus defined as a core component of the overall response of culturally diverse societies to the need to construct a means to induct learners into moral behaviour and values by means of rational educational strategies and experiences, including cognitive, affective and behavioural dimensions. Those concerns were located within present endeavours to construct what is known as 'multicultural education', and the interrelationship and synergetic effect of the two concepts was argued and illustrated.

This task of teaching to correct for prejudiced values, attitudes and behaviour was seen as a complex and difficult one for teachers to undertake: one which needs to be planned, implemented and evaluated on the basis of a knowledge and understanding of how prejudice is acquired and may most effectively be reduced. The process of acquiring that knowledge and understanding was argued to involve teachers in achieving a greater awareness of their own clarified and reflective value commitments. The book then identified a flexible model for systematising the process of prejudice reduction, elaborating the case for both whole-school and whole-curricular policies. The curricular rationale proposed comprised seven major elements encompassing both ideological and pedagogical dimensions. Based on a scan of the literature, these elements translated into a discussion of 12 key exemplary teaching approaches, their strengths, weaknesses and proven potential in achieving attitude change. From these approaches an overall teaching 'style', idiosyncratic to each educator, but comprising common trace elements may be constructed so as to incorporate value clarification and attitude and behavioural change. Finally the central role of material resources and continued professional development on a collegial basis have been discussed and, in this latter area, content, strategy and principles have been proposed. Overall the intention has been not to advocate a separate, add-on curriculum, but to enhance the existing teaching and learning opportunities so as to address more centrally, consciously and expertly, the elimination of prejudice.

While this volume has sought to pose a challenge to current educational policy, its many limitations should be recognised. First, the selection of material for inclusion has had, of necessity, to be limited to those more recent studies, researches and writings that seem to directly illuminate the task of the teacher. In the process, a great deal of earlier material and some contemporary work has remained unmentioned or implicit only in the work and findings of later authors. Second, many unresearched issues have been raised that urgently necessitate further research and conceptual development and there are still many unanswered questions. Third, the use made of the material cited inevitably reflects my own interpretation, however much I have sought in the text to represent as wide a range as possible of disciplinary approaches, theoretical perspectives and philosophical positions. Moreover, as I have attempted to simplify, organise and explain often complex material, phenomena and findings, there has been an inevitable process of 'flattening out' the bumps in reality. Fourth, the book concentrates on the schooling process and the role of the teacher in combating prejudice. Thus, while the wider sociopolitical issues and structural dimensions are not neglected, neither is the book an analysis of the political changes which are essential accompaniments to the educational changes proposed. Finally, I am unyielding to compromise in my conviction of the need to re-work the values underlying the covenant of democratic societies for a new generation: a generation in which all cultural groups are structurally included in the process of defining that covenant by means of creative discourse aiming at rapid evolutionary development in the fight against prejudice and discrimination by humane and rational means.

I have referred previously to the need for further research to sustain the introduction of strategies for prejudice reduction into the everyday life of teachers and schools and there are, in fact, a number of significant gaps in the literature. As Grant and Sleeter (1986) have convincingly shown, for example, there is a tendency to treat racial, class and gender groups as if they are homogeneous, and, consequently, there is a paucity of studies and writings that substantively integrate race, social class and gender. There is no doubt that this neglect of people's multiple group memberships is a major flaw in the existing research work on equality and thus also on prejudice acquisition and reduction. As Gilligan (1982) trenchantly points out, we cannot assume that psychology validated on males is automatically valid and applicable to females, nor, as Lightfoot (1976) argues in concluding a survey of the literature, is sexism synonymous with the life experiences of white middle-class girls.

Scholars are now beginning to highlight the way in which traditional sources, questions and approaches may be inadequate for characterising women's contributions to education and to question the way in which the current conception of education is organised around male experience, values and life paradigms. Indeed, the implications of the 'new scholarship on women and education' are, as Biklen and Dwyer (1986) argue, at the least, that the current structures of educational disciplines and nature of current methodologies are 'prejudiced' and need to change as generalisations about human behaviour are generated from women's as well from men's experiences; one could perhaps add — from white males' experiences. And in this respect what applies to gender is also valid for the other forms of prejudice and discrimination, discussed in this book. Certainly, the introduction of new equity strategies at all levels of the education system, to combat current gender, race, creed and social class biases, cannot leave educational research untouched if it is to be effective in contributing to the production of integrated educators as well as integrated persons.

There are other pressing issues too. How valid, for example, are the principles for beneficial interethnic contact, cited in this book, for more specific cultural contexts in societies and countries other than those where they were generated? What are the most successful pedagogical strategies to eradicate prejudice? Which are the best means of linking home and school, family and teacher, pupil and peer group in co-ordinated efforts to improve the attitudes of all and in increasing opportunities for minority students? How can new, more 'culture-fair' methods of testing and evaluation be achieved? How reliable and appropriate are the minority categorisations which we currently use to identify social need and educational response? What are the most effective means of enabling teachers to become more culturally aware and of supporting them in their combat against prejudice and discrimination? Are there ways in which basic socio-cultural and value conflicts make the space for creative change, just as they may act as the seedbed for the growth of stereotypes, prejudice and discrimination? What are the precise, generic, cognitive and affective components of all prejudices and how far are these susceptible to common strategies of remediation?

These and many other questions remain to be resolved. Nevertheless, there is much which represents firm, reliable evidence as a basis for common cause by educators against discrimination. While that task will not be easily accomplished, given the political will, the goal can be attained. Achieving that goal will involve pursuing many of the courses suggested for teachers in this book. They will have to rediscover their own culture and become aware of their own values, beliefs and behaviour; understand their own preferred modes of interaction and their verbal behaviour; know about broad cultural patterns and their specific manifestation and permeation in their local socio-cultural setting. They must transform their teaching and recognise new goals, methods and learning approaches derived from very different cultural presuppositions about reward, motivation, achievement and fundamental human values and relationships and introduce more democratic and co-operative learning strategies for their pupils and themselves. They cannot move forward without pulling back the shroud on their own professional performance through such techniques as peer observation and recognising new thresholds of accountability; designing new materials; above all, creating new values and visions in themselves and others. Such tasks cannot be achieved, however, without the necessary administrative and political support, including the appropriate resources. Administrators, local and national politicians and the public must also respond to the need, lending both material and moral support.

In my view, the key issue facing the school system of democratic societies for the rest of this century is to deal effectively and justly with the dynamic of increasing cultural diversity. At the centre of that task is the school's role in weaning pupils from prejudice and initiating them into beliefs and behaviour that are in moral accord with the core values of democratic society. Schools do not merely transmit these values, however, they contribute to them according to their own internal cultural logic and that of their communities. The relationship is reciprocal.

If schools are to undertake teaching for prejudice reduction — and it has been the argument of this book that they must — there is much to be done. Major changes are needed in social attitudes and priorities; there has to be tighter legislation more in tune with democratic values; new materials and resources are necessary along with more research; staff development for educators and administrators is essential. Yet, such policies are well within the capability of democratic societies to implement. For as long as they remain inactivated the question must remain about the earnest of the declared political will of society to creatively reconstruct democracy, to eliminate prejudice and discrimination and to create a just society for all citizens and a fair education for all its children.

REFERENCES

Aronowitz, S. and Giroux, H.A. (1985a) Radical education and transformative intellectuals, *Canadian Journal of Political and Social Theory.* **99**(3), 48–63.

Aronowitz, S. and Giroux, H.A. (1985b) *Education Under Siege* (The Conservative, Liberal and Radical Debate over Schooling). South Hadley MA: Bergin and Garvey.

Biklen, S.K. and Dwyer, C. (1986) The new scholarship on women and education, *Educational Researcher,* **15**(6), 6. Special Issue June/July.

Carnoy, M. and Levin, H.M. (1985) *Schooling and Work in the Democratic State.* Stanford, CA: Stanford University Press.

Gilligan, C. (1982) *In a Different Voice: Psychological Theory and Women's Development.* Cambridge MA: Harvard University Press.

Giroux, H.A. (1985a) 'Intellectual labour and pedagogic work: rethinking the role of teacher as intellectual', *Phenomenology and Pedagogy.* **3**, 20–32.

Giroux, H.A. (1985b) 'Critical pedagogy and the resisting intellectual: part II', *Phenomenology and Pedagogy.* **3**, 84–97.

Grant, C.A. and Sleeter, C.E. (1986) Race, class and gender in education research: an argument for integrative analysis, *Review of Educational Research.* **56**(2), 195–211.

Lightfoot, S.L. (1979) Socialization and education of young black girls in schools, *Teachers College Record.* **78**, 239–62, quoted in Grant and Sleeter (1986), *op. cit.*

Parker, W.C. (1986) 'The social studies teacher as curriculum agent', paper presented at the American Educational Research Association Conference, San Francisco CA, April 1986.

Name Index

Subject Index

Acculturation 6, 8
Acknowledgement of difference 24
All Faiths for One Race (AFFOR) 148, 149
All London Teachers Against Racism and Fascism
  (ALTARF) 148, 151, 153
American Association of Colleges for Teacher
  Education (AACTE) 16, 175
American Educational Research Association
  (AERA) 145
Anti-Defamation League of B'nai B'rith 58, 117,
  138, 148, 149, 154, 169
  Florida middle schools research 58
Antiracism xii, xiv, 11
  antiracist education 8–11
  antiracist perspectives 161
  antiracist teaching 161
  three 'o's of 9
  writers 10
  see also Prejudice reduction
Antisexism xii, xiv
Assessment 3, 22, 64, 75, 76
  culture-fair xvi, 181
  objective tests 76
Assimilation 4, 5, 10, 11
  alternatives to 5
  assimilationist strategy 8
  sub-processes 6
Assistant Masters and Mistresses Association 62,
  80
Association for Supervision and Curriculum Development (ASCD) 149, 154
Association of Teachers in Colleges and Departments of Education (ATCDE) 162, 175
Association for Values Education and Research
  (AVER) 131, 138, 148, 154
Attitudes xiii, 2, 22, 23, 48, 87, 90, 192
  determinants of change 114
  ethnocentric 34
  hostile 3
  interethnic 45
  legitimate 34
  maintenance 26
  moral 19
  positive civic 12
  prejudiced xv, 20, 24
  racial 48
  socially dysfunctional xi

towards school 26
unfair 3
unhealthy xii
Australia 5, 7, 117, 142, 150
  Curriculum Development Centre (Canberra)
    19, 29
  Human Rights Commission 150
  White Australia Policy 5
Authoritarian personality 33, 34
  authoritarianism 37
  criticisms of theory 34
Aversion 35

British Broadcasting Corporation (BBC) 48
Behaviour 20
  aims in prejudice reduction 93
  prejudiced 20
Bias 42
  in schoolbooks 42
Bilingual education 11
Blaming the victim 26
Bradford 61, 62
  City of Bradford Metropolitan Council 62, 80
British Columbia Teachers Federation 62, 63, 80
British Youth Council 149, 154

Canada 7, 62, 117, 120, 131, 135, 142, 150, 154,
  169
  British Columbia 150
    Council of Human Rights 150, 154
    Teachers Federation 62, 63, 80
  Charter of Rights and Freedoms 150
  Human Rights Commissions 150
  Komagata Maru incident 120
  Ontario Institute for Studies in Education
    (OISE) 124, 150
  school boards 169, 171
    North York 169, 171, 172, 175
    Toronto 169
    Vancouver 81, 169
  University of British Columbia 131, 148
    Western Education Development Group
      (WEDGE) 148
Capitalist societies 8
Cat and Mouse fantasy 43
Catholic Commission for Racial Justice 149, 154
Centre for Contemporary Social Studies 13